European Institute of Education and Social Policy

Trentham Books

WOMEN WHO TEACH IN UNIVERSITIES

by Margaret Sutherland

First published 1985 by
Trentham Books
30 Wenger Crescent, Trentham,
Stoke-on-Trent, ST4 8LE,
England

ISBN: 0 948080 00 0

cover design by Cal Swann FSIAD

Set and printed in Great Britain by:
The Bemrose Press Limited/Cheshire Typesetters, Chester,
England.

Contents

Thanks are due to many people and institutions for their help in the research reported here: in particular to the following:

The University of Leeds for study leave, and colleagues there who took on extra work to make the leave possible

The Commission of the European Communities for a grant towards visits to France and West Germany.

Professor D Anna-Liisa Sysiharju, University of Helsinki

Professor Dr Pirkko Saarinen, University of Oulu

M. Jean Auba, erstwhile Director, Centre International d'Etudes Pédagogiques, Sèvres

Mme le professeur V.Isambert-Jamati, Université René Descartes-Sorbonne, Paris

Dr Jacques Champion, Université de Grenoble 11

Professor Dr W. Mitter, Deutsches Institut für Internationale Pädagogische Forschung, Frankfurt

The late Professor Dr Walter Schultze, Deutsches Institute Für Internationale Pädagogische Forschung, Frankfurt

Professor Dr Ingeborg Willke, Ruhr-Universität Bochum

The Humboldt University of Berlin
The Karl-Marx University of Leipzig

Above all, repeated thanks are due to all the women in all the countries included who responded so generously to my enquiries.

INTRODUCTION
The Problem and the Research

The access of women to education has improved greatly in recent decades. Throughout the world there have been changes in the enrolment of females in primary, secondary and tertiary levels of education.[1] Growth of provision in primary and secondary levels in countries where formerly females were disadvantaged holds the promise of future improvements in access to higher education there. In countries where already there was equality at primary and secondary levels there has been direct growth in enrolment rates of females in higher education. It is true that not all the 'developed' countries yet show equality at the third level — the United Kingdom, for example, has only recently, in 1980, reached the 40% level in female entrants to universities:[2] but in some developed countries the 50:50 stage has been reached and in some there is even a slight tendency for women to outnumber men in the first stage of university studies. In some developed countries too there are signs that the second and third stages of higher education are being increasingly entered by women though in most, if not all, systems women are still clearly in a minority position at postgraduate levels. For example, in the USA, there is evidence of progress:[3]

	1964-65	1979-80
% of women among those gaining Master's degree	33.8	49.4
Doctor's degree	10.8	29.5

If equality in higher education is to be reached, there remains a final barrier to be surmounted, the barrier to teaching in higher education, especially in universities. For although teaching is widely regarded as a woman's profession yet in universities women remain in the minority among teachers and, most notably, women remain in a minority at the top of the university teaching hierarchy, at professorial level.

Since this phenomenon seems present in practically all educational systems, it seemed a good idea to investigate it by going to a number of European countries and in these countries talking to women who are university teachers.

The choice of countries was somewhat arbitrary. It seemed advisable to choose some where interviews could, if necessary, be conducted in the language of the country. This, given the investigator's own language competences, indicated France and Germany. Since the political systems of East and West Germany and their educational systems diverge considerably, choosing these two countries had

1

obvious advantages. France seemed a good choice for more than one reason: its educational and social traditions have some resemblance to those of Britain but at the same time it offers a good example of the continental university system. The fourth country included abroad was Finland. This choice admittedly was not determined by language factors: but Finland has the merit of having shown for some years[4] an equal percentage of men and women students in higher education and it was felt that the readiness of Scandinavian people to cope with the English language could be relied on. So these four countries — France, East Germany, West Germany and Finland — were chosen as having characteristics likely to produce useful comparisons with each other and with the UK. Four weeks were spent in each country: in each, two university centres were chosen and in each centre some 20 women teaching in university were interviewed. To provide comparable information, in the UK in each of two universities a group of 30 women was interviewed. Altogether 244 university women teachers provided information through interviews: that is, 60 women in the UK and over 40 women in each of the four countries visited.

Initially, a written questionnaire was tried out in one of the UK universities and, with modifications suggested by experience and by the peculiarities of different systems, circulated to women in the other UK university and to some of the women in Finland, in France and in West Germany who were teaching in the universities visited but who could not, through shortage of time, be included in the interview group. This was intended not only as a method of gathering additional information but as a check on the representativeness of the group selected for interview. But while some useful information was gathered in this way and while, on the whole, returned questionnaires confirmed the information gained from interviews, the percentage of returns in France and West Germany was too small to be reliable. No attempt was made to circulate the questionnaire in East Germany as there was not enough time to make the necessary application for permission and the poor return rate in France and West Germany had already been discouraging. Some further reference will be made to these questionnaires: returns were also obtained from the second UK university and from a small group of men in one of the UK universities, chosen to correspond in seniority and subject area to the women who had returned a questionnaire in that university. But the main purpose of the investigation was to discover through interviews what, according to women actually in the university teaching profession, are the factors which have influenced their own professional career and what seem to them to be the conditions relevant to the access of women to university teaching posts, especially at professorial level.

Some important points must be mentioned here. Firstly, that as research subjects university women teachers are ideal. Almost without exception, they were ready to cooperate in the investigation, even when they initially had doubts as to whether they wholly approved what they suspected its intentions might be. They were hospitable, offering refreshments of various kinds, according to the resources of their offices or universities, from the ubiquitous black coffee of

Finland to the fruit juice or mineral water of East Germany. Some invited the investigator to a meal, at home or in restaurant or cafe. They were ready to talk analytically and frankly about their own background and experiences. The result, for the investigator, was insight into much more than the specific topic. There were glimspes of a whole way of life in the countries visited — and some moments of sheer delight in the beauty of, e.g., modern Finnish interior décor or the calm tranquillity of a traditional French apartment, reached by way of a courtyard guarded by solid wooden doors and an ascent by a small and creaking lift.

Interviews were therefore pleasant occasions. It was decided not to tape-record them, partly because of the technical difficulties of doing so in a variety of settings but also because of the inhibiting effect which such recording has on some people — not to mention the inhibiting effect of having to replay in full at least once. Notes were taken normally as the interview progressed and these were re-read and amplified, and the data tabulated, as soon as possible after the interview, while the meaning of statements and their context were still fresh in mind. (It may be mentioned that in one or two instances in West Germany women asked me to stop taking notes when reference was made to their husband's occupation or views.) In Finland the interviews were inevitably conducted in English: in all but three cases, the Finnish university teacher was happy to cope with this language unaided: in three, a friend whose knowledge of English was said to be better was brought along to help out. This at some points produced the frustrating situation in which an animated dialogue in Finnish was finally summed up by the friend: 'Yes, she agrees'. In France and the two Germanies the interview was in the language preferred by the interviewee: in France, it was normally in French, except when the woman had special competence in English: in West Germany, two languages might be used, perhaps beginning in German and progressing in English as the woman gained confidence and re-discovered fluency in that language: in East Germany, apart again from those with competence in English, German was normally the language used. While the interviews were in conversational style, following the sequence indicated by the situation and the woman's interests and career, certain questions were included in each interview, even if not always in the same order. Inevitably, as the interviews proceeded more topics showed themselves to be interesting and relevant: where possible they were followed-up in subsequent interviews even though there was no possibility of having complete data on them. Hence no attempt has been made to give numerical weights or calculate statistical significances. The influences which affect women's careers in university are in fact so many and various that it would take several researches, each perhaps concentrating on one or two factors only, to arrive at a fully informed point of view. One could, for instance, make a detailed study of family histories, to discover the sociological influences important for women's careers and the psychological relationships within the family — e.g. the number of siblings, their careers, the importance of the father's interest and attitudes, modelling on or rejection of the mother's role. But, given the limitations of single-handed research, not all relevant factors can be included in one investigation.

Interviews, in any case, varied in duration, partly according to the circumstances of the interview — from a leisurely evening meal in the interviewee's home to a period fitted in during office hours and possibly interrupted by students seeking information or advice — as well as according to personality. An hour was the standard duration: few, if any, interviews were shorter than this: some were longer.

There was further valuable though incidental information about the physical and other characteristics of universities. There were the wind-swept, frozen expanses of the Bochum campus: the tower block of Frankfurt, its mixture of new buildings, busy streets, and older houses in quieter avenues: the rain, wind and snow of central Helsinki and its solid, well-heated buildings: the 'child's toy' new buildings of Oulu university, the clear sunlight, blue skies and sub-zero temperatures: the narrow streets of inner Paris or the new-built 'housing-estate' premises of what is still known as Vincennes: the wide and lavish roadways of the Grenoble campus with the magnificent panorama of snow-capped mountains: the solid dignity of old buildings in East Berlin and Leipzig's mixture of skyscraper tower and traditional old houses. The interiors of the universities also had information to convey: student notice boards and graffiti: office hours notices on tutors' doors, quiet little groups of students waiting patiently to see tutors at the stated times. Teachers' rooms themselves were highly revealing. Some had been provided with flowers, plants, pictures, posters or other decoration reflecting the owner's personality and interests. In others, the basic minimum of table or desk and a couple of chairs provided by the university had been left as it was, a clear indication that the teacher's working hours were not spent there. In some instances scientists and medical specialists preferred to meet in laboratory surroundings. There were one or two dignified and opulent book-lined studies. But the majority of interviews took place in rather similar working rooms — that is, when the teacher did have a room available for meeting with foreign investigators — or students — undisturbed. In some cases, junior members of staff had to prevail on the kindness of colleagues who shared a room with them to make themselves scarce while the interview went on. In one, resort was had to a departmental library: in another, to a minimally furnished general staff room which fortunately was at the time deserted by the large number of colleagues who had access to it. Accommodation thus indicated whether the university considered it important for junior or other teachers to have sole occupancy of a study or office: and whether it was expected that the university teacher, even if — or especially if — senior, would spend most of the week elsewhere, coming into university only for the basic required number of teaching hours. This view, it appeared, was still quite characteristic of some departments in Paris. It is tempting to decide which university merits the booby prize for the accommodation made available to staff: but this would be hard to award: in more than one country — the UK included — staff are lodged in cubby-holes of old buildings with antiquated painting or papering on the walls and some degree of dampness. The surroundings do not necessarily correlate with the attitudes of the university teachers: but again in more than one country there was something to be said for rooms in an old house which had been adapted — thoughtfully and efficiently — to university use. More modern university provision could be pleasant and functional also but in its less good and more common manifestations was somewhat utilitarian and austere.

A more important additional result of the study was increased awareness of how political events influence the life of women who teach in universities. The Second World War in particular has left traces intertwined in remarkable ways in the individual life patterns of the woman interviewed. There was the woman in Finland who on four occasions had had to leave her home, accompanied by her young children, uncertain if they would see it again or if it would be destroyed in the Russian army advance. There were the others in Finland whose native Karelia is now part of the USSR. There was the woman in West Germany whose father and husband had both been imprisoned in Dachau. There were the German women whose families had lost everything in bombardments or who had joined, literally, in re-building their universities. There was the East German woman who had spent the war as a Jewish refugee in Britain. From later political upheavals, there were those who had moved from West Germany to East: and the woman in East Germany who had been called on for extra efforts to help her professor cope with the extra work following the defection of two colleagues to the West. There was the Hungarian woman who had been separated from her young children for a period of some years while passport formalities and exit-entrance regulations were sorted out.

They are an international group, women who teach in universities. While most are natives of the country in which they teach, some have moved to a foreign country in youth and stayed there, possibly because of marriage to a national of that country: some have moved with their foreign husband to his homeland: some have pursued their own research interests and settled in the country whose language or civilisation they study: many have visited and taught in other countries. So in studying the profession of university teaching it is impossible not to be reminded of international problems or the international movement between universities, even today. There are remarkable instances of this scholarly immigration and emigration and admirable examples of individual ability to overcome, or at least to survive, the difficulties created in personal circumstances by international forces.

But of course the women interviewed *are* the survivors: the survivors not only of international complications but also the survivors of whatever difficulties lie in the way of women proceeding through the educational system of their own country, aspiring to further study, to university teaching — or even drifting into university teaching. This basic factor must be recalled as we note what talking to these women provided in the way of evidence about their career and circumstances. These are a select group. Even so, their evidence reveals ways in which women can be guided from or forced from the profession of university teaching. They are aware in many cases of the problems of women they knew

5

who have not entered or continued in university teaching. From their statements there may emerge no one clear-cut solution to the problem of improving access to university teaching for women but the interviews were rich in information not only about factual circumstances but also about the more subtle attitudes which can determine success or failure. Ideally there should be studies of the women who did not continue in university teaching (though some of the present group may decide not to do so): and there should be comparable studies of the ways in which men's careers bring them to university teaching and to high positions within it. The present study is simply a beginning.

Notes:

1   Unesco: *Higher Education: International Trends, 1960-1970* (Paris, 1975),pp.9-12: Unesco *Statistical Yearbooks,* passim.
2. *University Statistics 1980* (University Statistical Record, 1982) vol.1, Table C, p.7
3. B.Heyns, J.A.Bird:'Recent Trends in the Higher Education of Women' *in* P.J. Perun (ed.): *The Undergraduate Woman: Issues in Educational Equity* Lexington Books, 1982,p.54.
4. Central Statistical Office of Finland: *Position of Women* (Helsinki, 1980),p.28, Table 11.

Chapter One

Women Teaching in British Universities

It seems useful to begin with the situation of women teaching in universities in Britain.

The access of women to higher education in Britain has followed a pattern typical of that in many European countries. In the latter part of the nineteenth century there was a sometimes reluctant opening of the doors of universities to women students, an opening which was particularly controversial and fiercely fought over in the case of medicine. The two most ancient universities of England indeed resisted till well on in the twentieth century before admitting women to full graduate status. But in Britain, as in other countries, there was an initial period of enthusiasm, reaching its peak about 1927-28[1], followed by a time of stagnation between the wars and after when the first keen aspirations seemed to have died down and women settled to being a relative minority among undergraduates. For whatever reasons — and it is an international phenomenon whose origins merit further study — the 60s saw an upsurge in women's entry to universities. In 1965 the percentage of female undergraduates in the United Kingdom as a whole was 27.7: ten years later it had risen to 36.2: and in 1980-81, it reached 39.8.[2] Particularly interesting in this increase is the case of medical faculties where special factors had kept the entry of women students low: a quota system had more or less openly been applied to keep female entrants at 10 to 25% of the total admitted. The system was abandoned in the early 70s: thus in 1962 female students were 24% of the total in medicine whereas in 1980 they were 38.65%.[3] (In passing it may be noted that though the quota has been abandoned there are still mutterings of discontent from those who fear that 'wastage' among qualified women medicals will result in an under-supply of doctors in future. But this is a complex question to which we must return later).

But has the percentage of women among those entering universities reached its maximum? The qualifications required for acceptance into university must be taken into account. Here we find that there has in fact been an improvement in England in the number of girls taking A-level[4:] there are now equal entries by both sexes though the choice of subjects is still strongly sex-biased and boys are more likely than girls to take a larger number of subjects. In Scotland, among those leaving school in 1980-81[5,] a rather higher percentage of girls than of boys had attained three or more Highers in the Scottish Certificate of Education. One could therefore expect equal entries to subsequent university education. But a major reason for limits in the proportion of women entering universities has for many years been the counter-attraction of teacher-training courses in Colleges of Education. Much greater numbers of qualified young women than of qualified young men have opted for decades to go to Colleges of Education rather than to university[6]. There has been much speculation as to the reasons for this preference: some have suggested an initially greater enthusiasm for teaching, especially for teaching young children: in Scotland it was suggested that possibly a shorter course of training of three years in Colleges as opposed to three university years plus one in College attracted girls who were looking forward to early marriage. Possibly, it has also been suggested, girls have felt less confident of their academic abilities and have opted for what seemed an academically less demanding course. The reduction in the numbers of students allowed to enter Colleges of Education in both England and Scotland has thus been a change affecting females more than males. The situation had of course also been changed by the introduction of the B.Ed. degrees and the longer courses of study such degrees entail: the more recent abolition of the Teacher's Certificate qualification in England must also have affected those girls who might have wanted to avoid an academic degree course. As yet there is no clear evidence to indicate that the barrier to one form of higher education — its reduced number of places — has led to an increase in the entry of girls to university: but it may be that something of this kind underlies the steady, though not spectacular increase of university entrance applications from females in recent years. Changes in the economic and employment situations may now make university education seem a less reliable way to a rewarding career than it formerly seemed: this could affect both male and female decisions to apply for a university place. In all, however, it seems probable that the proportion of women undergraduates will continue to increase in the immediate future.

At postgraduate level too there has been some improvement in the representation of women. Statistics here tend to be unclear when total numbers of postgraduate students are provided, for the term 'postgraduate' may refer to those taking a one-year course of teacher education at university: women are well represented on such courses so an unduly good picture of women's presence among postgraduate students may result. What has to be considered is the total of postgraduates taking higher degrees and women's contribution to this total. In 1980-81 women were 35.4% of postgraduate students in general[7] but only 26.1% of those obtaining higher degrees. It may be that this situation will change or is in process of changing. Improvement has been noted recently in the USA, where the Carnegie Commission on Equal Opportunities in Higher Education[8], reporting in the mid-70s, found that from 1930 to 1970 the percentage of women obtaining doctor's degrees had remained remarkably constant and low: recent figures (already cited) show a marked rise — though not yet to 50%. Possibly there will be a move from such a plateau of higher degree results for women in the UK also.

Many factors must affect decisions to work for a higher degree but one may be the encouragement given by university teachers to their students to proceed to postgraduate students. Questionnaire returns from the two UK universities showed that the great majority of women respondents think male and female students are equally encouraged by their teachers to go on to such studies: and the men in the group responding to the questionnaire in one university also thought, with no dissentients, that there is equal encouragement. But a minority of women (25 out of 160) thought that men students are more encouraged to do post-graduate work than women students. One respondent thought that women are more encouraged than men. It should also be noted that some comments were added to the effect that in the present situation no student, male or female, is encouraged to proceed to postgraduate studies since these, apparently, would have no career prospects.

The matter of access to higher degrees is of course particularly important if more women are to teach in universities. There has been a considerable expansion in the numbers of female undergraduates in British universities. Women are less strongly represented at postgraduate levels but they do form a perceptible group there. Yet the proportion of women teaching in universities, and especially at professorial level, has altered little during the period of expansion. In 1980-81 the distribution of university women teachers in Britain[9] was:

	Percent female
Professors	2.64
Readers, senior lecturers	6.42
Lecturers, asst. lecturers	15.55
Others (e.g. research staff, usually lower paid)	34.24

The percentage of women in university teaching as a whole was 13.85.

This situation is to be compared with that in 1962 when women were 10% of university teachers: in 1965, when they were 10.6% and 1975 when they were 11.5%. The increase over 20 years has scarcely been dramatic. At professorial level similarly, in 1961-2, 2% of professors were women: in 1965, 1.4%: in 1972, 1.7% and in 1978, 2%. These percentages seem to be remarkably constant even if there has been some slight increase.

It must of course be remembered that with the increased number of students has come a great increase in numbers of university teachers, so that in fact there are now much greater numbers than formerly of women teaching in universities. Since women in a minority situation may be highly visible, this may well give the impression that the proportional representation of women is much better than it used to be. It is indeed suggested by women as well as men in universities that the increased numbers of women students will automatically lead to more women university teachers as these students become qualified. But there has now been a fair amount of time for the increased numbers of female undergraduates of the late 60s to work their way into and through university teaching and change still seems slow to come. The situation now is also rather unfavourable for the prospects of newcomers: the expansion of the 60s meant that many Chairs were filled by relatively young people who now, in effect, block the promotion chances of later comers. Possibly the spate of voluntary early retirements from Chairs will result in some widening of the bottle-neck of promotions to senior posts: but at the same time, it remains to be seen whether women are more likely than men to opt for early retirement. If the position of women university teachers was not altered radically by a period of expansion, is it now likely to improve during a period of retrenchment?

It should be remembered that the pyramidal structure of women's representation in university teaching, especially their low representation at the top of the hierarchy, is by no means unique. In France 1978-79,[11] this was the distribution:

	Percentage females
Professeurs	5.8
Maîtres de conferences	9.9
Chargés d'enseignement, chargés de cours	18.9
Maîtres assistants	29.8
Assistants	34.7

and in Finland, in 1980,[12] the percentages were (excluding teacher education):

	Percentage females
Professors	5.7
Assistant Professors	8.2
Senior Assistants	18.7
Lecturers	31.9

In West Germany in 1977,[13] the total percentage of women university teachers was 11% and just under 5% of all professors were women: among lecturers (a relatively small group) was found the highest percentage of women, 38%. Precise figures for the German Democratic Republic are not available but it is agreed there that the same pyramidal distribution exists: an estimate of the distribution by some university teachers was 10% Professors (possibly 12-15% in the most favourable university): 21% Dozenten, 25% Oberassistenten, and varying numbers of Assistents, ranging from 10 to 60% according to subject taught.

The British situation then is replicated in other countries. But how far is it affected by characteristics and conditions peculiar to the university system in this country? In the first place, are there features of the system of appointment to posts and promotion to higher posts which could help to explain the minority position of women?

Criteria for appointment and promotion

The university system in the United Kingdom differs from systems of other European countries by the vagueness of its criteria for entry to university teaching and for appointment to senior posts. Given the relative autonomy of British universities, there is also some divergence from one university to another and from one academic discipline to another. Formerly, entry was by appointment to an assistant lecturer post, possibly preceded by a period as a graduate research student giving tutorial assistance or demonstrating in the department. Such assistantships in the past were often in the gift of the professor and, in such cases, would not be advertised: they would be filled in an informal way, the professor approaching a promising recruit with an offer of employment. Tenure of an assistant lectureship tended to be for a period of three years, after which the assistant might progress to a full lectureship: again, the degree of formality associated with this appointment could be minimal. Even when the post was advertised, the holder of the assistantship had strong prospects of appointment if good relationships had been maintained within the department and the assistant's work had been satisfactory. The system now has become more formal and posts are normally advertised for appointment at lecturer level. Such appointments have usually a condition of a probationary period, normally a three-year probation. (It may be recalled also that until relatively recent times, appointments to lectureship in some universities were for periods of seven years, renewable at the end of such a period: in practice, the renewal tended to be thought of as automatic and the lectureship effectively was one in which tenure was taken for granted even if formally it was subject to reconsideration every seven years.) Since the Second World War the procedure of appointment has become more open: posts are formally advertised and appointments depend, normally, on the decision of an interviewing committee whose recommendation is approved by the highest university authority. Assistantships have been faded out, though the employment of graduates as tutorial assistants or demonstrators continues — provision of such employment indeed has come to be regarded almost as something the university owes its postgraduates.

Tenure till retirement age has become something which can be achieved by the British university teacher at a relatively early stage, in some disciplines even before achieving a second degree and in some certainly before gaining a doctorate. The recent financial crisis has led to a number of limited term posts and to a more fundamental reconsideration of whether permanent tenure should be given so early in the career or given at all. Whether some of the far-reaching proposals made about tenure will be implemented remains to be seen. But it remains of interest that until now tenure has been relatively easy to achieve — though of course the existence of the efficiency bar at a point on the lecturer's salary scale has provided one mechanism by which external pressure to work hard at teaching and research could be applied. (Again, the rigour of judgment at the efficiency bar varies from department to department and from university to university. Much can depend still on the assessment made by the head of department.)

What factors do determine appointments in British universities? The advertisement of a university post usually asks candidates to provide in addition to their curriculum vitae and such other comment as the candidates may think fit, names of three persons to whom reference may be made. If the qualifications and other characteristics of the applicant seem promising on paper, the appointing committee will take up these references. But there may also be enquiries to other people likely to know about the candidate. In some cases, some members of the committee are already familiar with the candidate's work or take the trouble to consult work the candidate has included in a list of publications. Especially when a Chair is to be filled, the committee may also consult people knowledgeable in the area to ask for names of those who would be suitable for appointment: people thus mentioned may be invited to meet the committee even if they have not spontaneously applied for the post. A short list of candidates to be interviewed is thus arrived at through consideration of information provided in applications, through informal consultation and through what referees — and others — may say about candidates. The choice of names for the short list thus depends on a considerable variety of sources. It may also be determined by the committee's perception of the particular needs and characteristics of the department. The information circulated to candidates about the post may correspond to a greater or lesser degree with this perception of what the committee or department is 'looking for'. All this clearly has the benefit of flexibility. The system is open to the 'outsider' or 'unknown' candidate who has simply to provide a sufficiently good curriculum vitae and adequate referees. But at the same time there are obviously a number of points at which subjective factors could prejudice decisions about calling for interview — and indeed could affect the kind of reference given by those consulted. These factors could be the result of rather good judgment of people: or they could be the result of personality clashes: or of discrimination against women — or of failure to think of women as suitable nominees, particularly for a senior post.

The questions asked at the interview also depend on the opinions and personal reactions of those forming the interviewing committee: sometimes the situation is approached fairly scientifically, an attempt is made to put the same questions to all candidates and to discover candidates' abilities not only in the academic field but in teaching. Some interviewers however specialise in the divergent 'off-beat' question or even in the 'hostile attack' technique. The extent to which the course of the interview is determined by the personality of the candidate also varies: some who seemed promising on paper contrive to 'talk themselves out of, the job. Naturally the members of interviewing committees form judgments as to the general acceptability of the candidate from their own point of view, even if not necessarily from the point of view of the department in which the appointment is to be made. (It is normally the case that the committee includes members of departments other than that to which the candidate is seeking to be appointed, though probably they will mainly be from cognate departments). Discussion in committees can at times show remarkable agreement in assessment of candidates' responses and behaviour: it can also reveal individual idiosyncrasies, projections, prejudices. Since the introduction of Equal Rights legislation there is probably a greater awareness that it may be unfair to ask women questions about their home life and personal circumstances which would not be put to men — e.g. whether the appointment would lead to constant travel from the married woman's home: whether the care of children would not make the candidate's work load too heavy. As we shall see later, women in the past have been disconcerted by such questions: but there is also the problem for women that a committee which does not put such questions may assume — wrongly — that it knows the answers and discount the woman's suitability for the post as a result.

It is thus sometimes difficult to determine, in a given instance, why the successful candidate has been given the post. In some cases the person appointed is clearly better qualified than the other candidates or has better or more relevant experience. In others, the decision may have been arrived at with difficulty, given almost equal qualifications — on paper: the reasons for the appointment may remain obscure to those outside the committee and even some members of the committee may remain unconvinced that the right appointment was made. Hence unsuccessful candidates may remain uncertain how to improve their future chances: they can probably evaluate their own qualifications, publications. etc., to some extent but — unless they are fortunate enough to be told — informally — by a committee member, what counted against them, they can only guess at the reasons for the committee's decision.

Some attempts in recent years by women candidates to challenge appointments by claiming that the committee was discriminating against women have mainly shown the complex nature of the decision-making process: it is extremely difficult to find firm evidence as to whether this factor was decisive.

Given these conditions, what do women actually in post think were the major factors in determining their *first* appointment in a university? The questionnaire offered a list of factors which could have been influential and asked for ratings of 'important', 'very important' and 'not important' for each of these. The results show that for the women replying the factors considered important or very important were reference from a professor or other university teacher and specialisation in a given subject area. Next in importance came performance at the interview: followed by class of first degree and possession of a postgraduate degree. But the reference and the specialisation were clearly seen as much more important than these formal qualifications. As was probably reasonable in consideration of applications for a first post in the British system, publications were not thought to be of particular importance.

Responses to a question about factors important in obtaining subsequent appointments were limited because many respondents were still in their first post. Replies obtained indicated that continuing importance is attributed to a professorial recommendation and to the field of specialism. Publications now appear high on the list: but performance at interview is still regarded as highly important also. Perhaps surprisingly, relatively little importance is attached to a postgraduate degree. And although folklore would have it that making oneself widely known through activity in professional associations is a way of obtaining advancement, this kind of activity is rated as relatively unimportant. It should be noted that various comments were added to responses to the question set by the questionnaire. Being known to people in the university through having worked with them earlier in some other place was regarded as helpful: so was the experience obtained in professional work outside the university, especially if it was relevant to new developments in teaching or research in the department in question.

So far, we have considered appointment of people coming from outside the university. The position may in fact be rather different when internal promotions to a senior lectureship, readership or personal (titular) Chair are concerned. For senior lectureships various universities have now made their conditions of appointment clearer: promotion is based on three criteria — research, teaching and administration. In some universities lecturers can nominate themselves for consideration for such promotion whereas in the past such nomination had to come from the head of department: thus though heads of department had to indicate why they were not nominating people who had reached the top of the lecturer's scale and an appropriate age, subjective factors could determine whether the lecturer was considered for promotion or not. Subjective factors may still enter, of course, in the head of department's assessment of the teaching and administrative work of the lecturer: and the assessment by a committee of a list of publications — or research grants obtained — is not necessarily wholly objective and reliable. Nevertheless the move towards a clearer statement of criteria seems likely to benefit women as well as men and may account for the fact that a fair number of women, while not foreseeing appointment to a Chair, feel reasonably confident of their chances of becoming a senior lecturer — at least, they did so feel until the economic crisis which has cut down the number of available promotions.

Promotion to a readership is dependent on ability in research and publication. Hence, the decision is made on the basis of reports from external assessors who evaluate the candidate's published work. Subjective factors may again enter into the decision to recommend a lecturer as suitable for this promotion. The choice of referees is crucial. But it is a non-competitive situation, the promotion is in terms of prestige rather than in financial payments: it may thus seem attractive to those who are mainly concerned with achieving recognition in their own field of study but would not want the administrative load often associated with a Chair. Readerships remain a somewhat anomalous rank in the university career structure. It is sometimes difficult to distinguish between the qualifications for a readership and those for a personal or titular Chair: except, possibly, in the greater financial rewards of the latter and perhaps in age differences. A readership could certainly help a younger candidate in applying for an established Chair. But it is difficult to equate the British readership with ranks in other university systems. Possibly the Finnish 'docent' comes nearer to it than other ranks abroad. The West German Dozent or Privatdozent rank would seem to have some resemblances to the readership insofar as recognition of high academic ability is concerned: but it is a rank that is disappearing in West Germany. In Britain readership remains a high rank to which only a minority of women ascend.

Promotion to an established Chair tends to follow the same lines as those indicated for a lectureship though there is greater emphasis on consultation with people in the field, a greater probability that some who have not formally applied will be invited to do so or to meet with the committee. Further, by the use of external assessors who will advise the committee and perhaps be present at the interview, there can be created something of a 'king-making' role for those considered the most expert or the most knowledgeable in the field: they are expected to know the most likely candidates — as well as the most likely to apply — and may indeed interview some candidates on more than one Chair-filling occasion.

This survey of the appointments system confirms the opinions given in questionnaire responses that personal recommendations are important. Support from the head of department or from a professor in another university is clearly influential in determining who is appointed even though the candidate's research performance and publication record also play a part as may the candidate's own personality as displayed at interviews. It will be noted that teaching ability is only indirectly assessed in the British system: it may be commented on by those giving references but it is likely to be overshadowed by what may appear to a committee the more 'objective' evidence of publications (committees are of course aware of the need to discriminate among publications, both with regard to the standard of the journal in which they appear and with regard to repetition of subject matter or multiple authorship).

Present procedures usually mean that women candidates are dependent on good recommendations from men, since the number of women academics holding positions at a level where recommendations are sought is small. It is highly probable that the interviewing committee will consist of men only — unless, in more recent times, a concession has been made by including one woman. Women in post at present have been appointed almost exclusively — often exclusively — through the recommendations of men. But of course it would be absurd to suggest that the sex factor is the most important or even important in the majority of cases. In making judgments of the kind required academics do try to judge reasonably and on the basis of the individual's merits, whether the individual is man or woman. Where prejudices enter into the situation they can easily be within-sex prejudices: they can — and sometimes quite importantly — be prejudices due to clash of personality or difference in academic — or political or social — outlook. In the appointment and recommendation of male candidates, it is frequently noticed that some men may be supported 'because the face fits', because they seem acceptable colleagues for reasons that are not basically academic. Thus if one is concerned about the criteria for appointments to posts in universities one may certainly note that subjective factors may be operative: but the sex factor may play a very minor or insignificant part in this subjective sphere. At the same time, the structure of the academic hierarchy does put women in the situation of being judged only by those of the opposite sex on a great many occasions. It is true that the presence of women on appointing bodies does not automatically entail support by these women for a woman candidate — they too will use their academic judgment and be affected by personal factors. It is also true that male candidates may think — or allege — that an attractive young female candidate has an advantage in appealing to male committee members. But in a system where the grounds of appointment are not always clear, candidates may be unsure whether sex discrimination has been operative.

Having looked at the procedures by which people become university teachers in British universities, we can now consider what the situation looks like from the other side, from the point of view of women who have been appointed and have been working in two British universities. What are the influences which have shaped their career pattern? What problems or what advantages have they encountered? To what extent do they think sex discrimination has affected them and to what extent would they attempt to change the present situation?

Characteristics of the group of women interviewed

Almost all the women had indicated on their questionnaire return that they would be willing to be interviewed: in a few cases the questionnaire had not been returned but a phone call discovered that in these cases the woman had simply thought that her reply would not be useful — e.g. because she was about to retire. An attempt was made to include women at different levels of seniority and in as wide a range of subjects as possible: beyond that, selection was random insofar as it depended on whether the woman answered a telephone call at the crucial time.

The type of post held was as follows

Professor	5
Reader	2
Senior Lecturer	8
Lecturer	45

It will be noticed that professors are over-represented, given their proportion in the university teaching population as a whole: this is because a deliberate attempt was made to interview all professors: two could not be interviewed because one was away on study leave, one at a conference.

The subject distribution was not proportionate to women's representation in the various subject areas, though it comes reasonably near to this: a special effort was made to include some women teaching in departments where few women are employed. Thus the distribution obtained was:

Arts	19
Social Sciences	6
Education	3
Law	4
Natural Sciences	11
Applied Sciences	5
Medicine and dentistry	12

Psychology is sometimes classified as an Arts subject, sometimes as a Science: in the present case it has been included in the natural sciences. In medicine, distinctions have not been made between clinical and pre-clinical departments. Since Applied Science is regarded as an area where few women are to be found, it should perhaps be specified that in this group were two women in Veterinary Sciences, one in Civil Engineering, one in Textiles and one in Food Sciences.

The age distribution was this:

25-29	7	45-49	5
30-34	9	50-54	4
35-39	14	55-59	3
40-44	15	60-64	3

The number of years of university teaching experience varied widely from one year to 34: the majority had between six and twenty years of such experience: but the length of teaching experience did not necessarily correspond exactly to age: some women had spent periods of eleven to thirteen years as research workers before being appointed to a teaching post and others had been engaged in other professional work, often in the health service. As others also noted, they had made a late start, one, for example, simply 'following my husband and children around' for seven years. In most cases university teaching had provided continuous employment once they embarked on it: but three careers had been interrupted by periods of unemployment ranging from three or four months to three years — that is, periods during which no suitable university job was available. Two had left university teaching briefly for a year in order to engage in further study. One had been away from university for a year and a half owing to her mother's terminal illness.

Since the matter of qualification can be important, we note that half the group did have the degree of Ph.D. or M.D. (one had both). Seven of the others had mastership degrees. Nine had a first degree only. Others had a first degree plus various Diplomas in their specialist area or Membership in the appropriate medical or other college or institute. Three had no academic first degree but two of them had been appointed to university posts because of the special knowledge they had gained in the exercise of their specialist skills over a large number of years and one had, exceptionally, taken a Ph.D. It has to be recognised, of course, that some of the group are still young and that some of them are in fact registered as Ph.D. candidates. On the other hand, one of the younger members of the group had already completed an 'orthodox' course of studies, taking her Master's degree one year after getting a first, and completing her Ph.D. two years after the Master's. She is in a science department. It is noticeable that where women have only a first degree — or a first degree followed by a B.Litt. or B.Phil. of an ancient university — they are in the Arts departments.

Pre-university influences

Entry to university teaching can be pre-determined in school days. What were the factors affecting women in the group in childhood and adolescence?

a) Subject choices

It might be expected that many of those who have achieved high qualifications would have been devoted to their special subject from an early age. In fact, it is a minority (16) who recollect a childhood enthusiasm for a particular line of study and not all of these have pursued that youthful interest. Perhaps the most common enthusiasm mentioned was for the study of medicine. Seven women recalled this as an early interest but for various reasons only two of them went on to a career in this specialism — one of these 'never wanted to do anything else' and the other made her mind up about the age of 13 or 14. Two, while attracted by medicine, were worried about having to deal with dead bodies — so opted instead for veterinary science! (One of these later thought of studying medicine as a fairly mature student but was 'talked out of it'). One failed to make up her mind to apply early enough in her schooldays and turned instead to Law. One opted for nursing, believing that she was not bright enough to be a doctor — and being also repelled by memories of a disagreeable female doctor of her childhood. And one was urged by her father towards science instead (albeit in a medical area). An interest in dentistry had determined one woman from her primary school days onwards: though another dentist had been frustrated in her wish to specialise in Physics by bad school teaching in Sixth Form and opted then for dentistry instead. It is interesting to find a widespread interest in medicine from early ages since this interest appears to recur in women in other countries also. While in some instances one might have expected external circumstances to prevent females from achieving the fulfilment of an ambition to specialise in medical studies, it is fascinating to see what other considerations have been influential for some girls.

Yet external pressures did deter some girls from following their early ambitions. One who had wanted to be a vet was told that women could not cope with large animals: so she specialised in Science instead. Reciprocally perhaps, one who had been keen on maths in her youth later turned to medical studies though two others who had always been keen on maths — one even from Junior School days — did in fact continue in that specialism. But one was lost to her first love of science, through bad counselling on the part of the school: she became a geographer.

Other early enthusiasms fitted more smoothly into the expected interests of a girl. Two were enthusiastic about languages and went ahead with this study. An adolescent preference for history was followed without complication. A decision of one girl at about the age of 14 to study Law was also well received, though in another case the choice of Law was discouraged by the school.

Family and school in fact were not always helpful when girls formed an early ambition to study certain subjects. One of those who became a vet did so against her mother's advice. Another who wanted to be an architect was discouraged by information provided in the family circle that such a career was not for women. The study of philosophy seemed to one family to be inappropriate for a girl but this particular girl persisted, even though she was uncertain, till she had done some university study, whether she was in fact able enough to cope with this subject. Yet a family background which supported interest in scientific studies was helpful to the girl who opted to study engineering at a time when there was only one other female student in the subject at the university.

b) Family background

Family background naturally proves to have been important in the early stages of career choice and continuation of study. Although only about one-third of the group had parents who were graduates, families were almost invariably supportive with regard to the daughter's higher education. In two or three cases admittedly the families were opposed to the daughter's choice of option but in almost all cases the families accepted with pleasure their daughter's entrance to university studies. In a few cases, the daughter indeed satisfied a frustrated ambition on the part of parents who would have liked to study at university but were not able to do so. Only rarely did entry to higher education come after a reaction against the parents' influence and wishes. Yet families were not always necessarily promising backgrounds for advancement into higher education. Five of the women came from 'one-parent' families through divorce, separation or death of the father or mother. One woman in such a situation could not, she felt, aim beyond training college since her mother was bringing up the family single-handedly: another similarly felt that with younger sibs to be educated, she could not aim at academic training. Both came later, as mature students, into university studies.

It should also be noted that four women specifically stated that they came from a working-class family though they did not define working-class. Others had parents in non-manual class III occupations. But all families had been interested enough in education to support their daughters through full secondary education and most through university education.

c) Schools

The influence of the school has already been shown to be important in the matter of choosing a future career. Yet it could not always have been easy for the school to advise since in many cases these women showed general all-round ability: the choice of a future specialism did not prescribe itself through exam results for in some cases the girl felt enthusiastic about a subject in which she did not gain her best marks. Some scientists were attracted by languages: some linguists by mathematics. And of course some of the specialisms ultimately studied are not school subjects and so it was not until university years that some women discovered where their major interests lay. Here we should perhaps except the study of Law which does seem to have attracted some school-girls — possibly by way of Perry Mason.

As for all-round aspirations, one woman, recalling her early enthusiasm for the study of politics — which faded with the beginning of university studies — recognised that her early ambition to be the first woman prime minister could not now be fulfilled.

d) Girls' schools or co-educational schools?

It is much debated whether girls' schools are more likely than co-educational schools to develop girls' abilities in mathematical or scientific subjects and to develop also girls' self-confidence. The majority of the women in the group came from girls' schools. This is not conclusive evidence of the beneficial effect of such schools since in the years under consideration it was common for grammar schools to be single-sex rather than co-educational. So the women's own comments on their schools are rather to be considered.

On the whole, those who came through girls' schools speak well of them. Their main weakness seems to have been in the expectation that girls would enter women's occupations only: two women went on to study medicine in spite of the school's advice. Another felt that in her school ambition was not encouraged and yet another, that some girls were certainly not stimulated to develop their abilities fully. One girls' school was reported as small and ineffectual, giving only a limited choice of A-level subjects: in two other cases, a marked tendency to push towards the traditional Arts subjects was reported. Yet one praised warmly the special tuition in her school when she made a rather late decision to abandon the scientific subjects her parents had urged her into and move over to language study instead and another praised her school for having 'all the frills' — a curriculum going beyond exam preparation. More often there was comment on the high academic standards — and social behaviour standards — set by the girls' schools: though again one woman felt that her school neglected the girls who were not going to proceed to higher education. There was also a general agreement that the girls' schools had given girls a chance to play all kinds of roles rather than bring them, as some women said co-educational schools do, into a situation where girls are expected to adopt the traditional submissive and retiring role which society expects of females. Two women scientists were indeed indignant about the failure of co-ed schools to give girls confidence in their scientific ability (having observed the progress of their daughters in such schools) and one social scientist commented that 'co-ed schools do terrible things to girls'. Yet one woman views with some amusement the male chauvinist attitudes which her sons report (with disapproval) from their boys' school.

There are in fact various opinions on the social aspects of sex segregation or co-education. While the main benefit seen in girls' schools is the absence of female stereotyping, two women recognised that lack of experience in dealing with males led to (temporary) complications in first year at university — it took some time to get accustomed to the other sex and to realise that they too could be stupid. Another recognised that her sister who went to a co-ed school had a wider range of friends of both sexes yet felt that she herself had sufficient experience of co-ed relationships in her own out-of-school hours to make good any lack of these in her girls' school. One who saw some advantages in her girls' school yet described it as 'a prison'. One who had experienced both co-ed and girls' schools reported that at her co-ed secondary school she did not work much because she was more interested — at that time — in boys: when her parents moved to another town, she transferred to a 'dull' girls' school and did give more attention to school work. Contemporary trends to send public school girls into boys' schools were deplored by another interviewee: this practice erodes standards in girls' schools without changing the boys' school ethos. One who had experienced both girls' school and mixed education believed that co-education will continue to present a problem for girls until sex roles are re-defined in society generally: at present boys are ambivalent in attitude if girls are really bright.

As to the question whether segregation or co-education produces happier schooldays for girls, it was crisply dismissed by one commentator: 'They're happy because they're young anyway. And is happiness the point?'

While the majority were clearly 'good' pupils at school, there were cases where rebellion had been evident. Two refused to follow the pattern expected by the school and tried other occupations — before, eventually, going to university. Others, as we have noted, disregarded the school's views about the subjects they should opt for. (Incidentally, one should note that no school was referred to as having provided good and effective vocational counselling: decisions seem to have been made very much on the basis of family influences and the girl's own preferences). One reported herself as having 'truanted' in her later years at school by signing-in then going off to do something other than attend the classes she was supposed to be attending.

Entry to university teaching

A number of the group began the interview by saying 'But my career isn't typical'. Their view was that they had strayed into university teaching by accident, sometimes relatively late in life. So it is worthwhile to consider what, if any, seems to be the 'typical' career pattern.

Initially it is useful to note a point made by various women medicals. For those training as doctors career ambitions are likely to centre on a consultancy: the future career is envisaged within the National Health Service. University work is a side issue: it may come as it were by accident through teaching associated with a Health Service post. Thus the focus for the newly qualified doctor is on achieving professional and practical experience, working for the appropriate membership of a professional body. Consequently those with medical training may enter university work at a later age than those in other disciplines: they may enter at a senior level: and some may in fact move into and out of university work or give some university teaching to medical students while themselves employed by the NHS. In fact one-third of the whole group had made what could be described as 'direct' entry to university teaching: that is, they had been appointed to a university post immediately after finishing their first degree or a Ph.D. A further sub-group of eleven had spent short periods in research before gaining a university appointment, periods of two to three years. So that about half the group could be regarded as 'career' university teachers.

Nine had been engaged in professional work relevant to their subsequent university post for periods of some years. Six had been research workers for extended periods of time ranging from 9 to 13 years. Seven had spent a period of time in other teaching, mainly school teaching, but in one instance teaching at a polytechnic, in two others, teaching at universities overseas. But some of these occupations had been preceded by a period of not working, apart from domestic duties: and for three there had been periods of unemployment when no suitable university post was available. One, as earlier noted, had stayed at home for a year and a half to tend her mother during a terminal illness.

Thus for about half the group, university teaching had been a settled career for most of their working life to date. For others, it had been an unforeseen and unexpected development. They had certainly not planned for it when they left secondary school. One of these had been brought up abroad, in Switzerland, in an environment where girls were not expected to proceed to higher education though her school had been encouraging: it was only after some years of commercial work that she attended an adult education college and made her way into academic studies and university teaching. Two others had opted for secretarial work after school, feeling that university studies would not be interesting; in one case a sister's experience of university studies brought realisation that possibly the university world had something to offer. Another who had postponed entry to higher education by spending a year abroad in various forms of work also finally came to the conclusion that university might be worthwhile.

In a number of cases the women had worked in the profession or occupation for which they had trained — as nurses or as doctors or social workers or as a vet or architect or textile designer. Only after amassing this practical experience did they have it brought to their attention that possibly their skills might be useful in a university post which happened to be vacant and which a friend or acquaintance knew about. Often it was with trepidation that they applied for the post, very unsure of their own ability to fill it. In other cases they applied for posts which were not in the subject of their degree but were posts in which their specialist knowledge seemed likely to be useful and to which they could adapt their qualifications, e.g. from History to Roman Law, from Physics to Phonetics, from Computer Science to Psychology. Thus personal advice from friends, or from someone in university teaching, encouraged making an application which the woman would not spontaneously have thought of. And even in the 'direct entry' cases one is reminded of the haphazard way in which some career commitments were begun: a woman was offered an assistantship to fill in a year while she waited for her husband to complete a higher degree, after which the couple intended to teach abroad. Another was asked to substitute for a young woman not much older than herself whose assistantship was temporarily available because of her pregnancy: and the former assistant did not return.

There is thus in many cases a lack of career planning of a deliberate kind. A post was accepted and events developed under their own momentum. Some older women now feel that they should have seen their situation in career terms at an earlier age but for various reasons they did not do so. Few if any seem to have been advised by a superior in the university as to how to advance in their chosen profession though in some individual cases help may have come from such a superior in obtaining posts or in carrying out research projects. Women who spent long periods as research workers might have received better guidance as to their careers and applied for university posts at an earlier stage. In one case, it is true, a university's ruling against married couples working in the same department was invoked as a barrier to a research worker's entry to university.

While research interests were obviously strong in these cases and excellent work done, conscious career policy might have led to earlier and more determined moves to a different kind of post.

Younger women are probably more aware today of the need to think about career prospects. Yet some of them are in a precarious position so far as university employment is concerned for they are on limited-term contracts of two or three years — some are already on a second period of such 'temporary' employment. (So too are two of the older women.)

Yet not all the group are convinced that they want to stay in university teaching. One of the older age group had already opted for voluntary early retirement and a second was contemplating a similar move. Among the younger group two or three, in their thirties, were asking themselves whether they did want to continue in this kind of work for the rest of their lives: one described academic work as 'a cop-out' not a *real* job like others: and another woman in the middle age range was leaving university work at least temporarily, partly because she felt that the university was too much concerned with research and publication and not enough with work in the socio-medical field.

It is perhaps appropriate to note here that the group, in their earlier years at least, had not been greatly concerned with teaching as a career. Only one had deliberately opted for school teaching. Others who had engaged in some school teaching for some periods of time had seen it mainly as a stop-gap. One who had wished to study Law was urged by her parents to go into school teaching which was a suitable job for a woman: though she did concede to the extent of studying Arts yet she went on to study for a higher degree in a specialist subject leading her to university work. One was resigned to becoming a university teacher because teaching seemed to be the only thing one could do with a degree in Philosophy. Another was simply horrified when she found that a university post she had accepted committed her to teaching a tutorial group. Yet in spite of a wide variety of initial reactions to the teaching component of university work, the group now show great interest in teaching, many have devoted much time and energy to producing new courses and to devising methods of improving existing courses. Yet this interest in teaching is certainly not at the expense of commitment to research. It is however part of the general job satisfaction which characterises the group — even if one of the older members commented that student background and general knowledge have deteriorated in universities recently, so teaching has become less satisfying.

Encounters with sex discrimination against women

We have noted that, to be appointed, this group must at least have surmounted triumphantly any barrier there might be against women entering university teaching — or they may have encountered no barrier to surmount. Have they in fact perceived instances of sex discrimination against women or suffered from such prejudice?

So far as students are concerned, we have already noted that the majority of the group think there is equal encouragement of males and females to proceed to postgraduate work. Yet a minority think males are more likely than females to be so encouraged. They themselves do not perceive great differences in the work of male and female students though a few thought that possibly females do work harder. Generally, in vocationally oriented courses, both men and women students seem keen to work steadily for their qualification and to show no great differences. Yet in Law, it was suggested, women perhaps set their sights lower, on family work as solicitors rather than on attempting brilliance as barristers. In Medicine women students might benefit from counselling to alert them to career structures and to look ahead, beyond the first qualification. One woman recalled that in her own student days in a women's hospital school there had been a curious lack of vision: women students were seen only as future general practitioners, possibly working part-time — but this had been back in the 50s.

In general, prejudice against women is hard to prove. Those interviewed had impressions on this subject — some of them definite, some of them tenuous, elusive: some were convinced that they had never encountered any prejudice against women: others were ready to affirm that their own career had certainly not been handicapped by prejudice against women. But although there were some few who would wholly deny the existence of prejudice, the sum of impressions from the majority would indicate that prejudice has existed, is diminishing but is still present. Possibly, said one or two, men are still prejudiced but have realised this is not socially acceptable so they keep quiet about it. Some others suggested that prejudice may be re-emerging as a result of the economic difficulties of the present. In the past, one woman had been reassured by her professor that it didn't matter if she lost her job, she had her husband to support her. Nowadays in that same department, men interviewing candidates for a post may tend to try to judge which applicant 'needs' the post — i.e. has a family to suppport: a married woman would not be regarded as in need in this way.

Yet there was general agreement that the university is probably more liberal than the outside world in its attitude towards women. Those who had worked in other occupations before coming to university teaching had had evidence of anti-women prejudices: one had suffered severely from this in her first job in industry where male technicians were not willing to work for a woman: another noted similar prejudices against women at a lower rank in industry than her own, though she did find regional differences in this respect. In commerce, one had found being a secretary rather restful: she had been brought up to consider women inferior and in offices female secretaries 'know their place'. Another had been faintly amused by seeing a token woman in the management of a publishing firm when the whole structure of the firm was heavily male dominated and male chauvinistic. In the medical profession outside the university similarly there had been experience of considerable prejudice against women. Within universities and outside university structures, however, it was noted that in some instances there could be prejudice not against women but against people who were not medically qualified but were working in a medical area: women might come into the latter category.

Within the university it was clear to many women that in committees 'the ground rules are established by men'. Men dominate in such committees, numerically, and metaphorically, because men are more often in superior positions. Common Rooms tend to be male dominated too. Generally, the university is a 'man's world' and the old boy network is influential.

If we survey the incidents which people did recall as possible instances of discrimination it has to be kept in mind that they were not regarded as major: they were not being retailed as deep grievances. They were simply episodes where it had seemed to individuals that being a woman was a disadvantage.

In student days, for example, one had been refused as a Ph.D. student by one professor on the grounds that married young women went off and had babies: she coped with this problem simply enough by finding another supervisor. Earlier, another had been refused permission to do a Ph.D. because she had only a 'war ordinary' as her first degree: more effort might have been made for a similarly handicapped man. One had been counselled to take a teaching post before completing the writing-up of her Ph.D. thesis: her male tutor said she could always complete it later, possibly while she was pregnant — she too was a young married woman at the time. (Admittedly the tutor himself had postponed writing-up his own thesis.) Another had missed some time through illness during her first degree final year: the advice given by a male professor as to what work needed to be done for the exam was misleading.

When making applications for posts two had been warned by their professors that they would probably not be appointed, one — in 1963 — because she was a married woman, and one, much more recently, because she was a young woman who might get married. This was not necessarily an indication of personal prejudice on the part of these professors: but it was a discouraging comment even if the professor was reading accurately the mind of his fellows on the appointing committee. One, however, was advised by her professor to withdraw from a shortlist because she was pregnant at the time: he said there was a good field, she might well be unsuccessful and he could arrange to have her appointment renewed so that she could try again for a permanent post in a year's time. She did withdraw: she was appointed on the second occasion — though she was again pregnant then.

Some of the group had been unsuccessful at interviews for posts but, as we have noted, it is impossible usually to judge the reasons for such failure and they did not attempt to do so. One observed that she had had four interviews: on three occasions she got the job: on the fourth, another woman was appointed. In one case, however, the woman had been convinced that the professor simply did not want to appoint a woman: on that occasion no appointment was made. In another case, the woman heard later — whether reliably or not — that the professor concerned simply would not have a woman in his department. One woman commented that her jobs came to her through people who knew of her work personally: when she applied for jobs she was unsuccessful, though in fact she has had a very distinguished academic career.

We have already noted that some professors had been slow to encourage a woman to move from a research post to a permanent lectureship: on two such occasions, the personal relationships had been excellent and the women did not see this as an act of discrimination against them as women yet it could have had its origin in the view that getting established on the academic ladder was less important for a woman than a man. Another woman had noted that in one case where a woman and a man candidate for a post seemed equally good, the man was given the lectureship and the woman offered a research appointment. One woman felt that she had suffered, possibly through circumstances rather than deliberate prejudice, in that she had been assured that taking on the wardenship of a student residence would not count against her academic promotion: but in the course of time this assurance was apparently forgotten.

One woman said she had observed that in many cases it is a female senior lecturer who runs the department and does most of the work while the male professor enjoys the prestige and goes off, without concern, to give lectures and attend conferences abroad. Meanwhile the female senior lecturer does not get on with her research and publications. But, she added, this is a choice which the female makes in such cases: the responsibility is hers.

There is thus little evidence of active discrimination against women in the experience of the group. Nevertheless, those who had achieved seniority did believe that there had certainly been prejudices in the past and they were somewhat astonished at their own success. Some of them shared with younger members of the group the view that to counter conscious or unconscious prejudices when appointments are made, a woman has to be better than her male rivals.

Again one recalls that these are the women who have been appointed. It is impossible to know whether others have been refused appointment because of discrimination against women.

Whether prejudice operated in overt action or more subtly, there were various personal interactions in which women were particularly conscious of being in a minority. Many had experienced the situation of being the only woman in their department or on committees but, after the initial strangeness of the situation, had adjusted comfortably to it. One remarked that in some gatherings being a woman meant that people took the trouble to talk to her socially, as a newcomer: a man would probably have been left to make his own way. But it was also noted that at such social gatherings there was a tendency to expect the woman to pour out the tea and generally fill a distinctively feminine role.

The solitary woman in a department seemed sometimes to profit by the chivalry of her male colleagues and rather enjoy the situation. Sometimes such a woman might feel that it would be pleasant to have a female colleague to talk to: but in some instances she could at least find female companionship among female technicians or postgraduate students. As one woman remarked, having a woman on appointing committees would not necessarily lead to women being appointed: some 'solitary' women in university departments come to enjoy their own rarity value.

Initially, however, the woman in university teaching may have more difficulty than a man in establishing her credibility. More than one woman found that when she was to address an all-male audience she took special care with her preparations, making sure notes, visual aids, etc. were in good order. One found that as a rather shy student in a male field of study she had tended to be over-looked during teaching sessions, she received less teaching than her male peers. There are even problems about dress: one noted that when she simply followed the current fashions for young women, it took quite a time before she could over-come the 'dollybird' image which her male colleagues and students formed of her.

There are too problems about gossip. A man and a woman working on a research project may be much in each other's company and may indeed develop a close relationship with each other: comment by colleagues may well misinterpret this relationship. Newcomers to a department, if male, may be invited out by their male colleagues: a woman is less likely to receive such invitations. Wives too may be somewhat suspicious of their husband's female colleague. But of course such problems affect both males and females in any social group. But one young woman did feel that because she was a young and reasonably attrac-tive woman in a department otherwise male, student speculation about personal relationships tended to focus excessively on her. There is too the irritation of paternalism when older men are dealing with an attractive young woman lecturer: possibly this attitude can be advantageous up to a certain point, it was recognised, but it remains unsatisfactory.

And of course there are the casual remarks made by men. There is the instance of men hearing of the appointment of a woman to a formerly all-male depart-ment and asking whether this person really can be qualified for the job. There are slighting remarks about women in general which most of the women feel they can take in their stride, very often considering them part of the general personality of individual colleagues rather than an expression of hostility or even of seriously held views. One recalled with some amusement the remark of a male colleague in one of her former posts: 'I've nothing against academic women really, I just wouldn't want to marry one'.

In departments where there was only one woman or women were in a very small minority, the situation might in the past have been affected by the anti-feminism of a now retired professor but in the present there was no policy against appoin-ting women and no unpleasantness for the lone females. Indeed in some cases the men in the department were positively anxious to give new appointments to a woman — partly as a 'token' but also partly because a woman seemed likely to be specially useful as a counsellor to students. (Certainly in some cases such a counselling role was attributed to the woman member of the department: women students in particular seemed to find it easier to bring personal problems to her: though men students also often appeared to find the woman member of a depart-ment more approachable). One woman who was the only female member of staff in her subject remarked that she had seen the applications for a post lately adver-tised in the department and she considered that the qualifications of the female applicants were really not so good as those of males so she could not honestly recommend trying to appoint a woman.

Those women who had participated in selection procedures had not perceived any discrimination against women candidates.

Two or three women thought that there *should* be discrimination against at least some women. They had in mind married women who apparently expected everyone else in the department to fit in with their domestic arrangements or who thought that they should be excused some departmental tasks — thus putting an additional burden on their colleagues — simply because they had family responsibilities. One young woman who was concerned that women should not be discriminated against was worried by such behaviour, especially on the part of a senior woman colleague since she felt it gave women generally a bad name. One instance she mentioned was a woman who took *three* months' holiday in summer rather than the one month which would have been regarded as customary. It was suggested in one discussion of discrimination that there is a kind of positive discrimination *for* women in the fact that at a time when many university teachers are worried about finding themselves redundant a woman can go off for a year of maternity leave in the confidence that her post will be waiting for her when she gets back. One woman said that she would be worried about appointing a young woman in the present circumstances when a post might be frozen or lost if its holder gave it up: so if a young woman decided to have a child and stay at home to look after it — and women with children should stay at home to look after them — the department was in danger of losing the post. She would not propose to discriminate against women: she would appoint a woman, all other things being equal: but she would feel more confident in appointing a man.

This matter of maternity leave and family responsibilities is one to which we shall return shortly for it is a major consideration and many women had much to say on the topic. But so far as discrimination against women is concerned it is clear that these university women teachers are not going round with a chip on their shoulders. If asked about it, they may bring to mind an instance in which discrimination may have operated against women though it is only exceptionally that they think they themselves have suffered by it in the university world. They consider that attitudes are changing and that such prejudices as there have been are diminishing — even if a few think they have simply gone underground and may, in times of economic stringency, re-emerge. At the same time universities continue to be mainly male-oriented in structure and in policy-making. Nevertheless, in everyday work, women are happy and accepted in relationships with colleagues and students (apart from an occasional minor irritation which may be as much a matter of personalities as of gender). For those in senior or isolated positions the role of 'honorary man' is easily accessible and has a certain piquancy.

Feminist Organisations

Given the foregoing circumstances and views, it is possibly not to be expected that many of the group would be active in feminist organisations. On the whole, the women interviewed were not so involved. In one of the universities a committee set up by Senate to investigate the position of women in that university had roused considerable general interest and some of those interviewed had been members of that committee. Thus attention had been drawn to various factors which can affect women's chances of progress in their careers. Some of the women had been and were actively engaged in trying to achieve provision of creche facilities in the university or had been engaged in setting up alternative facilities to solve child-care problems. A few were also participating in small groups concerned with the situation of women: but no one claimed membership of a major feminist organisation working for improvement of the status of women in general.

This does not indicate an absence of concern or general unwillingness in principle to be involved in work for the betterment of women's status. Certainly some of those interviewed regard themselves as strongly feminist in outlook. Some had been active members of a women's organisation at an earlier stage in their career. But a degree of disillusion with the activities of organised women's groups seemed to have affected those who were earlier active in them: one woman, not regretting her earlier participation but no longer engaging in it, suggested that perhaps a woman ought to do her 'national service' in such groups — i.e. give some period of her life to working in and with them, but only for a limited period of time. The most general reaction was that probably a woman works most effectively for the advancement of women by being very good at her job; thus convincing colleagues how effective women are in university teaching and providing a role model for women students. She may also be able usefully to advise women students about their career planning.

Reinforcing this view is the fact that the women already find their time very fully occupied. Those who have family responsibilities certainly would be reluctant to add another activity to occupy their 'leisure' hours: children and husband may already feel that the woman gives too much of her time to work and too little to them. Or work itself may occupy evenings and weekends. The woman may feel that she wants some time for other and more relaxing aspects of living: to spend time with her friends: to enjoy various hobbies — domestic, athletic, artistic, musical; to garden, to go sailing (this last was quite a popular diversion, though membership of a society interested in paddle steamers seemed unique). There is occasionally a suggestion that women are less narrow-minded in interests than men: certainly some of the group found outside interests important though others seem to be fully occupied with work and, possibly, family.

Allied to these counter-influences is the critical reaction of some women to what they perceive as aspects of some feminist organisations. They criticise the stridency with which demands are put forward; they think that some of the demands made are unreasonable and that sometimes excessive privileges for women are being claimed. Such aspects, together with the verbal aggression of some organisations, seem to them likely to be counter-productive, arousing hostility in men who would otherwise be helpful and sympathetic. No support was found for that interpretation of feminism which expresses hostility to men in general, wanting to re-create what is seen as a basically wrong world and blaming all defects on men.

Thus organised feminist movements are not supported by the group though a number have had temporary involvement with them and some still have a slightly guilty feeling that perhaps they should be more active. Some recognise that while the situation of women in general still needs reform, they themselves have been fortunate enough to enter a profession in which equal opportunities are given. Some point out that they themselves are liberated women. And a few take the robust view that if a woman is really determined she can achieve any position she wants, especially in university teaching.

Nonetheless there is considerable feminine solidarity in the group. They are concerned that women should have equal opportunities and equal rights: they hope that the situation will continue to improve in universities. The majority are quite clear that the stereotyped woman's role of housewife would not suit them. They want to have a career outside the home and they enjoy their professional work — though they would not wish to suggest that women who opt for the housewife role should feel guilty. While they would like to see changes in the male domination of university authority and government they find that with few overt instances of discrimination against women there are few clear lines of counter-action to follow. The solution of getting on well with the job continues to commend itself: and that is a solution likely to occupy fully the time and energy of any woman university teacher.

Marriage and Family

The possible influence of marriage and family in determining a woman's career in university has already been referred to more than once. There has been in university teaching as in school teaching a change in the attitude of employers to married women and an increase of the proportion of married women in employment. It is difficult to know how great the change in attitudes has been: one woman professor recounted how when she went for interview for a lectureship in the 50s she did not wear her engagement ring and she concealed the fact that she was going to be married in a few days' time: she was convinced that knowledge of her imminent marriage would have barred her from the appointment which she was in fact given. Another woman has noted that phone calls about women candidates today tend — if the woman is young — to include the question 'Has she a boy friend?'. There has also been the expectation that a woman will retire, if not on marriage, then certainly with the arrival of the first child: and in that university which had, until the 60s, a 'regulation' that a married couple could not both work in the same department, the expectation was that the woman would resign on marrying.

Although the university woman teacher is no longer expected to have to make an absolute choice between career and marriage there are obviously still some lingering attitudes — even among unmarried women university teachers — that she should be, at least for their younger years, at home with her children.

In fact it would appear that the proportion of married women among university teachers has increased. Sommerkorn, researching in 1963-64,[14] made a deliberate effort to include married women in her sample: she quoted a Robbins Survey of University Teachers as stating that only 34% of women university teachers were married, compared with 83% of male university teachers. In the present sample of women interviewed the marital status was as follows:

Single	24
Married	28
Divorced or separated	7
Widowed	1

The proportion of unmarried women here (40%) corresponds fairly closely to the proportion of unmarried women in the group of 160 who returned questionnaires, 38.5%, though one cannot be certain how representative the group of those who returned questionnaires was in this respect — the title Dr. in university lists conceals marital status. The proportion of divorced or separated women among those interviewed was perhaps a bit high — 11.6% compared to a questionnaire proportion of 7.5% — but the total numbers are small. One should perhaps note that three of those interviewed mentioned they were co-habiting and others may have been doing so though they did not choose to give this information. There was also one unmarried mother.

Even with this apparent increase in the proportion of married women — and one would of course need to have evidence from other universities to find if it is general (Szreter[15] has produced some evidence to indicate that it is) — the groups interviewed in France, Finland and East Germany included a rather greater proportion of married women. The sub-group of single women among university teachers would seem to be rather larger in the United Kingdom and in West Germany than in the other countries visited — assuming again that the universities visited can be taken to be representative of their country generally. The family sizes were these:

one child	8
two children	13
three children	3
four children	2

The distribution of the children's ages tended to be bi-modal, the majority being in the pre-school and 5-12 age groups: there were rather few teenagers but a sizeable group now in higher education or established in adult life. But conclusions cannot be drawn as to typical family size since some of the women have not yet begun a family and some may have an additional child or children. One could comment that the age of child-bearing is probably later for university women teachers than for the population in general: the figures for the interview group show the majority as having their children between the ages of 25 and

31

29: a few have had their children in the earlier 20s: six have had their children when over the age of 30, some indeed in the later 30s. It is certainly an important factor in such women's family planning when they have to decide whether to postpone their first child until they have acquired further academic qualifications or an established post: or postpone a second child because of a crisis in their department or unusually heavy demands on them in their work during the coming year. Three of the women did feel that they had perhaps left child-bearing rather late. But again social pressures come in. One young woman, deliberately waiting till she had completed a further qualification before having a baby, found that people did ask when she was going to begin her family.

Responsibility for children may also come through marrying a man who has children from an earlier marriage: university women teachers perhaps tend to marry rather later than average. Certainly two women in the group had acquired responsibility for teenage children through marriage and one, after divorce, had single-handedly brought up her erstwhile husband's son by an earlier marriage.

Children have to be cared for: and they make the organisation of meals and the running of the home considerably more complicated. While one woman had taken a break from work of three to four years when her first child arrived and one had been able to work professionally, part-time, at home (this was before she entered university teaching), others had their first child or later children while engaged in research work which made division of their time and attention easier. But in practically every case, some helper with housework, or with the children, or with both had been employed and was being employed. Eight women had employed full-time nannies and found this satisfactory, though one did comment that a trained nanny will undertake only a limited number of tasks in the house. Others had used the services of a child-minder: one indeed combined with other women in the university to employ a child-minder to look after a small group of children, having her home registered as suitable for child-minding. Thirteen had some form of domestic help, for varying numbers of days during the week, the helper sometimes helping to look after the child or children too. Another woman had had a series of au pair girls. As the children grew, two women found their university child centre very helpful: five sent their children to nursery school. At a later age, children in two families were sent to boarding school, not simply as a way of having them looked after but because the parents thought this form of education preferable to what was locally available. One woman had many problems solved by her husband's decision to give up his own employment and stay at home and look after their baby.

Employing people in these various ways was recognised as being expensive: two women commented that for some years their own earnings were completely spent in paying for the domestic help: but this 'investment' had been seen as satisfactory by both husband and wife. No great difficulties had been found in obtaining suitable help though of course there had been problems of choosing people who would be acceptable and compatible — one husband was reported to be particularly proud that his professional judgment had led to what proved to be the right choice from among various applicants. The present unemployment situation, it was noted, was likely to make it even easier to find women looking for work of this kind. Yet there was quite a lot of divergence in the amount of domestic help which women employed, depending partly on home circumstances and partly, so far as can be judged, on personal attitudes towards housework, cooking and the rest. One mother of four children remarked that women tend not to recognise how much modern machines and processes can help in coping with housework: women who are at home all the time believe that a house requires more time and effort than it really does.

This point of view was shared by some of the unmarried women. Their attitudes to work in the home varied. One found she was obsessive about housework and found domestic occupations rather therapeutic: but rather more claimed to do only such housework as was necessary and two of them had a 'cleaning lady' to help with this chore. Attitude to housework was at times ambivalent: one explicitly said that she felt guilty if she gave time to it and guilty if she didn't. These were the women who were living on their own. Others were living with parents or had lived with an elderly parent, more often the mother, until the parent died. This arrangement did seem to have some advantages in providing someone to cope with the housekeeping, until old age or illness made looking after the parent another demanding task. One woman commented ruefully on the years she had spent not only as a dutiful daughter to be called upon for company and help but as a dutiful niece or friend's daughter at the service of a succession of elderly people. As we have already noted, another had missed over a year of work outside the home during her mother's terminal illness. It was felt by some of the older women that society still expected them to be ready to give family assistance of this kind: and that they were also expected — since they were not married — to be free to give additional time to departmental duties, to administration, to coping with students. One remarked on the feelings of envy that the single woman can have as she pictures male colleagues going home to domestic comforts for which someone else is reponsible. But others were rejoicing in running the flat or small house that they had bought or were buying for themselves.

From what has been said about the employment of domestic help by women with families, it will be deduced that the husbands of university women teachers tend to be also in well-paid (relatively well-paid) occupations. Many are also in university teaching, a few in the same department. Others are in the learned professions, in medicine, law, dentistry, social work, educational psychology. A few are 'in business'. In many instances the couple met during their student days or through professional work. One woman remarked that she had been determined that the man she married would be one with a first-class honours degree (in the event she married a man with two firsts). Whether there has been equally conscious determination in seeking highly educated husbands in other cases cannot be known. But there is a general impression of assortative mating so far as level of education is concerned, whatever the original social class background of the spouses may have been.

On a more important level, although husbands were not very generally reported as taking an equal share of domestic responsibilities — though some were said to be interested in cooking and good at it — they were almost universally reported as supportive of their wife's career. Many women commented on their good fortune in having an understanding husband, though in one case a wife described her husband as a male chauvinist — to whom she was strongly attached. In another, a wife whose husband had had a previous marriage was discovering that in fact he did not agree with her that she should continue her professional work: she had thought they were agreed on this point before they married but now it appeared this was not so. Such a case serves as a reminder that women whose husbands feel strongly against a wife's career may retire and so fail to be represented in the group studied: one can study only the survivors — or those who have survived so far. Generally the group did not give the impression of being likely to have their professional career threatened by husbands' attitudes: but the situation is complex in that a woman who is concerned about her career is likely to take a prospective husband's views about it into account before deciding to marry (though, as in the case above, views may be misunderstood or misinterpreted). It should be added that cases of divorce did not seem to have been due to a clash of opinions on the career question: the circumstances of individual divorces or separations were not enquired into but career interests apparently were not causes of breakdowns of marriages: even though one woman thought her career interests — accepted by her husband — might have had some share in deciding her not to continue a marriage. One woman commented simply that she was not the kind of person who should have married — she was a 'loner'.

Husbands' and wives' attitudes are highly important with regard to one aspect of the university teacher's career — mobility. In the past it has often been assumed that the wife will move with her husband wherever his career takes him. Some wives in the present sample had followed this tradition. One noted that when first married she assumed that her own career was secondary so her first jobs (not university teaching) were determined by her husband's position: she thought about her own career seriously, she said, about ten years after she should have done. Another, because of her husband's moves, was now in her fifth job. In two other cases the husband's move to a university city had brought his wife into a university post which happened to be available and in fact suited her very well: but in one of these cases at least, the wife would expect to give up her post again if the husband's career plans required this (one later did so).

In general it was recognised that marriage did limit mobility for a variety of reasons, not simply because of an automatic decision that the wife would go where her husband's job was. In fact, some couples had reached an agreement that at the outset of their careers they would go wherever a job was first offered to one of them: and two husbands had been willing to change jobs to accompany their wives to another place — here it does seem to be important whether the husband is in an occupation where jobs are relatively easy to find. There is of course the possibility of commuting and for a period of three years one couple had survived this — the wife travelling considerable distances at the weekends to rejoin her husband. Thus couples living within travelling distances of other universities have an advantage, especially if both are in university work or even in the same subject area. But mobility for women — as for men — is also affected by the degree of specialisation within their subject or the popularity of their subject. Some subjects are taught in only a small number of universities (and such numbers may be further reduced if UGC or government policy persists in its present course) and some specialisms, in medicine for example, may have Chairs in only a few universities. Hence the number of places where promotion can be found is strictly limited. If these places are at a considerable distance from where the family is actually living — and where the spouse is employed — it may seem undesirable to apply there. Thus the woman — or the man — settles ambitions at the level of a senior lectureship or readership: and may occasionally be fortunate if the university awards a personal or titular Chair. An established Chair remains out of reach in such cases.

Economic considerations also affect mobility. Where married university women teachers are concerned, the family budget is adjusted (almost invariably) to two salaries. As more than one woman pointed out, it simply would not be sensible to make a move if it meant reverting to life on one salary: an increase in pay for one partner would not compensate the loss of earnings of the other. Yet if both partners are in university work or even in the same department, the chances that both will be appointed to the same university in another place are small (though there have been cases where a husband has made acceptance of a post conditional on the availability of a post for his wife). Job-sharing is not yet common: and it would not solve the economic problem. So, as one young wife cheerfully put it, she and her husband in the same department envisage working on peacefully and happily where they are until the time comes for a move to the local crematorium.

There are of course also concerns in some families about the effects that a move would have in the children's education. If the children are coming to a crucial point in school work, and are settled in a satisfactory school, a family move seems undesirable.

Children and career

Children in fact have a variety of effects on the university woman's career. We have seen how the practical side of child-care may be coped with by the employment of various kinds of help and by using creche or nursery school facilities. Domestic tasks may be similarly alleviated: but as various women pointed out, employing help or having a husband who takes a share in child-care and/or domestic work may not be a complete solution to the married woman's problems. The responsibility of planning and organising in these respects is going to remain with the woman. Even beyond these practical arrangements children do affect working hours and working rates. One woman recalled how, when her children were at school age, she had had to work late at nights to get on with her university work. It was a good time but hard. A young woman remarked that her life at present was lived in three-hour sections: she was breast-feeding her baby and her other work had to be fitted into this timetable. She was, she said, becoming quite expert in knowing what she could and could not do the day after a sleepless night. Another woman estimated that her first baby had increased the time required to complete her Ph.D. thesis from an expected 3 years to 4½ years. Others estimated that a baby slowed down work by a year. For another, her research seemed to have stood still during eight years while she coped with the immediate requirements of her university post and brought up her children. A less extensive loss of working time had affected one woman when her son broke his leg — her whole summer's work (i.e. her research and writing) was thrown out. The number of children obviously is important too: one young mother found she could manage well with one child: a second might be too much.

Yet in other cases, women seemed to have fitted in babies and the care of children with no perceptible interruption to work or research activities. The effect of caring for children may depend on the type of research the woman is carrying out. If she is working in Arts or social sciences or Law and can make progress by reading documents, then combining looking after a baby or young children for part of the day with reading and writing-up her work may be quite possible. But if she is engaged in scientific or medical research access to laboratory or clinical facilities is more difficult to arrange: it may be necessary for her to be away from home at specified times, for a considerable period of the day. In such cases, research is more likely to suffer — or the woman has to accept sharper limits on the time spent with her family. These factors seemed to have made a difference in a number of cases though personality also was clearly influential. Not all could be like one woman who said that she had simply been 'sufficiently ruthless, selfish and cruel' to ensure that her children fitted into the pattern of her own and her husband's way of life.

For the first months of the child's life at least, maternity leave is highly important. It has been the subject of much debate in many universities lately and although universities normally provide more than the legal minimum of leave there are considerable variations in the arrangements made by individual universities. But a good many of the women interviewed had had their children in years when maternity leave was not automatically or legally available. In times past such a provision would have seemed to some of these women unimaginable. Only the younger women in the group, having children in recent years, have benefited from the new arrangements. Even so, some of them have deliberately planned their babies for the summer months when it is easier for a woman to spend time with a baby without interrupting the work routine of her department — though again this obviously depends on the type of department. Exam marking, for example, can be carried out at home, even with a small baby to attend to. There are no regular classes to be taught (in some subject areas). Some of the women had continued working right up to a few days before the baby's arrival and had returned to work within two or three weeks. Yet of course planning to have the baby at a convenient time can prove ineffectual eventually if the woman has to rest or is ill during the months preceding the baby's arrival. When the baby has arrived, breast-feeding can be a complication in the return to work. If the departmental timetable is sufficiently flexible and colleagues are willing to re-arrange their timetables to help (some may do so grudgingly), there are no great problems: or, as at least one mother had done, the woman can bring the child into the university department with her. In such circumstances breast-feeding can continue as long as the mother wishes. Otherwise existing regulations for those returning to work after the stated length of leave would tend to limit breast-feeding to three months. One woman felt strongly that regulations should be adjusted to take this problem into account.

Maternity leave can be considered from at least two points of view, that of the woman concerned and that of her colleagues in the university. Most of the women who had had or would apply to have maternity leave were much concerned not to upset the smooth working of their departments: they were willing — indeed anxious — to continue with whatever work they could — advising students, marking, reading, writing — even when technically on leave. In some cases it was felt that colleagues in the university did not fully appreciate the amount of work that women had continued to do in such circumstances.

But such consideration for colleagues is not necessarily universal. Some women had noted cases where maternity leave had been claimed and used in what seemed a totally selfish way, to the detriment of colleagues. One extreme case cited was that of a woman who had a year off for maternity leave: returned to work for a term: and went off for a further year of maternity leave. The effects of such leave on colleagues must depend on the size of the department and on departmental structure. Ideally, replacement workers should be brought in by the university during such times — one former nurse noted how much simpler the situation was in that profession when replacements could be readily obtained: but money is not always available for such purposes in universities and if the woman is highly specialised in her skills or field of work, replacements are hard to find, especially for a short-term appointment. So while a woman has maternity leave colleagues may have to take on extra work: or a given research project may be delayed until her return. There is the further possibility that the woman may decide not to come back after a period of leave — or indeed may decide to resign when she has a child: and in such circumstances the post she has had may be 'frozen' or lost as a general economy measure. It is such considerations that led some women to claim that the demands made for maternity leave were counter-productive: they reduced women's chances of being appointed in the first place. And one young woman who was much in favour of maternity leave provisions yet admitted that, having seen the disruption caused in her father's department by maternity leaves, she could understand why he was unwilling to appoint women in future. An older woman who had suffered some disruptions of the same kind in her department — a technician's post had been lost because the woman went off and decided not to come back — felt that the campaign for maternity leave could backfire. Another senior woman felt that those women who opted for the year off imposed a considerable burden on colleagues, especially since staffing was already reduced to a minimum: men were becoming disenchanted with the situation, and sympathetic as she was to the maintenance of women's rights, she could not see what the ideal solution here is. On the other hand some members of the group pointed out that men too can be absent for various reasons and impose burdens on their colleagues. They were very strongly in support of maternity leave and were disposed to maintain that having had maternity leave should not affect applications by women for study leave — i.e. having had maternity leave recently should not put the woman to the back of the queue for study leave.

The complaint about selfishness in demanding maternity leave — a few of the women thought that it would be more fitting for the mother to retire from university work for a period of time while the children were young — extended in some cases to criticisms of married women who seemed to expect colleagues to take on various administrative and other tasks in the department while they hurried off home, allegedly to cope with their family responsibilities. Some of the women with children were much aware of such potential criticism and had gone out of their way not to incur it. They had been extremely careful not to claim privileges because they had children to see to: indeed one said that she had practically never mentioned her children while she was in the university. Yet one young married woman had observed that in fact it is more likely to be her male colleagues who light-heartedly, with no apparent guilt feelings, take time off in the middle of the day (from a department whose hours of work are rather rigidly fixed) to go and ferry their children to various engagements — or to have their car serviced — or to play golf. On the other side it was remarked occasionally that those who do not have children to cope with can be inconsiderate in the times that they choose for having departmental meetings in the university.

Social traditions and child rearing

These controversies bring to attention one of the important factors for the university woman teacher who has children: her own feelings about the amount of time she is or is not giving to them. Society traditionally has stressed the need for the mother to be at home, especially with young children. A few of the older women without children agreed with this view. And spontaneously a number of the women had in fact wanted to be with their children during the infant years: some were glad that they had been able to stay at home, or at least to work part-time, at this stage and one who had continued to work full-time rather regretted having missed so much of her children during the early years. One woman was at present holding a part-time post because when she began her family she decided that she could not continue to hold her job full-time. (This decision had seemed to some of her colleagues excessively conscientious: she could, they said, have 'adjusted' her work to her changed circumstances. She felt still that she had made the right decision though a change of head of department had meant that the arrangement originally made as to what parts of the work she would be asked to do had been altered and her allocation of duties was now less convenient than she had expected.) It seemed to her that the department had certainly benefited in having acquired — with part of her former salary — help which added up with her part-time post to more than one complete lectureship.

In earlier years, in the 60s for example, some of the group had certainly been made aware of the opinion of colleagues and acquaintances that they were not doing their duty by their children. Continuing to work was regarded as selfish and unfair. While attitudes in society have changed with respect to working mothers, the former view continues to be held by some people. Possibly it may depend to some extent on the neighbourhood where the family lives. In some opulent suburbs it may be regarded as odd that the mother goes out to work: in others where many professional people live — or among children's schoolmates — the fact that mother goes out to work is taken for granted: some children feel a certain reflected glory from their mother's professional achievements. (Though one woman had found that her daughter, comparing her with women who did not have a dual role, thought she had a much less attractive way of life.) Something may depend too on whether the woman's husband is in a profession or occupation where working wives are still not common. And in neighbourhoods where women stay 'at home' the working mother may sometimes feel a slight pang of envy for those who can enjoy morning coffees and daffodil teas: just as the busy working mother recognises that her way of life does not allow for the leisurely lunch-time drink in the common room or extended coffee break which some colleagues enjoy.

Social traditions may lead to guilt feelings — one woman commented that she had not yet met a working mother who did not suffer from such feelings. However sure a woman may be that she is doing the right thing in opting to continue her professional career, awareness of social traditions and expectations can make her question whether in fact she is right. Especially she asks herself whether the children have suffered by having a mother out at work. One recognised that her child would certainly have liked to see more of her during the school years. Yet the conclusion these mothers came to was that their children — so far as can be reasonably judged — had not suffered and were not suffering because of their absence. Their children had grown up well or were growing up well: they were pleased with their children's development. Some pointed out too that having a working mother can develop greater independence on the part of the children: they are less likely to be 'clingy', they learn to fend for themselves. One, however, had made a rule that at home she did not talk about her work: family conversation was on subjects of interest to the whole family.

Yet while a few suffered from feeling guilty in both environments — at home because they were not getting on with professional work, in the university because they were not at home — others remarked on their own ability to concentrate on whatever they were doing at the moment. As one said, on reaching the university, the home environment was forgotten. She was of course available if a crisis developed at home: but while she worked, her mind was entirely on work.

Individual differences thus affect women's reactions to their dual role if they are coping with both family and professional work. Caring concern for their children is common to all: but the amount of time women feel inclined to spend with young children does vary: some of them — as well as some of the childless women — felt they would be frantic after a prolonged period of time spent at home with a child: others would rather welcome this situation for a year or so This difference affected also their attitudes to maternity leave and the choice they would make in having a short or long period free from outside work. Personality too affected reactions to social pressures. All were ready to resist these when their own judgment strengthened their resolve to combine motherhood with an outside career: but some were more hurt or worried by them than others.

Individual differences also become important when the effects of good or bad health are recognised. Some women commented spontaneously that they were fortunate in being very healthy. It clearly does take good health and sheer physical stamina to lead the highly organised and disciplined lives which the dual role demands. The health of the children also is important since it is still traditional that mothers attend to sick children and this responsibility was accepted even if, in some cases, the husbands' occupations meant that they too could participate in looking after a sick child or simply keeping the child company.

Paternity leave was a possibility which had been discussed in one university or had come to the attention of some women interviewed in the other. A suggestion had been made that when both husband and wife were employed by the university 'parental' leave might be shared between them. But there did not seem to be great interest in or support for a general policy of paternity leave.

Causes of women's minority situation in university teaching

What were the reasons given for the minority situation of women in university teaching and at professorial level?

Perhaps one popular traditional explanation should be disposed of first. One woman did say that generally women are 'less brainy': one other thought it worthwhile to state explicitly that she did not believe the situation was due to any difference in ability between men and women. None of the others thought a possible difference in ability worth mentioning.

A small number thought that the situation might be due to earlier restrictions on access of women to higher education: consequently they expected and hoped that the situation would improve in future as the effects of larger proportions of female students reached staffing figures. As we have suggested earlier, this expectation is not very solidly founded. A few others pointed out that the proportions of women employed depend to some extent on the traditions and attitudes within individual universities — Oxbridge, for example, apart from women's colleges, was considered unlikely to appoint women — and on attitudes in different subject areas. Further it was suggested that cash restraints at present impeded a reduction in the backlog of women's appointments.

By far the most commonly cited factor, mentioned in one respect or another by half the group, is the effect of family responsibilities. These are seen as interrupting the woman's career, claiming time and energy otherwise to be given to research and publication: but also offering to women a powerful counter-attraction so that wastage through marriage and family was considered a highly probable explanation for the fewness of women in university teaching. Allied to this factor was a lack of mobility and a tendency to put the husband's career first and move with him. Socialisation of females through family and schools was seen as developing a wish to take on the traditional role of women by getting married and having children.

The next most popular explanation, mentioned by one-third of the group, in a variety of forms, was discrimination against women — this, despite the relative lack of personal experience of such discrimination. The university situation was seen by some as simply part of the generally depressed status of women in society: a greater number referred to discrimination — conscious or unconscious — against women in making university appointments, especially at the higher levels: or even in organising work within departments in such a way that male staff had responsibilities likely to lead to promotion. Discrimination was thought in some cases to be more likely among older male academics and administrators: attitudes might be changing among the younger. Discrimination was also perhaps rationalised by men by various arguments about women's lesser reliability in staying in post, domestic interests, etc. Hence, two added, women had to prove themselves well above average, better than men, in order to achieve higher appointments. The same discrimination might lead to less encouragement for women to engage in postgraduate studies. Certainly, one observer asserted, while a department might be willing to appoint one or more women, it would not be willing to appoint more women than men. The most extreme statement of the discrimination view was that the university is 'a bastion of chauvinism dominated by narrow-minded and over-specialised men'.

There were a few suggestions that women have different interests from men in their interpretation of work: they give more attention to student care, they are more interested in teaching than research, they are more occupied in administrative tasks. Four thought that women are less likely to be single-minded about their university work and three affirmed that women are more interested in outside activities than men, they are less narrow-minded.

But another large group of responses centred on differences in attitudes. In various ways the group suggested that women are less strongly motivated than men to apply for university posts and to strive for professional advancement. Sometimes this lack of drive was seen as simply that 'women are not determined'; 'women don't push themselves, they have to be pushed'. Or, as one alternative had it, the situation is due to 'the rationality of women in not wanting to overstretch themselves: men go on pushing till they end up in jobs they are not capable of holding'. Or, said another critic, women can fall into a laziness encouraged by the academic life style with its lack of *overt* pressure. One woman medical had noted a kind of slackening-off in women once they had achieved their first qualifications.

But in some instances this lack of drive or ambition was seen as due to lack of expectation of success: it could be due to fear of encountering prejudice against women. Or, according to two responses, women may lack self-confidence even if they are better than their male peers. There is also uncertainty due to awareness of lingering prejudices against intellectual women: they are thought not to be socially acceptable or attractive.

There were also a few references to the problems of female participation in male-dominated committees or informal groups. One who recognised that becoming known to and accepted by others in the subject area could be helpful pointed out that this could be difficult if family commitments made conference attendance difficult and if the woman really did not enjoy late-night drinking sessions. Two others felt that women were not really involved in the political life of the university.

The situation was however interpreted as not wholly bad by one respondent. A research assistantship can have positive attractions: continuing all one's life in the one profession might be a bad thing.

Altogether, although there were some minority views and some highly original responses to the request for explanations of women's minority situation, the main weight of emphasis is on the marriage and family factor, especially the family responsibilities for children: this factor operates both objectively in determining the woman's disposition of time and thought and subjectively in providing a counter-attraction to the woman's striving for success in her career. Socialisation of women to accept the wife and mother role is noted as having affected women's thinking. And there is the third aspect of marriage and children, that it leads to wastage from the profession.

Prejudice against women is also seen as influential, taking different forms on different occasions, being more or less overt. It is noteworthy that women who generally claimed to have suffered little or not at all from prejudice in their own careers were ready to recognise it as probably still affecting the situation of university women in general. (Whether the suggestion by one woman that more women on appointing committees would improve the proportions of women appointed is realistic can be doubted in view of earlier evidence cited: and also in view of the point made by one woman that analysis of applications and subsequent appointments in one university showed that the proportion of women appointed was equal to — possibly even a little greater than — the proportion of women applicants: though this was mainly with regard to appointments to first posts and did not include internal promotions).

It should also be noted that some women give 'objective' reasons for the situation.

Attitudes are also regarded as fairly influential and there is a considerable body of opinion that women, for various reasons, are less likely than men to push themselves forward to appointments, especially at a higher level in the hierarchy.

The pattern of opinions gained from interviews was repeated in results from the total 160 questionnaire returns. The women interviewed seem to have the same views as those not interviewed when it comes to explaining the minority situation.

Conclusion

To arrive at definitive conclusions about women who teach in universities one would need to study men who teach in universities also. Some of the factors which have emerged from talking with women (and looking at their questionnaire returns) might well prove to be common to both sexes.

So far as the women interviewed are concerned, a major impression is of the variety of work done under the aegis of a university and the variety of patterns of work which make up the life of the university teacher. There are the perceptible differences in physical surroundings, the impressive machinery of some departments, the typical laboratory surroundings of others, the nonedescript Arts seminar rooms, the hospital buildings, corridors, clinics of the medical and departments, the typical laboratory surroundings of others, the nondescript Arts teaching, small group, one-to-one teaching: student groups where women are in a minority, student groups where women are the great majority and the differences in interest and aptitude of students who have chosen a subject in which their sex is a majority or minority.

There are great differences in the social interactions of departments also. Life is very different in the small, closely-knit department where people know each other and each other's work, or in the research unit of a larger department where there may be similar cohesiveness, from life in the large, rather impersonal department where departmental contacts of a social kind are rare. But it should not be assumed that the size of the department is necessarily the determining factor as to whether people enjoy the companionship of colleagues. There are, too, enormous differences in the extent to which members of one department know people in other departments of the university.

For women especially there may be some isolation if they are the only female in the department, especially if their department does not link easily with other departments or is physically distant from other parts of the university. Women then may say that they cannot judge what are the characteristics of women who teach in universities because they know only one or two such women.

Entry to university teaching also shows great variations of pattern. A goodly proportion of the group of women interviewed had not come directly into university teaching: they were, again for a variety of reasons, late starters or had interrupted careers. Thus, while there are some who are career orientated and some who have become so, many have come into the profession almost by accident and have no great ambition to achieve advancement in it, so far as promotion to professorship's is concerned.

Yet this review of their responses to questions about the minority situation probably fails to convey adequately the very real enthusiasm they bring to their work and the devotion of some of them to their research work especially. They also think about their teaching, they are concerned to make it good and to improve it, they enjoy contacts with students and are anxious really to educate them. There may however be some differences in attitudes towards the value of university teaching itself according to the subject discipline in which the individual is engaged. For those in subjects in which theory is applied — in applied sciences, in medicine, in dentistry — there is satisfaction in the balance given by the practical side of the work, in results obtained by the exercise of practical skills as well as in the development of theoretical knowledge. In some of the social sciences

— e.g. in nursing studies or community studies — there may at times be an impatience with the abstract nature of the university approach and its concentration on theoretical studies whereas the individual is seized of the importance of using knowledge for the benefit of others. In the Arts, lacking the practical component, there may sometimes be less conviction of the importance of what is being taught, even if the individual teacher is enthusiastic about the subject and eager to convey that enthusiasm.

These obviously are factors which can be important for any university teacher, male or female. Common to both also is the factor of forms of alternative employment, the difference in attitude caused by having had experience of other kinds of work and — reassuring in times of crisis in the university — the knowledge that the individual's skills could lead to (or could not lead to) employment outside the world of teaching.

But again it must be emphasised that the direction of the present research entails neglect of the fascinating topic of the kinds of research interest which occupy women who teach in universities. With many there was discussion about their own particular field of enquiry: from this it was evident how seriously committed they are to research, how important this enthusiasm is and how fascinating is the work in progress. Some are recognised leaders already in their own discipline, others will be among its leaders in future.

As to the problems from which this enquiry started, the minority position of women in university teaching, we have discovered a number of explanations, even if the weight to be ascribed to each factor cannot be determined and may possibly vary from individual to individual and from subject area to subject area.

There is some evidence of discrimination against women; there is certainly evidence that women believe women have been discriminated against in the past and may be discriminated against in the present and in the future. There is the simple fact of being in a minority situation and finding that, quite naturally, the structure of universities and policy-making procedures are dominated by men; even if, according to some women, there is no great difference in the kinds of decisions and policies likely to be arrived at by representatives of both sexes.

Discrimination may be rationalised on the grounds of some women's commitment to domestic and family responsibilities as well as to their university work. Moreover, the claims of the family may mean that the woman has not in fact as much time and energy as colleagues to get on with research and publication (even if she copes fully and conscientiously with other duties). Combining the dual responsibilities of career and family calls for much determination, organisation, stamina and self-discipline: some women may opt out and leave the profession, especially as there are attractions in being with children, as well as social pressures, which may increase because of the present economic difficulties of the universities and which would rather favour this course of action. Thus the total number of women in university teaching suffers from 'wastage' of this kind: the total reaching higher ranks in the profession may be reduced because family cares reduce academic productiveness: women may be less likely to be appointed because maternity complications are envisaged: women may originally have received less encouragement to proceed because their future was seen in terms of marriage and family. There is also the mobility problem. Certainly there is growing awareness of the need to help women to cope with domestic responsibilities and arrangements for maternity leave have been improved. But the evidence does not suggest that the problems of the dual role have been solved.

There is some evidence to suggest that the attitudes of women themselves may make it less likely that they will enter university teaching and try to achieve advancement in that career. Some of those interviewed had originally doubted whether they were able enough: some had needed the prompting of a teacher or friend to apply for a post: some still would avoid 'the limelight' and be perfectly content with continuing as they are, even at lectureship level — they enjoy the work itself.

And of course we have been looking at the responses and circumstances of survivors.

But are these the only explanations? Do they continue to seem valid when compared with the information obtained from women teaching in universities in other countries where the career is differently organised, the qualifications different in some ways — and the proportion of women university teachers a little higher than in the United Kingdom? The evidence from other countries is now to be considered.

Notes:

1. University Grants Committee: University Development from 1935 to 1947 (HMSO, 1948) p.27.
2. Department of Education and Science: *Statistics of Education 1965* (HMSO, 1966), pp. 118-19: *Statistics of Education 1975* (HMSO,1977)pp.6-8, Table 2 *University Statistics 1980* (University Statistical Record , 1982) vol.1,p.7.
3. University Grants Committee: *Returns from Universities and University Colleges in receipt of Treasury Grant, Academic Year 1961-62* (HMSO 1963), p.22, Table 5: *University Statistics 1980*.
4. Department of Education and Science: *School Leavers, CSE and GCE, 1981* (HMSO, 1981), Table C13.
5. Scottish Education Department: *Statistical Bulletin, School Leavers* (HMSO,1983), p.5,Table 6.
6. Department of Education and Science: *Statistics of Education 1972* (HMSO 1974), Historical Tables, pp.2-3, Table A.
7. *University Statistics 1980* (University Statistical Record, 1982),pp.22-3, Table 6.
8. Carnegie Commission on Higher Education: *Opportunities for Women in Higher Education* (McGraw-Hill, 1973), p.89.
9. *University Statistics 1980* (University Statistical Record, 1982) vol.1, p.51.
10. Committee appointed under the chairmanship of Lord Robbins: Higher Education (HMSO, 1963), Annex Three, App.G., p.172.
11. Ministère de l'Education, Service des Etudes Informatiques et Statistiques: 'Les principales caractéristiques des enseignants en fonction dans les établissements d'enseignement supérieur -Année 1978-1979',(Paris,1979),Note 9-34.
12. Ministry of Education: Committee Report, June, 1982 (Helsinki 1982): quoted in letter from the Ministry.
13. C. Schmarsow: 'Women in Higher Education — Some Information on the Situation in the Federal Republic of Germany', *Higher Education in Europe,* Oct.-Dec., 1981, pp. 49-54.

14. I. Somerkorn: *On the Position of Women in the University Teaching Profession in England* (revised edition of Ph.D. thesis, University of London, 1969), p.29.
15. R.Szreter:'Opportunities for Women as University Teachers in England since the Robbins Report of 1963', *Studies in Higher Education* (1983), vol. 8, no. 2, pp.139-50.

Chapter Two

Equality for University Women Teachers in Finland

Finland gave women the right to vote in 1906, one of the first countries in the world to do so. In 1972 it set up the Council for Equality 'for the purpose of promoting social equality between men and women and preparing reforms in order to increase the equality between men and women'. In 1980, as part of the United Nations Decade for Women, the government adopted the National Programme of Finland for Promoting Equality between Women and Men. The programme[1] referred to six areas in which equality was to be developed: the first listed was Education and Culture. Within this area reference was made specifically to equality education through school subjects, to developing educational material, to tutoring and vocational guidance. Reference was also made to the need 'to decrease the segregation of fields of study on the basis of sex'.

Yet in some ways, Finland would seem to be already one of the most advanced countries so far as equality in upper secondary education and entry to higher education is concerned. Women in Finland generally have been found to have a higher level of education than men in Finland and, at university level, slightly higher than that of women in other Scandinavian countries.[2] And for much of the 70s there has been equality in the proportions of males and females completing upper secondary education.[3] At present, at the end of the basic nine-year comprehensive school, girls emerge with rather better marks than boys and continue in higher numbers into upper secondary. The OECD examining team found in 1981[4] that 'pupils in upper secondary schools are 60% girls and 40% boys'. This imbalance was said to be due largely to the choices made by girls and boys as to the courses followed: opting for the more intensive levels of courses in maths and foreign languages in the basic comprehensive school means that more girls are qualified to go on to upper secondary — though changes have since been made in the options system to make the boys' chances better. Then too there is a great stress on foreign language learning in the upper secondary school and this makes it more attractive to girls. Boys, it is said, opt rather for vocational courses.

Whatever the complications at secondary level, the situation has been established for some time now that there is equality — or even superiority on the part of women — when first level higher education is concerned. Equal percentages in entry to higher education have been reached for some years now. The percentage of women among those taking their first degree in 1978-79 was 54. Thus the question of access to higher education would seem to have been satisfactorily answered.

But in Finland as in other countries the situation changes when access to still higher level qualifications is considered. The percentage of women among those obtaining the second degree — the licentiate — in 1978-79 was 22.9: and of those achieving acceptance of doctoral dissertations, 15.5%.[5]

The Programme for Promoting Equality referred to a segregation in fields of study. In this respect Finland follows much the same pattern as is found in other countries. In upper secondary school, choices of specialisation showed,[6] in 1977, girls as 99% of those specialising in textile handicraft, 70% (which is really remarkably low) in Home Economics, 80% in French, 71% in Russian but 14.8% in Agriculture, forestry and horticulture and only 1.2% in technical handicraft. Similarly — and as a natural sequence to such biases in school choices — in higher education the following situation was noted in 1977:[7]

	Percentage female
Humanities, fine and applied arts	68.8
Teacher education	69.7
Economics, law, social and behavioural sciences	53.6
Engineering and natural sciences	30.7
Health and health related courses	59.1
Agriculture and forestry	26.2

It is unfortunate that engineering and natural sciences are grouped together since it would have been useful to know what proportion there was of women in engineering: the overall percentage is not particularly good even for natural sciences alone. Some isolated figures may add usefully to the picture. In 1977, 63.9% undergraduates in Chemistry were women: but at M.Sc. level in mechanical engineering, 6.3%.[8] In Helsinki University in 1978-79, the percentage of women in Maths and Natural Sciences was 46.58:[9] but in Oulu, women were 15.8% of those studying technology[10] and in Helsinki University of Technology, the percentages of women students were for electrical engineering 4.8, for mechanical engineering 8.37 and for technical physics 7.6.[11] Thus one finds a fairly typical picture of women in the majority in the humanities, in education and in social sciences and in the minority in maths, natural sciences and applied sciences — though the percentages in the latter area are rather higher than in Britian.

Thus it would appear that although in some respects equality has been achieved in the education of males and females, there remain areas where it is still to be effected — and, as we shall see, university teaching is one such area.

So far as society outside the universities is concerned, a 1980 publication by the Central Statistical Office, at the instigation of the Council for Equality, on the *Position of Women* gave a wealth of interesting information on women's situation in education, at work and in social organisations. The information with regard to public life shows women as rather more active than in Britain — at the time of the investigation, some 25% of members of Parliament were women and a similar percentage were elected to serve at municipal and communal council level. Yet obvious weaknesses in the position of women were also evident.[12] Women did not appear as chairmen of municipal councils and were only 2% of communal councils' chairmen: as committee chairmen they were again in a minority, except in such committees as could be considered interested in 'women's fields' — temperance, Adult Education, library and cultural committees.[13] In State Committees similarly the Council for Equality reported that in 1979 56.8% of these committees had no female members and the average percentage of female members was 7.1%. Typically, while only 3.2% of committee chairmen were females, 21.9% of secretaries were female.[14] Yet women have participated actively in elections to Parliament: 74.7 of those entitled to vote in 1979 did so, as compared with 76.0% of men; women were 52.6% of those entitled to vote — and 26.1% of the candidates were women.[15] There is then some way to go before equality at this level is achieved and informal discussions suggested that the prospects of a woman becoming a party leader, or Prime Minister or President were still remote.

Women's participation in trade unions or professional associations also shows something of the expected trends. The Kindergarten Teachers' Association had 95.2% women members in 1979 but 88.9% of the union's central council were women.[16] The Union of Textile teachers had a 100% female constituency but the Association of Teachers at Technical Institutes had only 12.6% women members, 5% women in the Union's central council and no women members of the executive committee.[17] The Finnish Association of University Professors had a membership of 45 women in a total of 680 (6.6%): there was 6.9% participation of women in union meetings and 4.2% female membership of the central council: and no women members of the executive committee in 1978.[18] The Association of University Lecturers (that is, of those employed at a lower level in the university hierarchy) had however a 51.2% women membership, 38.1% participation in meetings and 42.9% membership of the executive committee.[19]

Similar structures were observed in other professional organisations, the general trend being for the percentage of females among members to decrease in the central committees and especially in the executive committees. Thus, for example, the Teachers' Trade Union in Finland was noted by the Council as having a 64.5% female membership, 25.2% of women in the union central committee, 23.5% women on the executive committee.[20]

In political parties similarly, while women may be equally or at least well represented at membership level, they fall into a minority situation in the party councils.[21] The Liberal Party apparently gave most place to women in that 42% of the membership were women and 31.9% of the party council. (One excepts here the very small Private Entrepreneurs' Party which managed 33.6% women members and 33.3% women on the Party council).

Thus in public life and social organisations women in Finland play an important part but the figures suggest they are still, in various respects, underrepresented.

In Finland as in other countries visited, there was a general agreement that the university world is more liberal in its attitudes towards women's equality than is society outside the university. Nevertheless, differences in the position of women in university teaching are apparent: and there is the same pyramidal structure as in other countries, with the percentages of women being higher at the lower levels and diminishing as top level positions are considered. Figures for 1980 showed the following distributions:[22]

	Percent women
Professors	5.7
Assistant professors	8.2
Senior Assistants	18.7
Lecturers	31.9

Bias in subject areas is again indicated by the varying proportions of women at the different levels within subject fields.[23] Thus, for humanities the percentage of female professors in 1980 was 12.1: in Agriculture and Forestry, it was, remarkably enough, 10.5% — though the total number of professors here is the smallest for any subject area: Social Sciences had 6.2%, Medicine 5.4%, Natural Sciences 4.3%. There were no women professors in Technology — though one might perhaps note that at assistant professor level, 2.6% were women. If one adds together professors and assistant professors, the percentage of females alters slightly but not, probably, significantly: for humanities it becomes 14.7: for agriculture and forestry 15.2: for Social Sciences 8.4, for Medicine 6.9, for Natural Sciences 2.8 and for Technology 1%. The same order of female representation applies at the lower levels, when senior assistants and lecturers are considered: there women reach 41.1% in humanities, 50% in agriculture and forestry, 21% in Medicine, 20% in Social Sciences, 10% in Natural Sciences and 8.1% in Technology: thus the overall percentage of women at this level is 26.3 whereas the percentage of women at professor and assistant professor level is 6.7.

The university hierarchy

To realise how women or men may reach the various levels just mentioned we have to consider the structure of university teaching as a career in Finland. As in other systems, postgraduate students or, occasionally, students who have not yet formally completed their first degree, can be invited to work for a few hours a week as demonstrators or as assistants with practical classes. As elsewhere, this can be helpful financially to students who are trying to support themselves as they study. In Finland it is all the more important financially because, while students have to pay only a small tuition fee, they are less likely than British students to have a maintenance grant. What Finnish students can obtain is a part-loan, part-grant from the state: effectually, the state guarantees the repayment of a loan from a bank on which interest charges have to be paid even during student days. When the student has graduated the loan component has to be repaid in a period twice the length of the period during which the loan was received. Some students complain that the repayment of the loan comes at a time when life is particularly difficult, financially, for young people since they are probably, in the years following graduation, beginning a family and trying to set up a home of their own.

The initial step into university teaching would be, again as in other systems, to become an assistant in a university department: frequently, the department in which the student has taken his or her major subject will invite the student to apply for a vacant assistantship. The assistantship is intended for people who are engaged in postgraduate studies for the Licentiate (the second level degree) or the Doctoral degree. Formerly, it was for a period of three years but recently the period has been extended to five years and appointment as an assistant can be renewed for a further period of five years. The allocation of teaching duties of an assistant depends very much on the department in which the young teacher is but it should leave ample time for assistants to pursue their own studies. Occasionally, it may happen in a small department that the amount of work required seems to the assistant too great to allow for satisfactory concentration on personal work. But a crisis situation is developing with regard to assistantships. Departments may not have any permanent posts to offer the young teacher and similar posts in another university may be difficult to obtain. Consequently, in some departments there may now be assistants who have obtained the doctoral degree — which is regarded as making them considerably over-qualified for the post: their appointment, once they have obtained this degree, may be renewed for further periods so that in fact it becomes practically a permanent appointment. This is not a wholly advantageous situation for the individual: but it is also not advantageous for the development of the department since new, younger people cannot be brought into its staffing. Thus, as in other systems, the situation of the assistant in Finnish universities is particularly interesting and precarious. In some cases an assistant is a well qualified person who is regarded as practically a member of the department and may indeed have not only the doctoral qualification but also that of docent (to which we shall come later). In other cases, the assistant may, after the brief period of a first appointment, go out from university teaching into some other career. Moreover, some young people may be appointed as temporary assistants, filling in for someone who has moved, for a limited period of time, to a research project: or a gap further up in the department hierarchy may have meant a temporary move upwards for the staff on lower levels. Whether a temporary assistant will eventually find a permanent assistantship and from there go further up the university teaching ladder is always highly uncertain. It is true that there is the alternative of appointment as a research assistant, with no teaching duties: but these research assistantships also have no security of tenure to offer: the individual is dependent on finding a new scholarship or appointment when the first one runs out. There is also what may be a 'waiting room' appointment, that of amanuensis, appointed to do clerical and minor administrative work in the department. Some amanuenses combine this with research but time to do research depends very much on conditions within the department. At least the position is a way of being in touch with, being known in a department and ready to profit by a temporary assistantship if one occurs.

The grade of lecturer (Lehtorit) is of people mainly appointed to carry out teaching duties, having sometimes as many as sixteen hours a week. While enjoying security of tenure, the 'lecturer' very often feels that there should be official recognition of the wish to engage in further study and research: hours of duty should be adjusted accordingly. The union of university lecturers (it is noteworthy that in the Finnish university system there is not *one* association of university teachers but a number, each representing a specific grade) has been negotiating for recognition of research as part of the official duties of this grade.

The next position, that of Assistant Professor — or, as some Finnish university people prefer to describe it, Associate Professor (by analogy with the American system) — is a tenured post: the duties are teaching and research. For appointment to this grade there is a procedure very different from that followed in British universities, a procedure employed also for the appointment of full professors. Candidates submit six copies of their published works — i.e. journal articles, monographs, dissertations, books. The relevant Faculty then appoints three experts to read these publications, to judge whether the applicant is 'competent' to be appointed at this level and also to place the candidates in order of merit. The Faculty then considers the nominations proposed by the experts, and, if the experts are in agreement, will normally move for the appointment of the applicant given first place by the experts. Normally the Minister of Education and the President will accept the Faculty's proposal. But there are, from the British point of view, additional fascinating aspects of this system. Not only have the candidates to give a kind of trial lecture — of perhaps half an hour's duration — which is assessed by the experts and Faculty members (students may be present but have no voice in the assessment) but it is also open to any of the applicants to challenge (i) the suitability of the experts proposed as assessors (ii) the decision arrived at by the experts. A candidate might, for example, claim that one of the experts proposed by the Faculty was not really competent in the subject area in question or, later, that one of the experts had not been able to judge competently of the merits of people with research interests in a rather different sphere from the expert's own: or that the experts had overlooked certain features of importance in the candidate's work. When such challenges are made, the Faculty may nominate other experts in place of those to whom objections are raised. If the decision of the experts is challenged, the Faculty must reconsider the whole case — as indeed must the Ministry, if appealed to. Occasionally, though not frequently, the decision may be reversed after such reconsideration.

The full professor is normally head of department but where there is more than one professor in a department, the headship may be given to one in perpetuity or it may change from one professor of the department to another. The head of department is responsible for deciding the use made of the funds awarded to the department by the Faculty and for the use of resources, both of material and of personnel. The full professor is also a member of the Faculty Board and of other university committees.

It is further of interest that even if a candidate is not appointed to the post sought, the fact that the candidate has been found 'competent' by the experts, even if not placed first in their order of merit, is something which is recorded in the candidate's dossier and can be referred to on subsequent occasions when the candidate is making an application for a similar appointment.

Another interesting feature of the system of appointment-making is that candidates can ask for a period of time to improve their qualifications before the experts judge who is the best applicant for a vacant professorship. Normally, candidates would ask for and receive a period of one year — a 'respite' period for the improvement of qualifications. This means that they have that time available to complete writing-up some work on which they have been engaged, to get it published, or possibly, they may present it as an additional, unpublished research report along with their publications. Occasionally, applicants may not get quite as long a period of respite as they request — they may, for example, be allowed six months instead of one year. But this naturally produces a situation in which appointments take a very long time (by British standards) to make: a period of two or two-and-a-half years in proceeding to fill a Chair is not regarded as unusual. Apart from possible challenges and periods allowed for improvement of qualifications, experts do require a certain number of months in order to read appropriately carefully the various works submitted.

A further position of interest is the position of docent. To obtain this qualification, a candidate must normally have done some additional high level research after obtaining the doctorate. The candidate's publications are submitted in the fashion just described and a trial lecture has to be given. If the candidate's application is successful, then the candidate has the title of Docent and the right to teach in the university which has accorded the title. But this is not a full-time post within the university. The docent teaches for a limited number of hours during the year and is paid for the number of hours actually taught — the docent presents a claim for payment to the university. The actual number of hours taught by docents varies considerably from Faculty to Faculty: indeed it must vary because it depends on the need of individual departments for the special knowledge and teaching which a particular docent is able to give. In some cases, where a department cannot employ a specialist in a given subject area, the docent may be called upon to give regular courses of lectures each term or each year — for example, one might provide the teaching in child psychiatry when the full-time staff includes no specialist in this area. Where the department does not have such a need, the docent may give only a small number of lectures in a term, on the docent's special interest: but attendance at such lectures will not be part of the students' regular courses. Sometimes a docent may give only one or two lectures during the entire academic year. But if the docent does not teach at all during a period of one or two years the docent must apply to the university for exemption from teaching duties, otherwise the title of docent will be forfeited.

It must be admitted that among docents there can be differences of opinion as to what the required number of hours of teaching is. Certainly any payments made for teaching do not amount to anything like a livelihood. The system is rather one by which people who are active and eminent in their professional sphere can spread their specialist knowledge more widely. In the medical profession specialists may serve much as honorary lecturers do in Britain to bring knowledge derived from their practical expertise to university students. Similarly those engaged in the exercise of other professions can bring their outside knowledge into the university world. But it may also be the case that people teaching in one university or in one department may be docents in another. The title itself is regarded as an honour: it is said that the requirement to do some occasional teaching stems from the fact that some people outside the university might well enjoy simply having the title — and using it as a reason for charging higher professional fees — without bothering to give their knowledge to university students by lectures (paid at no very high rate). The title may of course also facilitate applications for research grants.

It is, as we noted earlier, a further anomaly of the situation created by lack of expansion in the universities and the consequent absence of posts at higher levels that some people employed as assistant in universities have already achieved the honorary title of docent.

In the Finnish university system one may note also that for many university teachers there is alternation of periods devoted to teaching in the university and periods devoted purely to research. Thus after a number of years as an assistant a young university teacher may become a full-time research worker and move from one project to another, earning a living by successive research awards. Then there may be a return to university teaching, possibly at assistantship level again or, perhaps more probably, at assistant professor level. For those who have gained the rank of full professor, there is the possibility of an award by the Finnish Academy of a research professorship which is held for a period of five years and which enables the individual to devote himself or herself purely to research for that period of time. During the absence of such a person as a research professor, other members of the department may temporarily move one grade upwards, having 'acting' rank on the higher level. Thus the appointment as a research professor can be doubly beneficial — in honour and in practical terms — to the individual and to the department.

All these factors tend to suggest that in the Finnish university system the emphasis on research noted in British universities may be much more clear-cut. The place of research and publication in the university career is clearly defined. On the surface it would seem as if the methods of appointment at the higher levels would lead to more objective decision-making: they are certainly more open to public scrutiny. Yet personal factors can of course enter into the process also since applicants for a post may well be known personally or by reputation both to the assessors (though assessors from other countries may also be used) and to the Faculty receiving the application.

The groups interviewed

The University of Helsinki, the oldest, largest and — many would agree — most prestigious of the universities of Finland seemed obviously an appropriate choice of centre. The University of Oulu, in the north of the country, seemed a good representative of the newer universities of the country. It would of course have been interesting to include the technical or commercial universities but in these, perhaps not surprisingly, there seemed to be relatively fewer women at higher levels of appointment. An advantage of the docent system is that women lecturing in one university may be docents in another: thus in any one university there is some interlinking of knowledge about other places. Certainly Helsinki and Oulu provide rather fascinating contrasts in physical conditions. In November Helsinki was a place of snow and slush, wind and rain, while Oulu offered clear blue skies, sunlight and white frost on the ground. In Helsinki interviews took place — when not in women's own homes — in the traditional university buildings, some of them imposing nineteenth century edifices, others indistinguishable from the city's business blocks. In Oulu there was a mixture of traditional building for Education, hospitality in social surroundings, and the new buildings, modern, decorated in primary colours — the child's toy building set, as someone unkindly described it. The sample was again obtained in a rather random manner, in Oulu by informal contacts mainly, women telling of other acquaintances or friends in the university who could be interviewed: in Helsinki, by some such contacts and also by phoning women listed on the University staff list. (Tribute should be paid, incidentally, to the ease and friendliness with which many of these women responded to an unexpected phone call in a foreign language). An attempt was made to be put in touch with women at different levels in university teaching and in different subject areas. Once again, no one refused to be interviewed, though in one or two cases it proved impossible to find a convenient time. Since interviews had, unfortunately, to be in English one or two women opted to have with them a friend who was, they said, more competent in English. In practice the friend's services usually did not seem very necessary. The cooperation and hospitality and interest in the enquiry were excellent, consistently.

The distribution of subject areas for the groups interviewed was:

Humanities	8
Social Sciences	7
Education	6
Behavioural Sciences	2
Theology	3
Law	2
Medicine, Pharmacy	8
Maths, Nat. Sciences	4
Agric., Forestry	1
Technology	1

Thus 42 women were included in the group.

The distribution of subjects represents reasonably well the grouping of women's contribution to university teaching. It should be noted that the agriculture/forestry and the technology areas were represented by women teaching aspects of nutritional science and thus still in traditionally feminine areas.

Description of the levels at which the women were employed is complicated by the fact already mentioned that when a Chair is vacant, or an associate professorship, it takes some time to fill — or a professor may be absent on a research professorship. During this time other members of the department temporarily have a higher 'acting' rank. Quite a few of those interviewed were in fact serving at the time of interview at a higher grade than the substantive appointment to which they would later revert. It was decided that the substantive grades should be used in describing the levels of appointments, which were as follows:

Professor (including one emeritus, one titular)	8
Associate professor	8
Assistant	11
Lecturer	8
Opettaja	3
Docent	4

(Opettaja is a rank in medical faculties: it is an appointment essentially for practical work, at lecturer level.) The docents were women who had in addition a full-time professional appointment outside the university: some of the other women interviewed were docents in other universities but have been shown here according to their full-time university appointment.

The age levels showed a fairly even distribution throughout the group — it is, incidentally, interesting that in Finland university calendars provide the year of birth of members of the teaching staff. (In East Germany too colleagues are well informed about the age of others in the department and may offer birthday congratulations when appropriate: thus, e.g., *Das Hochschulwesen* publishes the names of professors celebrating their 60th, 65th, 70th and so on, birthday.) This openness must certainly facilitate calculations as to when Chairs are likely to become vacant in Finland and what the prospects associated with age are for various competitors.

The age distribution was this:

25-29	3	45-49	6
30-34	7	50-54	3
35-39	7	55-59	3
40-44	8	60-64	5

Home and Family Responsibilities

Since, in Finland as in other countries, the importance of trying to combine family and professional life was recognised widely, it is useful to begin the analysis of information with the factors relating especially to marriage and children.

The great majority of the women interviewed were married: and almost all those who were married had children — one of the three married women with no children of her own had married a man with children by a former marriage. The distribution was this:

Single	9
Cohabiting	1
Married	28
Divorced	3
Widowed	1

The figure for cohabiting has been given separately because this is how the woman described her marital status but it may well be that other single women could have described their status thus. It is also faintly possible that 'married' was sometimes used to describe a stable but unmarried relationship with a man: but on the whole it is unlikely that the women concerned woult have felt inhibited about describing their status precisely and since it is customary for cohabiting couples to marry when they have children, it is probable that the 'married' figures are accurate. The number of divorces is possibly unexpectedly small since, in Finland, the divorce rates for urban marriages had reached 40% by 1975.[24] Cohabiting has also become more common during these years. For the 20-29 year-old age group in 1975, it was estimated that 11% of men and 9% of women were cohabiting. But, given the tendency of these relationships to end with formal marriages, one would not expect to find them largely represented among the — relatively — older women of this survey.

Of the married women, the family situation was:

No children	3
One child	5
Two children	13
Three children	8
Four children	2

Such a statement of the numbers of children masks differences in career and family patterns for women teaching in universities. A major difference that seemed to emerge in the group was that between marrying young, having children, returning to study and resuming an academic career when the children had reached school age (sometimes when children had reached the middle or later school years) and 'going straight through' by getting an assistantship just after the first qualification, obtaining higher qualifications and a secure post and *then* having children. Thus there was the example of one woman who had been a school teacher until her children were adolescent: she then decided to resume academic work and, after some initial difficulty in convincing the professor in her chosen field that she was a serious and competent student, took her licentiate, obtained a post in the department and, after ten years' further study while working in this post, achieved a doctorate and a high level appointment. Similarly two other women spent a considerable period in teaching in school — one in secondary, one in primary — and bringing up a family before, in one case, being appointed a lecturer in teacher education and working on towards higher qualifications and in the other, beginning study again and gaining a higher degree by research.

This process of children first, qualifications later, could be seen at a different stage in, for example, the mother of three young pre-school children who was, as an assistant, working for a licentiateship and — presumably — eventually would work for a doctorate. In this case the appointment was temporary: the strain of coping with work and study and teaching was considerable and could prove too great: there might also arise problems about moving to another place for academic appointment since her husband's occupation might not allow of his finding a suitable post elsewhere. How many in her circumstances will not survive as university teachers? Yet two women professors had embarked on a university teaching career even later in life, when their children were already adolescent.

On the whole, a continuous career in university work did seem more secure and more smooth-running. Women who were following it or had followed it seemed satisfied with the results. One, for example, had just achieved the rank of docentship (in addition to her full-time university post) and was just awaiting her second child, having had the first after obtaining her major qualifications. Another thought a professor's advice 'Get a doctorate before you get a daughter' had been sound. Another young, married, still childless woman, had likewise just achieved her doctorate and seemed to have good academic prospects. Two of the women professors had followed this pattern though possibly less with the clear intention of choosing it than because circumstances had made it the natural path.

But of course there is the intermediate path of combining having children with teaching in university and working for higher academic qualifications. Some women in the group had done this, or were doing this, successfully. Undoubtedly this pattern imposes very hard work on the woman concerned. One mentioned that during such a period in her life she had developed the habit of a work period beginning at 2.00 a.m., because that was the time of the baby's feed and she had found it easy to stay awake then and work in the quiet of the night — and the habit had persisted after the need to feed the baby had gone. Another slept for a couple of hours after her evening period of play with the children and was then encouraged by her husband providing black coffee at 9.00 p.m. to settle to a work period then. As one woman cheerfully put it, it *is* very hard work for a woman to combine children, teaching and academic study but at that stage in her life 'it seems normal'. Another said that only now did she recognise how overworked she had been in her days as a young mother.

Nevertheless, some of the women trying to combine young children with academic work did seem to be in a precarious position. They were under stress. Some might find that their husband's comprehension of the need to study would wear thin: there were also the threats of mobility problems, to which we shall return later.

Highly important in all these considerations was the factor singled out by some of the women — health. Many commented that they — and their families — had been fortunate in having good health: and a few further noted their ability to manage with relatively little sleep. Obviously, as was pointed out, a sick child is likely to demand extra attention from the mother.

For whatever reasons it was in fact a minority in the group who had 'gone straight through' by entering university work immediately after their first degree and progressing through the various positions in the hierarchy. Thirteen of the group had had this kind of career pattern, though even here two had had a year of school teaching immediately after their first degree. Eight had followed a somewhat analogous career by engaging in research work — with research grants, assistantships or contracts — over a period of some years before coming to a university post. Twenty-one of the group had had various periods of time in other occupations — mostly in teaching in schools but also in such areas as medical practice and market research — before coming to university teaching. There was probably a tendency for the 'straight run through' to occur for women on the science side.

Housework and child-care

The problems of looking after children had differed according to age levels of the women in the group. For the older women, in earlier times, it had not been as difficult as at present to obtain domestic help: as one pointed out, in the immediate post-war era Finland had still largely a rural economy, the move to urban life was only beginning and it was possible to find young women willing to look after children. When a woman was married to a man also in professional work the cost of employing help did not place too great a strain on the family income. While some women still employ domestic help and had found it without difficulty, for younger women it is now more often a matter of finding a child care centre in the neighbourhood where the child can find a place: or possibly of leaving the child with a child-minder who cares for a group of three or four children, possibly including her own. (This child-minding system receives public funding). In one or two such instances the relationship with the child-minder was said to have been very happy, the contact having continued for a number of years with an almost 'family' relationship building up between the child-minder and her charges. One woman had solved the problem very effectively by setting up a communal child centre in the block of flats to which she and her husband moved while their children were still young. Initially this received very little state aid but after the 1973 Act public funding became more extensive:[25] the centre has continued to flourish even though the founders' own children are now of school age and no longer need it.

Here perhaps one might note the resentment felt by a divorced woman that she had been given no tax relief for payment of a housekeeper while she was working and her children were young.

Apropos of child care, the system observable in Helsinki and found in other population centres in Finland of the 'park auntie' should be mentioned. It is a system subsidised by local authorities. The park auntie is a woman who looks after a group of children — babies in prams (from 6 months on) or pre-school children (up to age 6) — in parks, squares or children's playgrounds: she is on duty normally about three hours in the morning, from 9 to 12 and for two hours in the afternoon, from 2 to 4. The system apparently works well: children are cosily wrapped up for play during the winter months though if the temperature falls very low, the service is withdrawn: and of course individual parents can judge whether it is too cold for the child to be out. But the defect in the system, from the point of view of working parents, is that someone must collect the children and bring them home for the mid-day period.

Of course there was recognition in Finland as elsewhere of the advantage of having a grandmother willing to look after the children while their mother is at work and some women did have such help. But it should be remembered here too that the proportion of women in the work force in Finland is high: women formed 46.6% of the labour force in 1977, which is rather higher than the percentage in the other Scandinavian countries at the time.[26] It is true that rather more women than men are employed part-time (12% of women as compared with 3% of men) and a major reason for this appears to be care of home and children. Thus the trend for grandmother too to be out at work affects child-care problems in Finland as it does in East Germany.

Efforts have in fact been made in Finland as in other countries to increase the availability of day-care centre places: but although the provision of such places rose dramatically between 1960 and 1978, it has done little more than keep pace with the increase in demand so that the overall proportion of children provided for in this way has not shown the desired increase. There are still priority places for low income families, for one-parent families and other disadvantaged groups. In 1975, it was found[27] that care of children as used by employed mothers took the following distribution:

	Percentage provided for
Day-care centre (full time)	11.4
Day-care centre (part-time)	13.8
Child-minding	39.3
Servant, nurse	10.6
Relative	20.9
Other family member	4.0

Jallinoja comments that the increase in the proportion of child-minding from 25% in 1970 to 39.3% in 1975 probably indicates the effect of the day-care law of 1973 which granted state allowances for this service: from the administrative point of view costs in this form are likely to be lower than in others.

Sharing domestic tasks

The amount of difficulty which the working mother with children may experience naturally depends on the extent to which her husband is ready to share the tasks of child care and of housework.

There was evidence to show that there is a trend towards greater participation by men in such domestic responsibilities. Again, there may be a difference in perception between husband and wife — in Finland as elsewhere wives are more likely than husbands to say that wives cope alone with certain household duties. Some evidence,[28] based on replies by 340 wives and 357 husbands, has been published concerning the division of household tasks in 1977. With respect to some of the most common of these the findings were:

	Wife alone	Husband & wife	Husband alone
Preparing dinner			
replies by wives	76	11	—
replies by husbands	65	15	2
Daily cleaning			
replies by wives	78	16	—
replies by husbands	59	24	1
Weekly cleaning			
replies by wives	61	26	—
replies by husbands	44	35	—
Shopping for food			
replies by wives	53	31	—
replies by husbands	39	38	—
Small repairs at home			
replies by wives	6	16	36
replies by husbands	2	11	43

A variety of other alternatives — e.g. mostly wife or mostly husband — were offered (hence percentages do not total 100) but the above figures are the most important. It might be noted that the one other area where husbands took a major part is in the payment of regular bills though responsibility here was fairly divided with payment by wives and payment by the two together.

The situation however may be slightly different in the academic world from that in the population generally. In the group interviewed it seemed possible that this also was a matter of age levels, the older men being less inclined than the younger to take a full share in coping with housework and looking after children. One woman reported amusedly that her husband could just manage to cook an egg or boil a potato for himself; but her sons had been brought up to be much more competent in the house. One observed that her son had become rather more involved in doing household tasks after her daughter noticed that the tradition of daughters helping about the house generally while sons have only a small number of specific tasks leads to considerable inequality. It was generally agreed however that men are coming to regard it as natural to share in domestic work and in coping with children; women in the group had at any rate arrived at their own division of labour with their husbands — though one reported a current demarcation dispute as to who was responsible for taking clothes to be dry-cleaned. Even so, there was the impression that women still have the heavier share of housework, especially in the older generation. Yet some at least take it lightly: standards can be flexible — 'what we don't get done at the weekend just isn't done' said one philosophically. Housework seemed to present few problems for the single woman: some rather enjoyed it. And it seemed to one at least that the single man would be on equal terms with her in this respect since he would have the same tasks — and people are not invited home to meals so much in Finland.

As to child-care, the popular survey of customs in the country generally[29] showed that in 1977 the following attributions of responsibility for looking after children were made by a group of 110 wives and 91 husbands:

	Wife alone	Husband & wife	Husband alone
Feeding children			
replies by wives	43	32	1
replies by husbands	32	37	1
Dressing children			
replies by wives	40	41	1
replies by husbands	27	48	2
Putting children to sleep			
replies by wives	40	41	3
replies by husbands	22	51	3

The differences in perception between wives and husbands remain of interest but the tendency for the wife to be more heavily involved is still clear.

Another relevant duty is that of collecting the child from whatever day-care is being used. Here, in the group studied, it was simply a matter of which partner would be free to call for the child at the appropriate time. As to another rather important aspect, caring for the child during the night, there had been some attempt by some couples to share responsibility here. One woman mentioned with some pride that it was her husband who heard the child crying in the night. Another had arranged with her husband that they would take alternate nights to get up to tend children. But another woman was doubtful whether men are as sensitive to such crying as women are: though she and her husband had agreed to take turns in caring during the night, she was always the one who actually heard the child crying for attention — she thought that possibly there is some biological reason for women's greater responsiveness here. Disturbed nights obviously lead to physical weariness and again the health of mother and children can be an important factor.

Maternity leave and paternity leave.

The birth of a child is usually regarded as mainly affecting the wife's career. But in Finland some evidence of the involvement of both partners in caring for the baby is evident in recent provisions. Allowances for maternity leave have been increased in Finland during the last two decades from 54 working days in 1964 to 174 in 1974 and then to 234 weekdays (as of 1980); that is, some nine months, with one month before the birth and eight after. The allowance paid by government grant varies accoring to the income of the family. What is remarkable in Finland — as in some other progressive countries — is that there is also legal provision for paternity leave, since 1978. The number of days' leave taken by the father is deducted from the number of days allowed to the mother: fathers are allowed 6 to 12 working days or can be granted 24 working days at the end of the wife's maternity leave. It has been found in recent years (e.g. in 1979) that every eighth father took paternity leave but the number doing so was greater in South Finland than in North Finland, and greater in cities than in country districts. This interest or lack of interest in paternity leave may be related not only to the greater sophistication of families in certain districts but may also derive from the amount of allowance payable per day of paternity leave: if the man is earning high pay, then there is a greater financial loss if he takes the leave: so men may instead prefer to 'save' their annual holiday entitlement in order to stay at home when the baby is born. In addition to the allowances and days off, future parents also benefit by a state gift of a layette for the baby or money of equivalent value.

In the group interviewed many of the women had had their children before these provisions came into operation. None was particularly interested in the full length of maternity leave, many having opted — and having admired colleagues who so opted — for a very brief absence indeed (of some five days, in one instance). Nor were instances cited of husbands who had taken paternity leave. But one or two women did mention the complications caused for employers because of women's right to maternity leave and one at least thought that she could sympathise with an employer who would, for this reason, be reluctant to employ a woman worker.

Husbands

The importance of the husband's attitudes has already been made clear. Many women commented that they had a marvellously comprehending and helpful husband. It may in fact be the case that the husband's outlook depends on whether he shares or has shared the experience of doing academic work and studying for a higher degree. As in other countries, many of the women studied had husbands who were also in university teaching or in the university world. The majority of husbands followed some kind of professional career: few husbands could be described as non-academic. Husbands were stated to be in the following occupations: 8 in university teaching, three of them in the same department as the wife: 4 medicals, at various levels of the medical profession; in a variety of other categories — clergyman, teacher, vocational counsellor, banker, judge, architect, journalist, in market research, financial director of a large firm, manager in a firm providing civil engineering supplies, in an insurance firm, air traffic controller, painter, farmer. Eight husbands who were now following another career had at an earlier stage had a university post. In a few cases, the husband's occupation was not stated.

In two or three cases the point was made that the husband's financial situation had considerable practical importance for the women. It enabled her, one woman pointed out, to devote herself to work in which there was — at her stage in the career — no security of tenure: or it could enable the woman to accept a research grant which would not provide a good standard of living without the husband's income. In another case it was pointed out that the husband had deliberately chosen to give up his own prospect of a university career and had left a university assistantship in order to take a job with more security in which he could provide more satisfactorily for the family. This pressure on men should be recognised, it was suggested: where popular tradition regards the man as the breadwinner he may feel constrained to opt for a career in which financial prospects are secure: university assistantships, especially in present circumstances, do not guarantee future security. Yet in some cases it was the woman who supported the man financially while he studied: and in one such case reported, when it was the turn of the woman to be supported as she studied, the man divorced her!

Reasons for the minority situation of women in university teaching.
a) Family responsibilities
As has been already apparent, the woman's responsibilities for the family were regarded as of considerable importance. The reason most commonly given for the minority situation of women in university teaching and especially at professorial level was that women have to cope with families. This reason was advanced by 22 of the women spontaneously: others arrived at it as they commented on the minority problem.

The effect of the family situation was described in a number of ways. Some women emphasised the heavy claims made on the woman coping with both home and work responsibilities. 'I was so tired I forgot things' said one, recalling her years as a young mother, coping with children and her job. In addition to the physical strain there is the matter of divided attention. University work, it was pointed out, demands close concentration: the woman who has also to plan for the household or who is perhaps worried about a child will find it difficult to produce this concentration. One successful woman, commenting on this problem, said that she herself had the advantage of being able to switch off attention from the situation other than that in which she was actually present: she was, she said, in a way schizophrenic — during her time at work she could forget all about her domestic concerns (though of course this did not prevent her from taking thought for a sick child if the situation arose). Others however noted the guilt feeling or divided mind arising from questioning whether the child *is* being neglected — or university work being neglected.

The dual role means, for many women, that they make slower progress with studies for higher qualifications. Estimates of the differences in time required for qualification varied: one put it at a mere six months' delay in Licentiate studies while a woman had a child: others thought the delay could be a matter of years (and in fact, many of the women showed extensive periods of time between the acquiring of their first qualification and subsequent degrees). Thus women would be ready for higher appointments at a later age than men: this did not improve their prospects when a generation of brilliant young men had already been appointed to full professorial posts in their particular subject area.

On the more positive side it was emphasied that many women *want* to give time and attention to young children. Thus they may deliberately choose to withdraw from academic work for a while or recognise that it will have to proceed slowly while they concentrate on their family. In this women are less single-minded than men: they have wider interests.

Yet, it was also pointed out, men benefit in their academic career by the support and encouragement given by their families and in particular by the admiration which wives may show for their husband's academic achievements. But again, though some pointed out that not all husbands would reciprocate such admiration for academic achievements, many women did emphasise the importance of their husband's interest in their academic work and the support which he had given them while they worked for their qualifications. In one instance a husband had given up a full professorship in another university and reverted to a post of associate professor because his wife could not have a post in that other university and he recognised it as vitally important that she should be able to continue her academic career. Many husbands were reported as 'marvellously understanding'. Some, as a practical demonstration, cared for the children while the wife was abroad. Yet one young woman reported problems with her husband's view that as she took time out for her 'hobby' (of studying) so he could go off for hours on his hobbies. Another said that though her husband was sympathetic there was a limit to his tolerance — which might be passed if she decided on years of further study. And some of the successful women noted that lack of support from a husband was likely to interfere with the career of women they knew as colleagues or assistants.

b) Attitudes

It was held that another major reason for the minority situation of women may be found in various personal and social attitudes towards this kind of career for women.

Possibly women may be affected by the perception that there are relatively few women teaching in many university departments, so women may be less interested in the idea of this career. At the same time, some women pointed out that women are not in a small minority in some departments, they may indeed even be in a majority: one example given was that in Plant Physiology in Finland all three professors of the subject were women.

But women's perception of the possibility of a career in university teaching may be affected by attitudes in families and in schools which do not encourage the full development of female abilities — on the whole such attitudes seemed more likely to be found in families rather than in schools. One woman said she knew a number of women who were unhappy in their present situation because they had simply not been encouraged to go in for an occupation which would have used their abilities fully. Schools should certainly try to build up girls' confidence, said one woman: others thought that girls were by no means inhibited in giving their opinions in the coeducational schools. (These impressions of girls' contribution to discussion in schools may be misleading — sometimes the relative quietness of girls is simply not noticed. Certainly in one class observed — in language teaching — more questions were addressed to the boys, possibly because one at least of them was rather restless.) Opinions varied as to the effect of school structure on attitudes. One woman held strongly that girls' schools are better because positions there go by merit not by sex: girls are forced by lack of males to take responsibilities and they often have good models in females holding authority in the school. But another felt coed schools prevent over-valuing of males and avoid an aura of mystery about them.

Society generally, it was commonly felt, still tended to stress the need for achievement for males and not for females: females were not educated to feel they must be competitive or, for other reasons, females did not choose to enter into competition. Traditionally, it has been believed that females should be less assertive than males: this conditioning, said a number of women, is difficult to throw off in the university situation where it is important that the individual shows confidence in his or her own work and in putting forward individual opinions. One woman suggested that the traditional virtues of women — which some women do in fact possess — being open to others' points of view, ready to listen to argument and change an opinion where it seems reasonable to do so, are defects in the competitive academic situation where a tough defence of one's own views may be essential to obtaining recognition and prestige. Women too often have come to accept the traditional view of their role. And schools still, said a young woman, teach girls to be shy and nice and not critical: shyness makes you beautiful. It should perhaps also be noted that some women consciously used a 'feminine' approach in their work; that is, being charmingly reasonable, cooperative in dealing with colleagues. But perhaps it is a mistake to think of this as feminine charm — one woman remarked of her male professor that he listened sympathetically to what everyone had to say — then acted as *he* thought right.

There were some suggestions that women do indeed have different attitudes towards their own work: they are uncertain of its merits: they are too meticulous about detail to take the broad general view essential to professional research.

Women may also be less enthusiastic about the strenuous, concentrated work which is essential to successful research and consequent progress in an academic career — more than one pointed out the long hours, seven days a week, which are required for good research, at least in some disciplines. Women who have — whether innately or through social conditioning — less ambition than men and wider, more diffuse interests, may deliberately opt for work in which they can be less competitive and in which they can find time for family and social interests also. They may be interested in art, music, other leisure activities: and, generally, interested in living. Hence they may find other occupations more attractive than university work — school teaching, for example: one woman suggested that perhaps there are so few women teaching in universities because there are so many women teaching in schools. Similarly, women qualified in law may prefer to take up work in a law office or in the civil service because of the prospect of regular working hours and the relative ease of combining this with family care: or, said one woman, they may prefer to sit making out prescriptions for spectacles rather than engage in research in ophthalmology.

c) Prejudice

The question of prejudice against women reveals various complications. There has been in Finland considerable discussion of the equality of the sexes and, as we have noted, there have legislative efforts to remove the disadvantages from which women have suffered in the past. In general, the women interviewed were in agreement that all that can be done by legislation has been done. Some inequalities of pay remain but it is difficult to eradicate these fully, though progress is being made towards improvement. As one woman pointed out, Finland, unlike many other European countries, does not have an immigrant population ready to take over the lower-paid occupations: thus women in Finland may occupy such jobs. While women are willing to take up work which is poorly paid and has little prestige, inequalities in average male and female salaries will remain.

In fact, the detailed analyses of occupations and pay by the Council for Equality[30] show consistently lower median pay for females than for males, the below average levels of income coming frequently in 'female-dominated' industries. Moreover, 'the income gap between women and men does not narrow with the increase in education. In 1975 the difference between the median income classes of men and women with higher university degrees was 20,000 Marks, with lower second level education 5,000.' This differential can be observed at all levels of teaching, ranging from a difference between the range 40,000-44,999 for women teachers in university and higher education and 50,000-59,999 for men at that level to 35,000-39,999 for women at primary level and for men at primary level, 40,000-44,999 Finnmarks per annum. Only at kindergarten level, where women are 99% of the teachers, is equality achieved, the range for both sexes being 20,000-24,999.

Another instance of discrimination might also be mentioned, that of the refusal of the Lutheran Church to accept women ministers. This seemed to some of the women interviewed a deplorably unenlightened view, given the proven ability of women in pastoral roles. It means also that women students are unlikely to take higher degrees in the Faculties of Theology since a first degree is all that is required for the offices open to them in the Church.

There was general agreement in the group that the world of the university is more favourable in its attitudes towards women than is society at large. There was also some international comparison; women with experience of working in other countries considered, for example, that there was greater anti-women prejudice in the United States and in West Germany and in Japan (obviously much depended on the individual institutions in which the women had been temporarily working). Judgments of Sweden varied: two thought that the women's situation in Finland was better than in Sweden, one finding that Finnish men were more sincere than Swedish in recognising equality: but one woman held strongly that equality for women had made much greater progress in Sweden than in Finland.

Nine women were sure that there was no prejudice against women in the university in Finland. They had certainly never encountered any suggestion of it. Others, while stating that they had not personally encountered any anti-feminist feelings thought that such prejudice might exist in other areas of the university: 10 made this statement. Some of these women could think of specific instances where they thought prejudice had been operative: others said that traditionally there was prejudice against women in certain subjects of study. Opinions about Theology varied: one view was that no prejudice against women was found in that Faculty: another that, through lack of experience of academic women colleagues men in that Faculty tended to judge all women as having the same outlook as their wives: thus they could not comprehend women's interest in research and wish for academic advancement. In 9 cases, women thought that there might have been anti-woman prejudice working against them at certain points in their career though in four instances they could not be sure that this had really been so. As some pointed out, it is difficult to judge of the motives of an appointing committee: inevitably the individual's judgment of the strength of a case for appointment differs from that of external assessors. Other factors may enter into the situation: in two cases the woman thought that it might be her political attitudes — or what were believed to be her political attitudes — which had influenced the assessors adversely. In one case a woman's nomination for a post had been challenged at every stage by a male competitor: her nomination had been upheld and it could not be known whether the challenges were against her as a woman or simply against a successful rival. Yet to five women it seemed that being a woman had prevented their promotion on certain occasions or had meant that they had not been helped in forwarding a research project. On these occasions the woman had objectively not been able to advance in her career and the problem seemed to be that she was a woman.

The Finnish system appears to be remarkably open and objective in the making of appointments: the evidence of publications is there for all to see and judge. Yet subjective factors are inescapable: it may be difficult for assessors to decide precisely the weight to be given to monographs or articles compared to a book or books. The practice of joint publication makes it difficult to decide the contribution of the principal or subsidiary member of such a team: a generous supervisor who lets students' names appear first on such occasions, to help the student's career, may find that assessors subsequently undervalue her work as compared to that of more assertive male supervisors. Further, the Faculty making the final judgment may have a clear impression of the personality of the candidates. Women are possibly in a Catch 22 situation: many feel that they have to act more aggressively than they would otherwise wish in order to be noticed and recognised: yet the reputation of being an aggressive personality may make them less likely to be accepted as future colleagues or members of a research team. The grape-vine even of student opinion may have conveyed to members of a Faculty how different teachers actually perform in the teaching situation, their care for their students or their neglect of teaching while they improve their research standing. Thus — as in other countries — it is not easy to judge whether the belief that a woman has been discriminated against — because of being a woman — is justified.

Certainly some women asserted that women have to be better than men to be appointed: 'A woman has to prove herself' said one, in situations where a man would simply be accepted. One commented that women professors may be accepted because they are too small a minority to seem threatening: more of them might revive prejudice. One or two women commented that once a woman has been appointed at a higher level the situation changes and life becomes easier. The woman has less need to fight for her position: indeed the fact of being a woman may mean that she is particularly welcome as a member of committees or as the 'token' woman to be appointed or to appear on some public occasion. More than one woman in a top position noted how unashamedly people would invite her to participate in some activity or organisation 'because you are a woman'.

But another woman professor commented that when she was first appointed, there had been one or two who tried to see what limits would be set by a female head of department: they adjusted quickly when she made it clear that she was in authority and had definite views as to what the decision-making processes would be. Another professor commented that there could occasionally be a sort of problem when it appeared that she was favouring young male assistants: she was trying to encourage their progress because of their academic abilities but gossip was ready to give other interpretations to the situation. It was of course agreed that a male professor who advances the career of a young woman is likely to meet with similar misinterpretations of his actions.

Certainly — inevitably, given the structure of the profession — many of the women owed their academic progress to the support and encouragement given by male professors. In the great majority of cases they had been encouraged to do research, offered assistantships, encouraged to apply for higher posts or research grants by male academics. In these cases there had certainly been no anti-women prejudice at work: they had been treated precisely as would any good promising student be treated, irrespective of sex.

Yet even the helpful male professors could reveal some discriminatory feelings. One woman who had been the first woman to be appointed assistant in a certain department heard that the professor grumbled — though not to her — that it was all women who wanted to have assistantships now. In forms of address, one very greatly admired professor hesitated to use the same friendly, familiar form to women assistants as he would to men: another similarly was observed to find detours round the directly friendly form of address: one always used the feminine Mrs or Miss title when talking to women colleagues even if they were entitled to be addressed as Dr. These idiosyncracies were not taken as serious defects — the admiration and friendship for the men in question remained very great: nevertheless these forms of behaviour did mark a different interpretation of roles. Women who had been the first female assistants or professors in their subject areas had certainly met with a considerable amount of social comment: they had been regarded as oddities. 'Fancy a woman being a professor!'said one friend. And a superior asked, 'How is it, being a female professor?' These women had been able to live this down; they have become accepted as individuals among their colleagues; the tradition that female assistants or professors are acceptable in the subject area had been established by them (and, some felt, they had served as models for other women, encouraging them to apply for such appointments). These social reactions had no great effect on the women — they were in many cases amused by them. At the same time, they did have some effect in making the woman aware that from the social point of view she was unusual. In society still one woman avoided the title of Professor, using simply Doctor.

Social interaction with colleagues in the university is another area where prejudice may be expected to have undesirable effects. Some women did think that male cliques can form and women can be excluded from the informal decision-making which can take place in social gatherings. Earlier there had been discussion as to whether the sauna, segregating male and female colleagues, was an activity by which females could be excluded from informal decision-making. But one woman commented that it would be ridiculous to try to abolish this segregation (e.g. as had once been proposed, by introducing stylish robes for the occasion): she herself found that drinking beer *after* the sauna was an occasion in which males and females could participate happily in discussions. Again, another woman had the impression that earlier there had been a tendency for men to meet each other in restaurants or pubs in the evenings and talk there about departmental or university affairs: women, who less often went to these places, were excluded from this informal relationship. But now the situation seemed to have changed as women were more likely now to meet male colleagues in discussions in pubs and restaurants. One regretted that a change of accommodation for the department had meant that now she was less likely to meet male colleagues casually at lunch time: she did regard this as the loss of an important way of keeping in touch with what was going on in the university and in her subject area. It seemed that at least some women were consciously considering whether the casual meetings of everyday life in the university meant that they were excluded — without conscious intention — from situations where male colleagues might have discussions leading towards important decisions; they had some concern that this might be so.

At the more formal level of participation in committees or other decision-making bodies there seemed to be no feeling of under-representation. Those who were on university committees tended to find them a not very acceptable demand on their time, though the necessity of attending them was recognised. Yet occasionally women suggested that on such committees it was necessary to modify their natural way of speaking to speak more assertively — even pitching their voice lower — in order to be attended to; to make their approach generally rather more aggressive. It was noted that women themselves have a tendency to elect a man as chairman on committees even where the majority of members are women: this may be because they feel men will be flattered by such a nomination — and indeed may expect it — rather than because they think a man will be a better chairman. Some women indeed believed that for committees in which 'real' work had to be done and realistic proposals had to be made — e.g. for changes in curriculum — women were more satisfactory members.

Some perception of prejudice was reported with regard to membership of committees and representatives outside the university. As we have noted, women are in fact under-represented on the committees of various professional and governmental bodies. Similarly, women were, it was pointed out, neglected when participation in seminars and conferences was being organised. Instances were cited of two recent occasions, in different fields of study, where women who were expert in the field had been given little place. Men had been invited to be the main speakers and to form the great majority of the final panel: women had appeared only in subsidiary roles, possibly as chairmen of sub-groups during the proceedings or as deputising for a male professor. One woman remarked that perhaps in Finland there was danger of too great complacency: it was assumed that equality had been achieved — and so public conferences could be organised with blatant disregard of the right of women to be given an important role in them. Yet other women thought that such countries as the United States shared this attitude: it was less likely that women would be invited to serve as visiting experts or speakers even when the women were as well qualified to serve in this capacity as male colleagues.

An interesting case of possible lingering of prejudice was indicated in the tendency noticed in some male research students and assistants to seek guidance in their work from male professors rather than from females. It was difficult to be certain if such actions were really motivated by prejudice — or by social inhibitions — since the approach might be because of a belief — objectively justifiable — that the male was more knowledgeable and interested in the particular area of work. It might also be a matter of getting to know the abilities and helpfulness of a woman who has recently been appointed to the department: when she has been in post long enough to become known this trend may disappear. Similarly, perhaps, women students also are gradually becoming accustomed to seeking guidance from a woman — they too may have to learn to accept the idea that supervisors are not necessarily men. This problem clearly depends greatly on the area of study in question: it is unlikely to occur — or be suspected of occurring — in departments where there are many women members of staff.

The attitude of women to the whole question of prejudice and the minority situation of women in universities does depend greatly on the composition of the staff in their own department or in related departments. For those teaching in languages, philology, education, the initial reaction is sometimes to query whether women are in fact in a minority — though a little reflection leads to acceptance of the fact that even if numbers are approaching equality at the lower levels, especially in assistantships, the majority of professorial appointments are clearly held by men. In such departments, women as university teachers are regarded as normal: relationships with male colleagues are long since established and perception of sex differences is likely to be unremarkable. In other departments where a woman has for years been the only female in the department the question about minority situations causes no surprise. Yet in such cases, women did not feel that they were treated differently from their colleagues or by their colleagues because they were women. Normally such women felt fully at home in the department, by no means isolated or 'odd woman out'.

It was also difficult to find any conclusive evidence of an anti-women bias in any one department or field of studies. Tradition had it that certain studies were likely to be biased against women: women in other disciplines suggested that this might be the case: but women working in the fields where bias was said to exist did not have feelings of being discriminated against. There were certainly differences between the percentage of female students in certain fields of study and the percentage of female staff but these could not be traced to a policy of discrimination.

d) Attitudes to promotion

It should be recorded that so far as the minority situation at professorial level is concerned, some part of the explanation might indeed be found in the attitudes of women themselves. Some indicated that they did not think it particularly important to become full professors. One indeed was in process of deciding *not* to apply for a full professorship in another university even though her prospects of obtaining it seemed excellent. She preferred to stay in a university where she was enjoying her work and where she had many friends. Two others had similarly decided against moving to another university to become a full professor since they preferred the place where they were — it seemed to them a pleasanter and more rewarding place to be.

Others found the work load of a full professor unattractive. It was said to demand too much attention to administrative commitments, it reduced the time available for research: it might also reduce time available for social life. Two at least felt that they would prefer to continue in a post where they were expected to devote themselves extensively to research and where they would not be bothered by administrative details. One expressed herself horrified at the amount of administrative work which the (female) professor in her department had to contend with. It was agreed that the post of full professor does carry considerable prestige in Finnish society: but such prestige was not necessarily a matter of importance for the women concerned. And financially the differences in pay did not seem important.

The amount of power exercised by a professor seemed to be estimated differently in different departments as did the amount of influence the policy of the professor could exercise over the work and conditions of the individual. On the whole it was suggested that with more democratic structures in universities nowadays power was not necessarily an important consideration — though this might depend on the area of study and the method of allocating research resources within it. One woman professor certainly welcomed the possibility of transferring the responsibilities of head of department to one of the male professors for a change. She felt that she herself had been rather 'put upon', left to get on with the administrative chores while her male colleagues had a much easier life, going off to conferences or visits elsewhere. But one younger woman was deterred by a professor's teaching responsibilities: she preferred research and liked teaching only in small groups: so she'd postpone applying for a Chair 'until a few weeks before I retire'.

Some women were thus clearly not interested in moving to a Chair. Another said that she might well become a professor at an age later than that customary for men achieving professorial status: but she would have lived on the way there. Men, it seemed to her, were likely to pursue a blinkered, undeviating path to getting to a Chair as soon as possible. But two or three of those who had returned to academic work in later life commented that at their age there simply was no prospect of getting a professorship. It was also pointed out that much must depend, objectively, on the woman's subject of study. In certain fields — e.g. languages — the situation was regarded as buoyant. In others where there were very few Chairs in the subject — and it must be remebered that Finland has a small population so that, although the provision of universities is generous by international standards the total number of universities is small — then the chances of a Chair becoming available were very slight. One woman said candidly that she would not apply for a Chair because there were 10-15 people better qualified than she was. It was not that she was diffident or afraid of applying

— she had applied for an associate professorship, but she recognised she would not be among the best applicants. *O si sic omnes.*

It did not seem as if problems of mobility much affected women at this stage of appointment to higher levels. As has been seen, reasons for not moving were preferences for the present position rather than the difficulty of moving a family to another location. Yet in earlier stages of their careers some women had engaged in heroic commuting from one part of Finland to the other — though the very efficient internal air services make this perhaps more easy in Finland than might be expected by outside observers. Teaching in a distant university is also easier because it can be arranged that teaching is on only two or three days in the week. Docents may move from one university to another for part of the teaching they give during any one term or one week. Altogether, there were few cases where mobility seemed likely to impede future access to a Chair though there had been the case already noted where a husband sacrificed his appointment at a higher level because his wife could not move to his university — presumably that couple decided that commuting simply was not a solution — though geographically the distance looked acceptable. But at other stages in their careers women's progress had been affected by mobility. One woman remarked that in coming to her present place of employment it had been a question of 'change job or change husband' and she had opted for the former course of action, going with her husband to the place where he had obtained a high appointment: yet, given her subject qualifications, it had not been a problem to find a suitable appointment for herself in the new place of residence.

The point was made by one woman with whom the lack of enthusiasm for becoming a professor was discussed that one cannot be sure what the motivations for behaviour really are: there might, she suggested, be some degree of rationalisation in women's decision that they did not want to become professors.

e) Ambitions

Yet one did not have the impression that many, if any, of these women had deliberately set out to achieve the top ranks in university work. They had been enthusiastic about their research; and naturally considered it important to have their research published and recognised. But of those who had been appointed professors there were some for whom it had 'just happened'. As they themselves noted, it had been a matter of being in the right place with the right qualifications at the right time; or of taking one step which led to another and so on. (Though against this must be recorded the situation of one woman who felt that she had been given professorial status a number of years after it was due: of another who had yet to receive such recognition for her work and felt that, if she had been a man, colleagues in the Faculty would have stirred themselves much more vigorously to this end: of another whose women colleagues thought she should before now have been given the rank of professor.) Admittedly an all-out careerist who has been devoting herself single-mindedly to achieving a chair in the shortest possible time will not necessarily admit this in discussion. But an impression of single-minded pursuit of success did not emerge from the academic career of any of the women interviewed. For many of them the entry to university teaching itself was a decision made some time after working in other occupations: it was not the ambition of their childhood or student days. In this respect it should be mentioned that although some of the women came from families in which it was taken for granted that the daughters would go to university, others were first generation university students. Three women did have fathers who were university professors and could thus have formed their ambitions on this model: but this is a small number and the situation did not seem to have been like that generally. For many women, their youthful perception of themselves in their future working life was as school teachers, medical practitioners, market researchers: a change to another career may carry with it acceptance that late entry reduces promotion prospects.

However, in spite of these changes of career, there did not seem to be cases in which a youthful ambition or choice of subjects had been thwarted. One, admittedly, had earlier wanted to study metallurgical chemistry and had moved into biochemistry partly because of availability of opportunities there. One had set out with the ambition of being an engineer and had in fact worked in a factory, then in its chemical laboratory — in a situation of being very much the solitary female in a man's world — before her interest in relationships within the work situation led her into the study of sociology. Parental influence had guided one towards pharmacy, her own developing interest modifying this initial orientation towards biochemistry. Entry to university work had come about for one who was originally intending to follow a career in the civil service planning department: some degree of frustration with the limits set by extraneous factors in planning coincided with an invitation to take a university post where, she was told, she was needed. One, however, had made a detour through teacher education before reverting to her childhood enthusiasm for the study of plants.

Schools did not seem to have been influential in determining choice of work except, possibly, negatively in that in some cases it was reported that girls at school mainly thought of going in for teaching and were encouraged in this. In a negative sense too, the closure of schools during the Winter War of 1942 had meant a break in education for a few of the group who were then in upper secondary levels: but this temporary interruption of educational provision did not seem to have had lasting consequences.

Noteworthy also was the fact that some of the group had been equally good on the Arts and Science side while at school so that choice of career had depended on factors other than ability in a given subject. One, indeed, had initially been keen on maths and possibly on studying architecture: but had 'drifted' into language studies instead because she found them easy and teaching was regarded as a practical choice for girls. Moreover, she was engaged to be married at that point and the choice of a career did not then seem all that important.

In general, those who had had scientific interests — or medical, for there were some of the group who early decided that they wanted to be doctors — seemed more likely to have followed a consistent line of career and study: those in the social sciences, education included, were rather more likely to have come through other types of work and to have preceded their higher degree qualification by following other occupations for a period of years.

The children of the women interviewed, if at the appropriate age levels, now also seemed to be following preparation for graduate professions. One, somewhat cynically, said that if she had had a daughter she would have advised her to go into a 'masculine' area of study since the prospects and eventual salary would be better there.

But on a wider view, so far as the younger generation in general was concerned, a number of those interviewed commented sadly on the lack of openings in university work: in pure mathematics, for example, it would seem unhelpful to encourage students to work for a doctorate since employment prospects for them would be so bad: classical languages offered similar problems.

As to future ambitions for themselves, a number of the group, as we have noted, did not envisage professorships. They would, with enthusiasm, hope for — or continue in — a post which would enable them to continue with their research work. Most would also look forward with enthusiasm to continued work in teaching students. But some aspects of professorships seemed unattractive. Even so, some of the younger members of the group did look forward to reaching that level if practical considerations of available posts in their subject made this realistic and also when they themselves were expecting to acquire higher qualifications and more research experience in the next years. One, however, was proposing to move out of university life, back into more practical work in her subject, and was welcoming this return to the 'real' world, the university being, she felt, a bit alienated from ordinary life — though she did not rule out a later return to university teaching. University teachers, she felt, exercise *indirect* influence: in application of their professional skills outside the university, they can have direct influence on individuals or on social developments.

Feminist interests

While there was a strong feeling for the importance of equality for women in almost all the groups interviewed, there was relatively little militant feminism. In general there was the feeling that through their work, women had done and could do much to reinforce the acceptance of women in the universities and could encourage younger women to form ambitions for their own future careers, possibly in university teaching. Again, many women felt that their already crowded schedule of activities did not leave time for other pursuits: but some were members of feminist organisations.

It should be noted that two of the women interviewed had been engaged in research on feminist topics so were particularly well informed about the progress of the feminist movement in Finland. But neither wanted to be one-sided in her approach: and one specifically mentioned that she did not want to be 'typecast' as a specialist in feminist topics only.

Membership of professional organisations, being a representative of their grade on union committees was also an indirect way of advancing the rights of women and a fair number of the group were involved in such activities. It should be noted that others were also involved in politics outside the university, one as a city councillor and two as councillors or candidates at commune council level.

Conclusions

The group interviewed represented a wide variety of academic subjects. To some extent, there was the typical clustering of women in certain fields of study but there seemed to be no evidence of especially strong anti-female attitudes in any one faculty. The distribution in subject areas seemed due to personal choices as well as to earlier social factors in school and society. The majority had not themselves consciously met with discrimination against them because they were women but the majority were also ready to recognise that prejudice against women might exist even within the universities and that the traditional attitudes against women die hard.

Many had not come directly into university teaching after their first university qualification: some had entered only after extensive periods spent in other work and in bearing and rearing children. It was generally accepted that care for children and family is likely to be the major reason for the minority situation of women in university teaching and at professorial level. Lack of mobility might affect some women's careers but this did not seem to be a major factor.

Another major reason for the minority situation was found in various attitudes held by women themselves. The social role of non-assertiveness in women may well affect behaviour in some academic situations and in drawing attention to the excellence of work done by women. Even in the Finnish situation of open procedures for appointment to top posts, some subjective factors may still come into play. It was emphasised that education in schools should do more to encourage girls to develop their abilities fully and to develop self-confidence. But the very great influence of the family in determining attitudes was also stressed.

It was noted that there are also certain objective factors which may make advancement in a university career less probable. There is the age factor — the age at which women enter university teaching and the age by which they acquire necessary qualifications in higher degrees or publication of research. (And one woman commented that age is something particularly noted in women candidates — 'Oh, at that age..!' might be said where it would not be said of a man.) But other objective factors which would affect men also are to be found in the situation of stagnation or contraction of posts available in the universities: once posts are filled, promotion chances may be blocked for years; and the relatively small number of universities means that Chairs in certain areas of study are very few in number.

Here one could perhaps note the remarkably wide experience of teaching or research in other countries evident in the life histories of the women interviewed

— work in the United States, W. Germany, the USSR, the UK, Australia, Greece, France, Hungary, the Sudan — and of course, Sweden which, from the Finnish point of view, would scarcely count as going abroad. Thus, although they might not have experience of teaching in a variety of universities in their own country, and the total numbers of universities is small, the university women teachers in Finland could not be said to have a limited, parochial outlook.

The group interviewed were generally well aware of the demands made for equality for women and sympathetic to these demands. While they felt that their society had made considerable progress in this respect and was still making progress, they could see areas in which progress was still to be made — in industry and the Church, most notably. Within universities, there was acceptance of the view that although some old-fashioned prejudices might still linger, women did have good prospects of advancement. There remained, however, the problem of family responsibilities and while, here also, women felt that a great deal of progress had been made towards sharing of these responsibilities fairly between husband and wife, some dominant responsibility for children inevitably remained with the women. Women themselves are actively engaged in research on the feminist movement and on the larger topic of the evolution of family life in Finland.

Research indeed emerged as a dominant interest in the lives of these university women teachers: enthusiasm for their subject was widely evident; and being able to make progress in the development of knowledge in their subject was generally regarded as the most important goal to aim for, a goal more important than personal advancement to posts of formal responsibility. Though some women would not themselves aim at top positions, there were others in the group who would hope to reach them in due course and there was a general belief that as women were now more numerous at the lower levels of the university teaching hierarchy, in future there would be greater representation of women at the top levels also.

Notes:

1. *National Programme of Finland for Promoting Equality between Women and Men,* (Helsinki, 1980).
2. I. Kandolin, H. Uusitalo: 'Scandinavian Men and Women: a Welfare Comparison', Research Reports, (Research Group for Comparative Sociology, University of Helsinki, 1980), No. 28, p.17.
3. Central Statistical Office of Finland: *Position of Women* (Helsinki, 1980), p.26.
4. O.E.C.D.: *Reviews of National Policies for Education: Finland* (Paris, 1982), p.85.
5. *Position of Women*, op.cit., p.37, Table 15.
6. Ibid., p.25, Table 8.
7. Ibid., p.29, Table 12.
8. Ibid., pp.30-34, Table 13.
9. Central Statistical Office of Finland: *Statistical Yearbook of Finland,* (Helsinki 1980), p.338.
10. Ibid., p.339.
11. Ibid., p.340.
12. *Position of Women*, op.cit., p.154, Table 93.

13. Ibid., pp.155-6, Table 94.
14. Ibid., p.77, Table 31.
15. Ibid., pp.150-1, Tables 88, 89.
16. Ibid., p.164, Table 97.
17. Ibid., pp.165-6. Table 97.
18. Ibid., p.164, Table 97.
19. Ibid., p.166, Table 97.
20. Ibid., p.164, Table 97.
21. Ibid., p.169, Table 99.
22. Ministry of Education: Committee Report, June, 1982 (Helsinki, 1982): quoted in letter from the Ministry.
23. Ibid.
24. E. Haavio-Mannila, R. Jallinoja: 'Changes in the Life Pattern of Families in Finland', (Department of Sociology, University of Helsinki, 1980), Working Paper 13, Chap.3, App. 5-6.
25. Ibid., p.58.
26. *Position of Women,* op.cit., p.172, Table 101.
27. E. Haavio-Mannila, R. Jallinoja, op.cit., p.60.
28. Ibid., p.107.
29. Ibid., p.108.
30. *Position of Women,* op.cit., p.99 and pp.178-9, Table 103.

Chapter Three

Do they order things differently in France?

France has produced a woman President of the European Parliament. At the time of the research reported here a woman, Alice Saunier-Seîté, was Minister for Higher Education. A woman, Hélène Ahrweiler, was elected President of one of the most prestigious universities, Paris 1, serving first from 1976-1981. Yet France does not generally enjoy the reputation of being an advanced centre of women's liberation. It is only recently that women have continued to go out to work after marriage and the beginning of a family. In the provinces it could still seem odd for a woman to work if she did not really need the money for her family. Abortion is more recently legalised in France than in Britain and the period during which it can be carried out is still shorter than in Britain. Equal pay is not yet established by law though it exists in the civil service, which includes teachers. France does, however, have a Minister (female) for Women's Affairs. So how do girls and women fare in education, since society generally has made some advances towards equality but shows some retardation?

In some respects the education of women in France has offered considerable and extensive opportunities since the reforms of the 1880s when the Ecoles Normales Supérieures were constituted to educate women teachers for the girls' lycées which were to be strongly developed: both the secondary education of girls and their access into higher education benefited by this move. At the beginning of the twentieth century, in 1900, female university students were very greatly outnumbered by males, as they were then in European countries generally: they were a mere 3%.[1] But this proportion increased gradually, reaching 25% by 1930 and continuing to increase in the post-war years to arrive at 45% by 1967-68 and 49% by 1980. If one looks simply at the proportion of girls succeeding in the baccalaureate examination which is the entrance qualification to universities, it would seem that the share of women students will in future be greater than that of men.[2] In 1979-80 there were 138,701 female candidates for the baccalaureate and 103,307 males: the overall pass rate for females was 67.1 and for males 64.7. A similar superiority of females has been evident in the pass rate in subsequent years, though the percentages vary from year to year.

But the overall total is not enough evidence. If one looks at the subject areas in which candidates are entered for the baccalaureate[3] it is evident that there is considerable sex bias: thus in Series A, which offered options in classical languages and modern languages, music, plastic arts, the percentage of female entrants in 1979-80 was 77.6: in Series B, economics and social sciences it was 64.6%:

in Series C (the prestigious option recognised as being best for future prospects in university and employment), specialising in maths and physical sciences, the female percentage fell to 37%: in Series D, maths and biological sciences, it was 55.1%: in Series D,[1] agricultural and technical sciences, girls were decidedly in the minority at 28.2%: similarly Series E, sciences and technical science, at 4.3%. If entries for the technician's baccalaureate are considered, the same picture of sex bias emerges: girls provide 11.9% of the total entries in options in the industrial sector though they are strongly represented in other options, e.g. medico-social sciences, with 98.7% of entries and strong proportions in some commercial options.

It should be recognised that there is nevertheless a good representation of girls in some forms of higher technical education, in the IUTs, (the university institutes of technology which offer a two-year diploma qualification) and the STS, sections of higher technical studies which, though attached to lycées, are regarded as part also of higher education.

When it comes to the choice of courses of study at university, there is again sex bias. Women opt in large numbers for the Arts subjects which have no very clear vocational value: though there is now a move towards practically equal proportions of male and female entrants into Law and Medicine. But straightforward entry into university after the baccalaureate is not the most promising course for the ambitious. Those who are high fliers and anxious to secure entry into a good career will rather — if their marks are good enough — return to a lycée to spend two years in the preparatory classes which teach for entry to the competitive examinations leading to the Grandes Ecoles, those institutions of higher education which have a clear vocational outlet to careers in science, technology, engineering, industry, commerce — or to teaching at upper secondary or university level. Once entry has been achieved, the student benefits from maintenance grants and has a fairly secure future for although the rank in order of merit in the examinations to be faced in the Grande Ecole may be important in some cases, there is a relatively low failure rate in most. (The preparation for the agrégation is another matter.) It has indeed been argued that entry to university is a second-best option: while the government may be anxious to secure a well-educated cadre of specialists through the Grandes Ecoles to keep government services and industry functioning efficiently, the fate of university graduates is of less importance. Now although the Ecoles Normales Supérieures offer equal entry prospects to male and female candidates preparing for teaching (in upper secondary or university) in Arts and Sciences, the other Grandes Ecoles, notably the Polytechnique, with its scientific-technological specialisation, are much more definitely male-oriented. It is only in recent years that the Polytechnique has received any women students, a situation only partly explained by its original function of preparing highly skilled scientists for the armed forces and its correspondingly military regime. In the Grandes Ecoles under the direction of the Ministry of Higher Education,[4] men students numbered in 1979-80 10.7 thousand and women students 1.2 thousand. (In the Ecoles Normales supérieures the proportions were, however, 1.7 to 1.1.) These disproportions are evident in the numbers of male and female students who are to be found in the preparatory classes of lycées: there, in the public sector, in 1979-80, were 22.4 thousand male students and 10.8 thousand females. It is of course true that the proportion of females to males will still look good if figures for universities and Grandes Ecoles are combined since the latter account for a much smaller total population. But from the point of view of the future careers of females such differences are highly significant. It is also a matter of interest that the Ecoles Normales Supérieures which were formerly single-sex institutions are now becoming coeducational. Given the varied opinions that have been expressed in England about the effects in Oxbridge colleges of a similar change, one wonders whether this move will necessarily be helpful to females or whether the argument that they may achieve higher academic performance in an all-female institution may have some force. (It could be noted in passing that in 1982 the best overall performances in the baccalaureate examination[5] were achieved by girls' lycées — though there admittedly a number of other factors such as neighbourhood and social background of pupils have to be taken into account.)

The University Teaching Profession in France

The way of entry to university teaching in France is much more clearly defined than in Great Britain and the qualifications more explicitly stated. This remains true even if the structure of higher education in France has changed more markedly than that of Britain in post-war years and the access to different levels of university teaching has also been changed in nature. Under the old system, the initial degree was the licence, (first degree) followed by a diploma of higher studies, mastership: possibly agrégation and ultimately the state doctorate, the 'doctorat d'état'. (A university doctorate existed and does exist but is regarded as a much less important qualification, often taken by foreigners.) For the title of 'state doctorate' indicates a fact important in higher education in France that although this and other qualifications are taught for and examined by the universities, the award is given by the state. This means, among other things, that the state has considerably more influence over the courses and teaching provided by the universities since the refusal of the state to 'validate' a degree or diploma reduces the value of that qualification in the eyes of the student and potential employers and so can lead to the closure of certain university courses. (Additional control is of course exercised through financial support.)

The new system (with some variations according to whether the area of study is Arts, Sciences, Medicine or others) is that of an initial two-year period of studies leading to a University Diploma (DEUG): this is followed, if the student does not leave the system at this point — or is not eased out of the system at this point — by a one-year course for the licence, followed by a second year for the mastership: in the next two-year cycle there are diplomas (diploma in higher specialised studies, with a practical orientation, diploma in advanced studies with a research orientation — the DESS and DEA), followed by the doctorate of the third cycle (doctorat de 3e cycle) which is a very different kind of doctorate from the state doctorate and regarded with some disdain by the older generation of academics though it may serve some useful purposes as qualifications for junior members of the academic teaching profession.

The state doctorate remains the highest (though reform proposals in 1983 suggested its abolition) qualification in most areas of study. But the demands made by it vary according to the subject area of the candidate. In Arts or Social Sciences subjects, estimates put the time required for such a thesis at 8-10 years of devoted study: the thesis writer must, it is claimed, abjure all holidays, all social activities and consecrate himself or herself, during every available minute, to the thesis. Normally too the writer will not publish during this time of gestation: whether because such publication would be premature or because ideas might be taken over by others is not entirely clear. It is true that the doctorate can also be awarded 'sur travaux', i.e. on the basis of works already published but now unified by introductory, linking and integrating sections: but this is regarded as a less reputable mode of acquiring the degree and is less common than the traditional one. In Physical Sciences, the thesis is less lengthy: it can, it is estimated, be coped with in some 6 years: and although it is exacting work, possibly the fact that it may depend largely on work in a laboratory may mean that leisure is less heavily encroached on than in the case of Arts candidate. In Law similarly, the thesis may be less weighty: it is estimated as taking 4 or 5 years. Medicine is different from the other disciplines: a similar state doctorate is not embarked on, though a thesis is the normal completion of studies in medicine, taking a shorter space of time in the final year of medical studies.

The agrégation is distinctive of the French educational system and, some would say, of the French academic acceptance of competitive examinations. There are in fact two agrégations, one which leads to teaching in upper secondary or university (in the old days it was the qualification required for an established teaching post in a lycée) and one which leads to promotion in Law, Politics, Economics, Management Studies, Pharmacy (formerly in Medicine also but there it has been replaced by a list of qualified candidates, a system which also is characteristic of the French approach and will be outlined later.) In both agrégations there is an examination of a very high academic standard: the competitive element is introduced by the fact that only a limited number of candidates, depending on the number of posts for which people are required, will be declared 'agrégés' or accepted. The teaching agrégation does carry with it the valuable award of tenure — a guarantee of a post for the working life of the holder — though this value is somewhat reduced, from the individual point of view, by the obligation to go where the post is available. (One can sympathise with the young married woman with a young child who learns that one of the appointments to be made as a result of her agrégation exam is in Madagascar. Even within France, the post offered will not necessarily be in the place where the candidate would wish to live.) The first of these two agrégations will normally be taken in the mid- or later 20s, when the candidate has performed successfully in university studies up to first degree or higher diploma level. Those attending the Ecoles Normales Supérieures are more likely to be successful than the 'external' candidates since, in addition to being highly selected for academic ability, they have the benefits of specialist tutition and the stimulation of others working at the same level for the same examination. Many candidates obviously will not succeed at the first, second or later attempts: so the age level of entrants can extend upwards. The second type of agrégation is taken by people who have already made a beginning on their professional career, so the entrants are likely to be in their late 20s or in their 30s when they present themselves. From the point of view of British academics, the sheer number of hours over which the examination can extend — 8 hours in the Law agrégation, for example — may seem simply horrific. There is, it should be noted, the possibility of a subjective element in the judging since, although there is considerable weight attached to written work, there is also the confrontation with a 'jury' of experts in the subject area: and, as is widely recognised, an oral examination does make it possible for personal factors and individual prejudices to manifest themselves, even given the scholarly objectivity expected of and sought after by highly educated academics. At the same time, the agrégation system can be said to have advantages over systems in which hurdles to be surmounted on the way to qualification and higher posts are less clearly defined.

Entry to teaching in higher education in France has in the past been sometimes as much a matter of individual chance and opportunity as in Britain. The first level, the assistantship, could be opened by an invitation from a professor to someone who had worked with him in another university or to a former student of the department in which the post was available. Another possibility has been that of research assistant, as part of a research team supported by the Centre National de Recherches Scientifiques: the Centre not only has laboratories of its own but supports through grants laboratories in other establishments. Many university teachers spend a number of years in this kind of research post before moving over to a post involving teaching.

But the situation with regard to assistantships was radically altered in 1979. Earlier, the expectation was that the assistant was appointed for a period of three or five years during which time the assistant would make progess in writing a thesis — a state doctoral thesis or a 3^e cycle doctorate. The assistantship was renewable but the aim of one holding such a post was to be placed on the list of those competent to be maître-assistant, the next higher level, a 'career grade'. Being placed on this list (LAFMA) gave, even if not officially, some security of tenure and the expectation that when a post became vacant at the maître-assistant level the assistant would be promoted to that level. This list was suppressed in August 1979: appointment as an assistant became subject to an initial 'concours' (competition) in which candidates present information as to their qualifications and are interviewed in the university to which they are applying: the names of those candidates whom the university wishes to recommend are sent to Paris where, later, the promising candidates are interviewed by a 'jury' of the Central Council for Universities (CSU). There was no guarantee of renewal of the initial appointment gained in this way: so those becoming assistants in these circumstances realised — or should realise — that in five years' time they might have to look for employment elsewhere. The new system had evidently been planned to reduce local nepotism and to prevent excessive inbreeding: but it caused considerable resentment, not least among assistants who found themselves not receiving the expected renewal of their appointment but having to compete for the post they had been enjoying. The prospects of finding alternative employment at the end of five years — if no further university post is available — obviously differ according to the discipline: in Law, for example, the assistant may have the possibility of entering the magistracy: or a scientist may find openings in industry. The Arts specialist, however, may have no cognate outlet except in secondary teaching — where already redundancies are occurring and, as has been noted, the place of appointment for an agrégé might not be the place the candidate would choose.

It should be noted that being placed on LAFMA was not necessarily such a difficult problem as obtaining other qualifications. The main criterion was having made a reasonable amount of progress in the writing of the thesis: in some instances a certain number of pages — say 200 — was regarded as being a safe qualification. One has the impression that in the past a number of theses may have remained at this interesting stage for many years after the access to the List had been secured.

The maître-assistant level, regarded as the career grade in the French university system, is in fact a relatively recent creation, established only in the 1950s as an intermediate grade between the formerly all-powerful professors and the assistants dependent on their patronage. The maître-assistant has tenure in the sense of being 'titulaire' and an established civil servant. But the maître-assistant has not the responsibility of teaching the 'cours magistral' (giving formal lectures to large groups of students) which is the perquisite of those holding professorial rank. Thesis supervision can be done by the maître-assistant but examination of theses remains the function of the professor. If a state doctoral thesis had not been completed, the maître-assistant was expected to achieve this task if he/she hoped to advance to the next grade in Arts and Science: in Law, Politics, Economics, Management Studies, Pharmacy, the next problem will be to succeed in the appropriate agrégation. Success here led to entry on the list of those competent to serve as maîtres de conférences (LAFMC): but again the decision about appointment has been taken over by the central Consultative Committee of the Universities and the former division between maîtres de conférences and professors was blurred by the designation in 1979 of all at these levels as being part of the 'corps des professeurs des universités' (the body of university professors).[6] This general designation also obscures the former distinctions between professors 'with Chair' and titular professors 'without Chair'. But within the new class of professors there are still subdivisions: there are two ranks for 'exceptional' professors: below that is a grade, subdivided into nine levels, of 1st class professors, and below that again, the six levels of the 2nd class professors — the first level in this class being equivalent to the former maître de conférences grade. All those in the professorial groups have the 'magistral rank' — i.e. are held competent to deliver formal lectures and engage in examining at the highest levels.

It should be noted that there are alternative routes to some of the higher grades. In those disciplines having an agrégation there is also the 'long route': one-ninth of the posts at the maître de conférence level are reserved for maîtres-assistants who have been teaching for ten years and who apply for appointment: competition to gain promotion in this way is keen, even if the requirements for appointment are less demanding.

It has been argued that university teaching in France proceeds on the cooptation principle since candidates for appointment or promotion are judged uniquely by teaching staff of universities: even although appointments may be formally ratified by central government officials. Universities have clearly had considerable influence on the career of their staff members, since judgments have in the past often been made by a local committee; hence the emphasis in the reforms at the end of the 70s on appointments being made by a central committee. It should be noted also that from the point of view of the individual, promotion up to maître de conférence level could run very smoothly within one university. But appointments to a chair can lead to mobility problems. In Paris especially first appointments at chair level are not given in the central Paris universities: thus newly appointed professors may have to spend some years commuting to a university in a more or less distant part of the country. Such commuting is made possible by the limited formal requirements of a professorial post: traditionally (since a regulation of 1840) a professor has given only three hours of 'cours magistraux' per week: though of course there are additional duties such as examining, coordination of courses, guidance to students: research activity and supervision of research. But it is possible for professors to concentrate their work on university premises within two or three days: so it said that certain train services to and from Paris are full of professors stopping off at various intermediate stations to attend to their teaching and administrative work in provincial universities.

It is also possible for teachers at all levels in university to teach in other establishments as well. In the case of maîtres-assistants and assistants it may be argued that they do so because they need the money gained by work in other establishments of higher or further education: but many have also a considerable interest in their students in these other places and are seriously involved in this 'outside' work. Here one notes also a distinctive feature of French universities compared with British: the permanent staff could not cope with all the teaching load in French universities — there is thus a great deal of provision of teaching by the assistants who are not on the permanent staff in Arts disciplines (though they may be so in Science or Pharmacy or temporarily state employees in Law, Politics and Economics). But established staff may also work 'supplementary' hours, i.e. hours additional to the number required of them as a duty of their post: and such hours are paid for from the university's budget. In addition some teaching is provided by chargés de course or chargés d'enseignement who are not part of the permanent full-time staffing of the university.

But in 1983 a comprehensive new law on higher education was introduced. It defines clearly the objectives of the first, second and third cycles of higher education and proposes new structures and qualifications for the teaching staff. The intention is that in future there will be two main categories, maîtres de conférences and professeurs, corresponding to the existing categories of maîtres-assistants and professeurs. Entry to the junior category will require a doctorate of the 3rd cycle, selection being made 'on dossier' (curriculum vitae and publications) by a committee drawn mainly from the Comité Supérieur des Universités (CSU) which is to propose a list of 3 to 5 names for final decision (for approval by the Minister) by a committee of the establishment and specialists (CES). This final proposal to the Minister is to be accompanied by a statement of opinion by the council of the institution where the post is to be held. The Minister is to decide in cases where opinions might be in opposition.

Appointment as professor is to be from those already maîtres de conférences or others who have a 'habilitation' or qualifications considered by the CSU to be equivalent. In addition, 'mobilité thématique ou géographique' — evidence of mobility in thematic or geographical respects - is to be a qualification: this condition is intended to reinforce one of the new objectives stated for higher education, that of international cooperation. There is also to be a 2/9 quota of entrants from those who have been qualified maîtres de conférences for at least 10 years and from foreigners or other researchers and teachers.

Other proposals for reform relate to greater coordination between the Grandes Ecoles and the universities. Moreover the hours of teaching allocated to professors and others are to be increased. There are indications of intention to have feedback from students as to competence: of periodical re-evaluation of research work. Interestingly, staff are referred to as 'enseignants-chercheurs' — teachers-researchers. But perhaps the most remarkable reform proposal is the apparent decision to do away with the doctorat d'état and replace it by a 'habilitation', an evaluation of the individual's research work, by an appropriate central committee, a qualification possibly valid for only a limited number of years. A new doctorate may eventually be created. There are, as we shall see, many complaints about the existing state doctorate: but as yet the alternative's effects cannot be judged — and naturally there have been protests from the holders of the doctorate.

Advancement in university teaching has been and seems likely to continue to be a matter of accepting and fulfilling some clearly defined conditions: in some subject areas taking a competitive examination — the agrégations: getting on to a list of those recognised as competent for the next level in career grades. Subjective factors could, as has been indicated, enter even into the examination situation but the academic requirements have nevertheless been clearly defined. It is of interest that teaching ability has not been included largely until now among the conditions of appointment (though reform proposals do stress it): the agrégation procedure certainly includes a kind of test of some teaching skills in that it calls for the exposition of the candidate's knowledge to the 'jury': and indeed the Arts/Science agrégation has been, during much of the development of school education, the test of ability to become a teacher in academic secondary education. But it was precisely the unsatisfactoriness of the agrégation in selecting people to teach in lycées that led to the introduction of the alternative form of teacher qualification, the CAPES, in the 1950s. So one can scarcely consider the agrégation as giving proof of competence in teaching skills. The performance of assistants and maîtres-assistants might conceivably influence a university committee's decision to recommend them for the LAFMA or LAFMC but again the important criterion there has been progress in research, or in academic studies. In this context it should be recalled that until very recent times there has been no great emphasis on the importance of teaching methods in the French universities. The traditional method has been, as we have been noticing, the 'cours magistral'. In the conditions of the formal lecture to large groups of some hundreds of students, the kind of interaction thought important in good teaching simply is not possible. The disturbances of May 1968 drew attention to the demands of students for more satisfactory learning conditions. Progress has been made, by a variety of methods, in allowing for more realistic teaching situations: in supervised laboratory work: in seminars. And the university teachers are, at least theoretically, available at stated office hours to see students who wish to consult with them. There has also been an increase in the provision of teaching resources, including the employment of additional staff or provision of additional teaching hours by permanent staff. Even so, much as various French university teachers enjoy teaching and engage in discussions with students, they would not think of their ability as teachers as contributing materially to their advancement in their professional career. The criteria remain ability in research and in scholarship. Whether 1983 reforms change this remains to be seen.

Since the new system of reference to a central committee in Paris, the CSCU, was intended to make the appointment system more equitable and prevent the operation of prejudices within an individual university, it might be mentioned that the CSCU has consisted of 12 sections, 62 commissions and subsections each relating to an area of study. Each section and sub-section has had nominated and elected members, the number of nominated (i.e. government nominated) members being equal to, at most, half the number of those elected. The committee has consisted of representatives both of the professorial rank and the rank of maître-assistant; the regulations concerning nominated and elected members applying to both. But on these committees, possibly because of the smaller numbers (relatively) of women at professorial and maître-assistant level, the number of women is small. One instance quoted was a commission with 32 full professors of whom 3 were women: at the maître-assistant level, there were 4 women among the 23 representatives. Of course the presence or absence of women on such committees may make no difference whatever to the chances of appointment of women candidates: but it is possible that awareness of the minority position of women in such circumstances may affect both candidate and jury.

Nevertheless it must also be noted that Marguerite Cordier,[7] looking at the decisions made in the 1970s by the predecessor of this committee, the CCU, in deciding about admissions to LAFMC, found that women had, proportionately, been treated as well as men. For example, in the years 1973-75 the proportion of female candidates was 22% and the proportion among those admitted to the

List was 22.8: in Science the proportion of applications by women was 12.5% and the proportion admitted was 11.2%. Her conclusion with regard to Medicine, where the agrégation was replaced by a List system with a curious two-tier structure, was that although precise data were not available for both parts, the evidence did seem to suggest that once admitted to the list, women had as good chances as men of being appointed to posts. She noted also that greater numbers of women applied for inscription than had formerly applied for the medical agrégation: but this could, of course, be a reflection of the greater numbers of women medical students in more recent years.

It will be recalled that the representation of women among university teachers in France is rather higher than that found in the United Kingdom. At professorial level, 5.8% are women: maîtres de conférences — 9.9%: maîtres-assistants — 29.8: assistants — 34.7.[7] The overall percentage is 24.7 though, again, there is the characteristically greater frequency of women at the lower levels of appointment. In future of course the change in designation of the higher ranks will mean that discrimination between 1st class professors and those ranking lower will be more difficult for those not having access to university staff lists: it is therefore of interest to note that at present the proportion of women is higher in the lower professorial ranks than in the top levels.

The Group of Women Interviewed

In choosing a group of women from whom to obtain information about their experience of university teaching as a career for women it seemed inevitable that Paris should be one of the areas where interviews would be carried out since Paris has been the mecca of university students and staff for so long and since such a large proportion of the university student population of the country is concentrated in what are now the thirteen universities of Paris (a sub-division of the University of Paris was made after the 1968 upheaval). At the same time it was not possible to obtain lists of all women teaching in these thirteen universities, select some and arrange to interview them. So the group of women interviewed in Paris was determined largely by personal contacts, by one woman passing on names of colleagues or acquaintances or by introducing them to the investigator. But an effort was made to get in touch with women in different subject areas and at different levels of the teaching hierarchy. It also seemed desirable to make contact with women teaching in a number of different universities rather than concentrate on only one or two since the universities do differ in traditions, though there is overlap in the subject areas they teach. Some still have the prestige of long tradition, as, especially, has Paris 1, Sorbonne-Panthéon; other new universities have received much publicity, especially Paris VIII, known as Vincennes where it was first lodged, celebrated as a highly innovative university in its early years of existence in the early 1970s, criticised bitterly by traditional academics for lowering university standards and depicted at times luridly by the media as a centre of drug pushing and other anti-social activities. In the event, women teaching in Paris 1, (4), IV (1), V (5), VII (1), VIII (3) and XI (1) were interviewed as well as one formerly teaching in Paris, but recently appointed to a post in Lille. It seemed also useful and valuable to interview also representative women in the Ecoles Normales Supérieures and one of the very rare women members of the Collège de France since they too are teachers in higher education. It was found, incidentally, that some of the women in the group also taught for other institutions of higher education so they were able to enlarge the picture beyond that of university teaching alone.

As counter-balance to Paris a provincial university seemed appropriate. The university, or rather the three universities, of Grenoble seemed a good choice since Grenoble is a well-known, well-established university, sub-divided after the 1968 reforms and recently moved to more extensive premises on a vast new campus on the outskirts of the city. Admittedly it would also have been pro-fitable to visit some of the new universities to see whether they were new also in their attitudes to the employment of women. But, given limited resources and time, it seemed that a long-established university, offering a wide range of teaching in different subject areas, including medical teaching, would give a promising research area. Grenoble, various people mentioned, is a place which attracts people and in which they happily remain, and, given its geographical location in the South-East of the country, it seemed to be independent of some of the factors attracting people to Paris. 27 women teaching in Grenoble were inter-viewed, 9 from Grenoble I, the university of science and medicine: 12 from Grenoble II, the university of social sciences: and 6 from Grenoble III, the univer-sity of languages and literature.

For the total interview group of 46 women the distribution of subject areas was this:

Humanities (including languages, philosophy, sociology, psychology, history, geography and education)   30
Natural sciences (including physics, chemistry, biology, maths, zoology, com-puter science)   8
Medicine (medical biology, pharmacy)   3
Law   3
Economics   2

It did not appear that the situation of women teaching in universities was greatly affected by the subject taught, though there were differences in the qualifica-tions required. There were obviously more women in some subject areas than in others and the distribution of subjects within the group reflects this to some extent. But attitudes to women did not seem to be subject- specific though some women assumed that there would be such a difference: they might say, for example, that in Natural Sciences or Medicine there is a more traditional or reac-tionary attitude to women: but such views were not confirmed by the women actually working in these departments. Thus perception of subject- specific attitudes to women seems always to be with regard to a subject other than one's own.

But one curious reaction was noted. In some instances women queried the state-ment that women are in a minority in university teaching: then, on reflection, admitted rather hesitantly that posssibly overall it was so but in their own area there were lots of women. In fact, in one UER (unit of teaching and research) which was in this way claimed to be full of women the ratio of male to female staff was 16 to 14. In another case, a university which was claimed to be full of women teachers had 44 out of a total staff of 136 — which makes 32%. Evidently women teachers are highly noticeable in their environment, to other women as well as to men. Within individual research teams the proportion of women was sometimes much higher: indeeed some small teams were, partly by accident, entirely female. But again there is confirmation of the finding that when women become more than a small minority, the belief that there are quite enough women around develops readily.

Two further points may be made about the characteristics of the sample of women interviewed.

1) The subject distribution showed a great predominance of women teaching in the humanities. For the country as a whole in 1978-79,[8] the percentage of women among those teaching in higher education was, for humanities (Lettres) 33.9%: Law, 21.6%: natural sciences, 19.8%: medicine, 20.2% and for pharmacy, 45.2%. If one considers simply those at professeur level and maître de conférences level, the percentages diminish considerably and pharmacy no longer seems such a model of near-equality: the professorial representation there is 10% (near to humanities' 9.2%) and at maître de conférences level, 20.5% compared to humanities' 19.9%. But of course the total populations employed in the two areas are very different in size, pharmacy accounting for a mere 3.8% of all those teaching and humanities for 22.9%. It must be recognised that the group inter viewed contains rather too many representatives of the Arts and social science subjects and too few in medicine and natural sciences and Law. Since, apart from the different qualification structures, there did not appear to be great differences in women's career prospects according to the subject studied, this may not seriously have affected the data gathered from interviews.

2) The other point concerns the level of appointment of the women interviewed. It was not always possible to discover to which category of professorial rank the woman belonged but overall there were 23 women professors in the group: of these 12 were full professors, class 1: 8 were professors of the second class, who would have been described as 'without chairs' or maître de conférences under the old system. There were 15 maîtres-assistants: 6 assistants: one chargée de conférences: two directors of an Ecole Nationale Supérieure. The group thus had more people holding appointments at the higher level than the British sample had, even allowing for the rather greater proportion of women among professors in France. The discrepancy arose partly from lack of access to lists of university staff. But, given that a main interest was to discover why women are a minority at professorial level, there were certain advantages in talking to as many women professors as possible.

It should perhaps also be noted that not all the group were born in France or in French territory. One woman was a native of Poland, one of Greece, one of Belgium, one of the USA and one of Germany. Hence their school and early university education had not been in the French system. But since their higher studies had been in that system and since they were now well established in the French system and had acquired French nationality by marriage, it seemed reasonable to include them. University teaching is traditionally international.

Choice of Career

One has again the impression that in many cases the career development of the woman occurred by accident. In some cases admittedly, perhaps among the younger women, there had been a determination to advance in university posts but for many entry to university teaching occurred without much earlier planning, possibly because a post happened to be available or someone suggested the woman should try for such a post; or a professor (male) urged the women to continue with further studies. Certainly some of the women had been clearly motivated to pursue research after achieving their initial qualifications: but this was not necessarily linked with a plan to gain university teaching posts. In other cases, years spent in other occupations — and possibly partly devoted to rearing a family — meant that the woman entered university work at a relatively mature age.

Schools seem to have exerted practically no influence on the secondary school-girl's choice of studies or career. No one interviewed suggested that there had been effective educational or vocational guidance in her school: nor had such guidance been expected. (Though one woman is now very conscious of guidance possibilities, being engaged in innovatory work to give guidance to university students as to career possibilities and prospects.) Decisions were made by the girl herself or by her family. In a number of cases the family tradition of work was influential: many were daughters of teachers — at primary, secondary or higher education levels: in some cases, both parents taught. In these cases, the girl's progress to higher education or to Ecole Normale or Ecole Normale Supérieure was expected by the family: though some such teachers' daughters decided not to teach, or at least not to teach the same subject as mother. Family circumstances also affected the girl's choice of further education after school. One whose father had died young was brought up by her mother to be as brilliant academically as her father had been. Others whose mothers were widows took the economic situation into account when opting for certain studies, avoiding those which would be long or would involve a year abroad — e.g. one chose to study the French language rather than the English.

Generally, the social background of the women seems to have been middle-class though there were some also from lower middle- or working-class families. A few (3) began by attending Ecole Normale to become primary school teachers then, as they demonstrated academic ability of a high level and developed the wish to study further, were promoted to entry to the Ecole Normale Supérieure or themselves sought bursaries for further study at university. One woman from a non-academic background commented that she had no part in deciding that she would proceed to higher education: although her family were not well-to-do when her father learned from the higher primary school that his only daughter was gifted he decided that she should move to the lycée and again took the word of the teacher there that she should next go the ENS and train to be a lycée teacher.

Many in fact did aim at the Arts/Science agrégation. But there seem to have been differences among the 22 who in fact were lycée teachers for some part of their career, for periods ranging from 2 to 20 years. Some, after attending classes préparatoires and the ENS, taught for only a short time in a lycée before gaining an assistantship in a university and going on from there. (One woman commented that in those earlier times women who gained the agrégation were not usually appointed directly to a university post as men might be: a woman had to teach in a lycée at least for a year or two first, in order to give proof of her good intentions.) Other women had seen teaching in a lycée as the summit of their ambitions. In such cases teaching in a lycée went on for many years until some chance altered the woman's plans: one had returned to Grenoble for a visit and heard of an available university post: one was invited to take a post by a professor under whose direction she had worked earlier: one feared that she was getting into a rut by teaching top lycée classes only: one was encouraged by her professor to work on a doctoral thesis while teaching: another was returning from work overseas and unwilling to go on with lycée teaching especially as she feared being sent to an unattractive area of France. In other cases a husband's appointment to another city led to an offer of a post to the wife or to her perception that she could apply for, and succeed in, university work.

As one notes again, the agrégation does seem to provide a useful kind of insurance policy in its provision of a guaranteed post for the rest of the agrégé's career. If a woman decides to try university teaching after teaching in secondary school she has this comforting knowledge that if the demands of research and thesis-writing prove excessive she can revert safely to an occupation in which she has tenure — even if she cannot be sure that she would like the location of the post offered. In the present situation in universities in which promotion from untenured assistantships is precarious and the renewal of assistantships much less certain than it was earlier, this guaranteed fall-back gains in value. (Of course these considerations apply to men also: and indeed men may be more mobile than women in accepting a move to posts in other parts of France.)

The choice of subject specialism had not always been straightforward: many of the women changed orientation in the course of their careers. Some — a minority — continued from school through higher education, possibly with some years in research, to their present university post in the same subject area. This clear progression was evident on both the Arts and the Science sides: it was found for teachers of English, Physics (3), History, Biology, Sociology, Greek, Chemistry, Philosophy. But others had been diverted from their original choice. Medicine, as in the British sample, proved to have attracted a number of the group: in one case the girl's father had thought the career, especially preparation for it, unsuitable for a woman so she had gone to Pharmacy instead. In others, the length of time required to complete medical training had been a discouraging factor: so one opted for Biology, one for Psychology and one for

Law. In two cases a beginning was made towards acquiring medical qualifications but one young woman had decided that the preliminary science studies did not really interest her, one was discouraged after a year in medical studies by the realisation (this was some years ago) that women were not looked upon with favour in the faculty and that the chances of specialisation in psychiatry, which she.was much interested in, were not good: she too moved to Psychology. Yet in another instance the girl had wanted to go in for nursing: her mother was opposed to this career and would have preferred her to be a teacher, as her mother was: but the girl was against teaching (and is rather amused to find she has come to teaching students despite this early refusal): she opted to study Medicine instead.

Maths also has been a subject which interested and attracted some of the group. In the past, it was necessary for girls to move to a boys' lycée in their final years of secondary education if they wanted to specialise in this subject: in one case the girl's father opposed this move (as he also opposed her preference for Medicine) so she became a pharmacist. In another, the woman did study Maths and took a first degree in it but subsequently moved to Philosophy and then to Psychology. One found it hard to choose between Maths and languages in which she was also a good pupil: but her parents considered that Maths offered better career prospects so she went to that side. One who had problems in getting into the university Maths course she wanted moved to Economics instead and became enthusiastic about that subject. Another continued with Maths in the classes préparatoires but, realising that success would mean moving to study in Paris, chose instead to enter the Arts faculty in her home university. Another found it difficult to get a bursary to support her through Maths studies after a period of training as a primary school teacher: so she opted also for psychological studies which eventually led to expertise in the teaching of Mathematics. In view of much that has been written about the relative scarcity of women in Maths studies in universities, it is interesting to find how, in various ways, girls' interests in this area were diverted to others. One Maths enthusiast however developed her interest to specialise in computer sciences.

In view of the relatively late development of Psychology as an independent branch of study in French universities and of the recent evolution of some branches of Psychology itself, it is not surprising to find that women now teaching in this area moved to it through Philosophy and, in some cases, were engaged in the creation of the courses they now teach. The social sciences generally, having been newcomers to recognition in higher education, inevitably have attracted people from other disciplines. Similarly, the relatively late recognition of methods of teaching as worthy of study at university level has meant that, in particular, specialists in languages have now moved to this area; though for them there are still difficulties in having topics of theses recognised as appropriate for one or other academic department.

Two other facts can be perceived as affecting subject choices. One is that in this group, as in the British group, there are people with good all-round ability. From the point of view of their teachers at school, various specialisations in higher education would have been appropriate for them. The decision depends in such cases on the individual's choice: if she is an all-rounder in outlook, that choice will be difficult and may be made through family pressures or external circumstances rather than a distinctive preference for one particular field of study. The other fact to note is that in some cases family counselling seems to have depended on consideration of future employment. One woman hesitated between pharmacy and biology: but her parents thought the latter could lead only teaching and that employment prospects might be better in pharmacy: so she chose that. One engaged in much reasoning as to whether she should go on to Arts studies since science was precluded by her weakness in Maths: but the employment prospects in Arts seemed relatively poor and since Law seemed to her to call for much the same qualities as the study of literature — reasoning and analysis! — she opted for Law. Yet another, hesitating between languages and Maths, was advised by her parents to choose the latter. One who was interested in English studies was — as we have noted — worried about having to spend a year abroad (her mother was a widow) so she chose to specialise in French. Another prospective linguist felt the career prospects were not good there so she opted for Law. In such cases the implied assumption frequently was that the girl's future would lie in teaching: decisions as to her employment prospects were taken with this in mind: entry to *university* teaching was not — in these cases — seen as a probable career. In other cases the influence of a parent who was teaching in higher education did affect the girl's choice of subject and her ambitions: e.g. the daughter of a professor of sociology sought a post in research at the CNRS.

In only two cases did there seem to have been a clear early decision to enter university teaching: one of the older generation was — she said — predestined to this by her home background: another, among the youngest in the group, had perceived this possibility during her student days and had set out deliberately to acquire the necessary qualifications. But early commitment to research had been evident in the employment some of the group sought with the CNRS. Eleven of the group had been full-time research workers in this way for periods varying from one to two years to 15 years.

Even so, many women comment spontaneously that their present position is very much due to the concatenation of circumstances: they consider that they had good luck in being at the right place with the right qualifications at the right moment. The expansion in universities in the 60s contributed to a considerable extent to such happy 'accidents'.

Looking at the background career information given in interviews, one can distinguish what can be regarded as 'clusters' of characteristics defining some types of women university teachers. One type is the woman who has followed much the same career pattern as a man might be expected to follow. Beginning by studying a science subject, she attends classes préparatoires and qualifies for the ENS. There she takes her qualifications, including the agrégation. She begins her doctoral thesis, having a part-time post as an assistant in teaching at the ENS or a CNRS post: she becomes a chef de travaux then maître de conférences and eventually a full professor, serving as directeur of her department for a number of years. Concurrently she has married and had children, some of them during the period when she was working on her thesis. Her husband is probably a university professor too. They have been able to employ domestic help so housework has not been a problem for her: her children, if any, are being brought up to take their share of domestic tasks. This pattern can be varied slightly by some years in a laboratory supported by the CNRS before entry into full-time university teaching. There may in some instances have been some slowing down in professional advancement during the years when the children were young: one such woman noted that she had specifically asked her professor to let others go ahead of her for a few years. Other notes the very tiring time they had when the thesis was being written, possibly by working late into the night, with young children to be cared for at the same time. Some in this sub-group are childless: one or two separated or divorced. Others have not yet reached the top professorial rank. But in this cluster there seems to be a special commitment to the subject and enthusiasm for research in it; which can also be associated with enthusiasm for teaching it.

A second type is found among women who have gone first into secondary teaching, with the agrégation. There they have continued to work on their specialist subject. A chance occurrence — discussion with a professor, for instance — brings them into university teaching. They are enthusiastic teachers. Not all of them will complete their doctorat d'état: they will register for it and some have written enough of it to get on to the LAFMA, before that list was suppressed. Others are quite clear that they do not think the doctoral thesis is worth the effort. They consider that their teaching function is important and enjoy contacts with students. They are also enthusiastic about their subject but they feel that their own interest in it cannot well be served by accepting the straitjacket of a formal thesis in the traditional manner: nor do they think the outcome of the many years of work would be read: nor would the preparation of the thesis be beneficial to themselves or their students. They are content to remain as maîtres-assistants for the rest of their career, the more so as the professorial responsibility for delivering cours magistraux does not seem to them an attractive prospect — they consider this a bad teaching method. Nor are they attracted by the administrative responsibilities of a professor. They deplore the time spent in committees — and not for the merely practical reason that they would prefer to be at home, especially towards the end of the afternoon.

But some in this category do enjoy administration. There is a sub-group here who feel that women can bring to the tangled personal relationships of departmental committees a reconciling and soothing influence. They think too that they have themselves a good common sense in dealing with administrative matters. Some have exercised these talents as heads of department (directrices d'UER) and have enjoyed the experience even if, as some comment, it is necessary on such occasions for a woman sometimes to adopt a more aggressive personality to 'mix it' in debate with aggressive males. (One, however, noted that in the Conseil de l'Université women did not speak up much; or challenge the views put forward by dominant males. She was unusual in noting that women tend to speak less than men on such occasions. In the less formal Conseil d'UER situation this difference might be less marked.) In this sub-group the very energy spent in administration may affect adversely the career prospects of the woman. The three years as head of department, by election, may mean that her own research, publications or thesis are neglected and this undoubtedly reduces any prospects of promotion she may have. It is possibly an unfortunate coincidence that the early 70s, with their new democracy of the university establishing new units of UERs and determining domestic policies, offered to women the chance to be actively involved in this decision-making at a time when some of these women would have been establishing their academic reputation. The present freeze, with the reduction of posts available, may mean that time lost in administrative and decision-making participation has made some women too late to gain the rewards of academic work even if they now complete doctoral theses.

Obviously these general categorisations are impressionistic. Individual cases show divergences and variations. Yet the overall impressions do emerge. Another overall impression is that in only a minority of cases does there seem to have been the wish to become a professor and occupy a position of authority. Even among those women who have achieved the highest positions there is the view that each has simply gone ahead and done the work that came to hand: 'Je n'ai jamais voulu faire carrière: j'ai fait mon boulot'! They have coped intelligently and effectively with each stage as it has presented itself. They have worked hard at their subject: they have given all their effort to carrying out their research and to doing the work they had to do. In some respects they do feel themselves to be representatives of women in their present positions and in these positions of authority they do try to help other women to succeed by ensuring good education for them and by making sure they are not overlooked when appointments, e.g. to committees, are made: but they have not set out to be feminist models.

It could of course be argued that statements made in an interview are affected by considerations of what is socially acceptable. Consuming and selfish ambitions might be present but concealed. Yet it is remarkable that the same point of view is repeatedly expressed, at least with every appearance of sincerity, in a situation where some degree of ambition would surely be socially respectable. These statements too are compatible with other statements, shortly to be discussed, about women's motivations in general and their attitudes to careers. The work which women may have had to put into reaching their present positions by non-academic manoeuvring is also beyond objective assessment in interview circumstances. One did mention the importance of having a 'patron' who can exercise political influence within the university: but in this she was unique. Others who recognised gratefully the 'pushing' received from their professors were clearly referring to the encouragement given on the academic side rather than political manoeuvring.

Marriage and children

From what has already been said, the influence of marriage and children can be important. In considering these aspects the age distribution of the sample interviewed is clearly relevant: it was as follows:

25-29	1	45-49	11
30-34	1	50-54	6
35-39	4	55-59	7
40-44	12	60-64	3
		65+	1

Thus the group is, as might be expected, given the greater proportion of those at professorial level, rather older than the British sample: the main grouping is of women in their 40s as compared with the main grouping in the UK of women between 35 and 45.

In the British group the proportion of unmarried women was quite high at 40% though there are indications that the trend is now for more women university teachers to be married than formerly. In the French sample the distribution showed only 28% unmarried:

Single	13
Married	26
Separated, divorced	5
Widowed	2

One cannot, unfortunately, tell whether this group reflects the general pattern of marital status for women teaching in French universities. A rapid check of the list of female teaching staff in one of the Grenoble universities indicated that 9 out of 37 were given the title Mademoiselle: if this is a reliable indication of marital status it would give a percentage of 24 unmarried: which would seem to confirm the interview group impression.

The family situation was this:

One child	9
Two children	9
Three children	8
Four children	5

One of the children was adopted by a single woman: and one of the single women had a child of her own. Thus the number of women who had pursued or were pursuing a university career without the complication of a child to attend to was small. And, as before, we must note that the families listed were not necessarily complete.

Yet the domestic aspects of looking after a family do not seem to have presented a major problem for the women interviewed. In almost all cases they had employed domestic help, possibly supplemented by the help given by grandmothers in three or four cases. Certainly the cost of such domestic help was something to be reckoned with but since both husband and wife were gainfully employed paying did not seem to be too difficult. (It is perhaps worth noting that an article in *Informations Sociales*, 1980,[9] noting the increase in the percentages of women with children going out to work since 1962, calculated that the wife's contribution to the family budget diminished spectacularly when expenditure on domestic help and child care was taken into account: at the same time, the compensation to be obtained from later financial benefits — pension rights, higher salaries — seemed to justify what was superficially an economically unrewarding situation.)

But the type of provision to be made for the care of young children was not self-evident and a variety of attitudes was expressed here. Students could be useful in fetching children from school and settling them to homework before mother returned from work. Au pair girls were occasionally recognised as useful. But the question was whether to employ someone in the house to look after children or to send them to a creche. Some women were critical of (mainly younger) mothers who simply sent children off to a creche: someone in the house, giving personal attention to the child, seemed preferable. Some had in fact been exceptionally lucky in finding a resident help or a daily woman who stayed with the family for many years and who could be entirely relied on to cope with the household while the woman was at work. In other cases it had proved a problem to find domestic help who could be relied upon and would not go off to other employment.

This reliance on paid domestic help did not by any means imply that the university mothers were content to leave the children to be looked after by others. Their relationships with their children were universally recognised as highly important. In various cases, women commented that the early childhood years especially are precious and pass quickly: some felt that even if it meant a slowing down of academic progress, time must be made available for being with the children. But others mentioned that the need for a good relationship does not lessen as the children get older: adolescents can, in some ways, be more demanding than young children. Usually children seemed to appreciate and admire their mother's work though one daughter did complain when her mother's promotion reduced the time that her mother could spend with her. In Paris especially, it was pointed out, children are likely to be living in an environment where it is customary for the mother to have a career of her own and peer group opinion expects this of mothers. Children who become university students may feel proud as they realise their mother's academic standing or find references to her publications — though there may be some embarrassment if the child becomes a student in the mother's department. In one instance, the possibility of the child being 'complexée' by the parents' academic brilliance was discovered: but the young woman student had overcome this problem.

The importance attached to this relationship meant that one woman had doubts as to whether someone employed to look after the children might in fact have too great an influence on them: but she was alone in mentioning this concern. But one, not French by birth, felt so strongly about the relationship with her children that she had not been willing to leave them to be looked after by others: only for a brief period of two years had she employed domestic help, while her children were at the pre-school stage and she was a school teacher: she had been tempted to give up her university work later, when her adolescent daughters seemed to need her attention. She was now, she thought, probably the only woman teacher in the university not to have domestic help.

Separation, however brief, had worried some mothers: one recollected how her heart was torn as she went out and her baby daughter looked sadly after her from the playpen. Yet others noted the benefit for children of acquiring some degree of independence from their mother.

Husbands' attitudes are clearly an important factor. While many husbands were reported as being encouraging and supportive with regard to their wife's career, it was not common to hear of a husband who took his share of domestic work. The standards of house-keeping expected by the husband did however seem to show quite a wide range. Some wives felt that they must ensure that the husband's comfort was not reduced because the wife was out at work. Two explicitly recognised that, given their husband's family background, a high degree of comfort in the home was expected: they saw to it by employing the necessary domestic help. In other cases, the couple were agreed on simplifying housework and standards of living. One woman admitted that her husband had been spoiled by his mother, having been brought up in the traditional view that men were ministered to by women: she had not seen any possibility of changing this outlook in his case but her children had been brought up in a different tradition. Some women commented that they themselves rather enjoy housework: it gives a useful equilibrium to engage in practical as well as intellectual activities.

In the care of children, husbands did seem to play a rather greater part. Here most accepted a shared responsibility: in one instance husband and wife had agreed that each should be responsible to attending to one of their two young children during the night: it was therefore a matter of getting up according to which child was needing attention.

The situation obviously is rather different for women, divorced or single, coping with children single-handed. Yet no great difficulties were reported here — apart from possible delays, which are to be discussed later — in academic work while a young child has to be cared for. Emotional disturbances of children after a divorce had been a problem: but this too had been coped with.

Again, it has to be recognised that the women interviewed were those who had managed to cope with work and marriage. They knew of others who had not been able to combine the two. One referred to the fate of a woman colleague whose husband had accepted her career only with the proviso that the normal running of the household must not be affected: his view of the 'normal running' had included arranging a dinner party the night before an important examination for the wife. The woman had eventually withdrawn from her university post. In other cases also there may be a conflict between marriage and career which is resolved in this way. In one university it was possible to discuss such a decision with a woman who had earlier given up an assistantship post and the writing of her thesis because it seemed incompatible with attention to her home and child. Now, in her mid-thirties, she had returned to work in an administrative post but was finding that it did not satisfy her interests: she was wondering if it might be possible to begin study once more and even to make a new start on writing a thesis. Such a career pattern might have been easily possible earlier: but in the present economic climate and with the disadvantage of being at a 'mature' age — the government setting age limits for assistantships now — her prospects of returning to university are not promising. She may well be typical of a considerable number of women who have, in the past, held university assistantships only to give them up because of family pressures. Conflicts may of course also be resolved in favour of the career but there was little evidence of this situation except that two of the divorced women thought that possibly their absorption in work, and the circumstances imposed by their work, might have contributed to the break-up of their marriage. Other divorcees did not give such indications: and of the two just cited one had married very young which in itself might predispose to divorce.

The husband's occupation is likely to influence considerably both his attitude towards the wife's career and the possibilities of providing for additional domestic help. Husbands who are themselves academics understand much more readily the demands made by university teaching. In seven cases the husband was a university teacher in the same or in a related discipline: in others the husband taught in a different area of study. Most other husbands were graduates, in graduate professions. Relatively few were not academics. Thus the couple could enjoy discussion of their work or research interests together. And in a number of cases the moral support given by the husband had been important for the wife's career: the husband had, on various occasions, helped the wife to decide to apply for a post or to publish work or to continue with, and complete in good time, a doctoral thesis. In two or three cases the woman suggested that she might well have given up writing her thesis, or failed to work for further qualifications, if her husband had not urged her to go on: — though in the majority of cases such additional motivation had not been necessary, the woman being in herself sufficiently determined to go forward.

The difficulty of finding posts for two members of a family in one institution did not seem to have arisen to any great extent. One woman did note that at an early stage in her career her promotion had been delayed because her husband had been promoted that year, in the same university: and it seemed to the — possibly misogynistic — members of the relevant committee that two promotions in the one family in one year would be excessive. But in other instances no problems arose about appointing a couple: in some, indeed, they were welcomed. The situation in which husband and wife have different areas of specialisation within a subject obviously had made it easier for both to be appointed to higher ranks though for the sample interviewed it was mainly in science or medicine, rather than in the humanities, that both husband and wife were professors in the same subject area. The mobility problem generally seems to be rather less in France because of the tradition of commuting from the place of residence to the university where one works. There were certainly some heroic examples of commuting — e.g. from Paris to Bordeaux — at some period during the woman's life. Again, the traditional requirement of only a limited number of teaching periods per week for professors and less emphasis on pastoral functions and 'community involvement' in the French university have made it easier for a university teacher to limit the amount of time actually spent in the university: thus commuting is facilitated.

When this matter of university women teachers having husbands in the same or a similar occupation is considered, the comment of one eminent woman is worth remembering. She had found in her work with young women graduates that marriages were not likely to last if the woman married a non-graduate man, one whose educational level was inferior to her own. Possibly the marriage could last if the woman's ambitions went no higher than teaching at secondary school level: beyond that, prospects were not so good. Yet this, she suggested, may be an interesting case of sex bias, the acceptance of traditional sex stereotypes: if academic men can successfully maintain a marriage with women whose educational level is below their own, why should academic women not marry happily with men whose education is less than theirs? The situation is admittedly complex since in the past women have received less higher education than men: educational level may not correspond to the real competence of the woman. There is also the question of the effect of higher education on personality, beliefs, way of life and there is the question of how and by whom decisions are made within a marriage. But the observation of this woman in France ties in with the finding of Kelsall et al.[10] in the UK that 'graduate women were much more likely than graduate men to have a highly educated spouse'. It is also conceivable that men and women choose their spouses for different reasons. Certainly there is a tradition of expecting the husband to be better educated — possibly more intelligent than the wife — and a recent investigation in the DDR[11] showed traces of this attitude still among the younger women studied. One may recall too the comment of the woman in the British sample who had been determined that her husband would have a degree with first class Honours. If there is this tendency of highly educated women to seek husbands at the same level, it could also account for the view expressed in more than one country that for young women the university has in the past been a place in which to find a suitable husband. (One must emphasise that this tradition is said to have disappeared but possibly because there is now less conviction that marriage is the only career for a woman rather than because of belief that the level of husband's education does not matter.)

Thus far, the attitudes and beliefs of the women who were married, with children, have been reported. The beliefs of the unmarried women are also noteworthy. Some of these thought that they could not have coped with marriage and children as well as a university career. Yet one unmarried woman had deliberately chosen to accept the additional load of an adopted child though she recognised that the adoption process had held up her thesis for at least a year. Unmarried women who were uncertain of their own ability to cope with the dual role did in some instances also recognise that they had colleagues who were coping — so evidently it was possible to combine the two roles. Yet they suggested that for some of these colleagues the strain was considerable. One thought that in her department it was only single or separated women who managed to complete their thesis. (Yet this correlation is by no means proved. And in the case of one childless couple, the woman remarked that as they had lived for ten years with her husband's thesis — newly successfully completed — she did not think they could stand the strain of another thesis, her own: so she was renouncing.)

Altogether the group provided evidence that, whatever the complications and strains of the dual role, some women have mastered these circumstances admirably: they have reached a high academic position, they have a happy marriage and children apparently about to embark — or already embarked — on good careers. University teaching does, as many women remarked, present some great advantages to the woman also busy with family responsibilities. There is a fair amount of flexibility in deciding exactly at what hours the woman has to be in the university: it may also be possible to re-arrange times of meetings with students if there is a family emergency: it may even be possible to change the time of year during which a certain course will be taught, if the woman is going to require maternity leave (the obligatory leave is six weeks before the birth, ten weeks after, though for a third child the leave is extended so that the mother can have ten weeks before and 16 after the birth). Granted that colleagues may not always be entirely cooperative about adapting to the married woman's circumstances — e.g. may refuse to come to a group meeting at her home while she is pregnant or may continue firmly to have departmental meetings in the late afternoon — the work of university teachers still has much to commend it from the point of view of the married woman with family cares. At the same time, secondary school teaching, if the woman is an agrégée and has to teach only 15 hours a week, can have even greater advantages since hours when she is not actually teaching are less heavily encroached on by class preparation and especially by research work.

Nevertheless there was an overwhelming consensus as to the effect that child-bearing must have on a woman's career. To some extent, the effect may depend on the stage at which children are produced. There were opinions in favour both of the postponement of child-bearing and early child-bearing. For postponement it was argued that if the woman has her thesis out of the way she has more time to give attention to children: her position is established and less 'leisure' time need be given to research work. Moreover, at the higher levels of appointment the woman is more master of her own time: the hours of required teaching are fewer at professorial level. Alternatively, some argued, if child-bearing occurs at a relatively early age — during university first degree studies, or just after — then the children will have reached what could be considred a less demanding age while the woman is still young enough to embark on a thesis and devote much effort to her academic work. Two of the women appointed to a professor-ship about the age of 30 had in fact married young and combined having children with writing their theses. One of these noted that being at home during the latter weeks of pregnancy offered a particularly good opportunity to get on with the thesis. But others who had married immediately after completing their initial studies and begun their family soon after, had had relatively large families so that child-bearing had alternated with acquiring higher qualifications. The cases of early marriage, early child-bearing, thesis, promotion were rare. More com-mon were the instances of years combining raising children with trying to acquire higher qualifications, promotion coming rather late — or even entry to univer-sity teaching coming late.

Many women recognised that their children had slowed down their academic progress: though sometimes they themselves had deliberately decided to enjoy their children while they were young. Many considered that children are the main reason for the minority situation of women in university teaching. At this stage, they believe, many women decide to withdraw from academic work and devote themselves to their family. A few commented that at present some women still feel that their identity is established through their family: to be successful, women must have children. Added to this pressure is the common view in society that a woman who does not attend to her household is odd: she is not fulfilling the role expected of her by society. And this same social tradition protects the man's time in the family circle if he wants to spend his leisure in academic work: it is characteristically the woman's role to have his meals ready, see to his comfort and keep the children out of the way while he works in peace at his thesis. Women seldom enjoy such conditions in the family home. But, some women pointed out, the traditions of society do impose on the man the duty of being the bread-winner for the family: thus there seems to be justification for supporting his efforts to better the standard of living of the family by achieving his higher qualification. In some instances, the husband's acceptance of this traditional role may mean that he decides *not* to continue in academic work but to go out into industry or commerce to earn more for the family: and then, possibly, the wife may enjoy the luxury of engaging in academic research later.

The dual role undoubtedly demands a great deal from the woman. Repeatedly it was stressed that the woman must be able to organise her time and her work. She must have the self-discipline to give her various tasks the right attention at the right time, to make a timetable for herself, and the family, and stick to it. Something also depends on her ability to detach her attention: some women find that they can 'switch over' to academic work when this is appropriate and forget temporarily the domestic problems which are also calling for attention. Some women can work in the home while the children are playing: others cannot. Those who achieve early a good academic position appear to be especially characterised by this kind of control over their thought processes.

Allied to this discipline, as many women spontaneously pointed out, is health. To cope with all the demands on her, a woman must have the good fortune to be healthy, not only in the particular circumstances of pregnancy but also in day-to-day living where physical stamina and energy are important. Some women admittedly have coped with health problems, miscarriages or difficult pregnancies as well. But those who have, for instance, managed with taking only 5 or 8 days off to have a child do seem to be at a great advantage.

Given such factors and the high demands of an academic career on the one side and the social pressures of women's traditional roles on the other, it is perhaps not surprising that women opt out of the academic profession or settle for a relatively low rank within it. As one woman explained 'Les femmes se lassent' ('Women get tired'). Yet as another put it: 'Il ne faut pas lâcher' ('one mustn't give up').

It must be added that it is not only married women who have family responsibilities. Two single women interviewed had to attend to ageing parents whose illness or simply increasing age and debility demanded hours of attention. Two others, as we have noted, had also a child to attend to.

A further point made was that in the university demands may be more often made of single women than of married women. The latter may not be asked to cope with administrative chores because it is felt that they have to deal with domestic affairs instead. The single women, on occasion, felt that they were therefore looked upon as being especially available to cope with administrative or other departmental tasks which were time-consuming and demanding but which in no way would contribute to their academic advancement. Such complaints could be seen as balancing the views of some married women as to the lack of consideration shown by departments — as one put it, men can sit there confident in the knowledge that they will be provided with an evening meal whenever they get home, women have to cope with putting together that meal after a protracted meeting; or departments arrange meetings for Wednesday, which is the day when mothers of young children want to be available for children who don't go to school that day — but this reason cannot be advanced by a woman for failure to participate in meetings arranged then. The matter of who teaches evening classes can also be a source of difficulty though in some departments it seems to be settled harmoniously, men accepting such hours with equanimity, married women avoiding them.

Maternity leave

Reference has already been made to some aspects of this provision. In the group were many women who had had their children before the advent of compulsory provisions like those of the present day. Despite current attempts to provide well for working women who are having children, quite a few of those interviewed were vague as to exactly what provision is now made and to what extent it was compulsory. This, however, may depend on the subject area in which women are working for in some branches of science, for example, the employer has a clear responsibility to ensure that the pregnant woman is not placed in a potentially dangerous situation by working in an advanced state of pregnancy.

It was recognised by some women also that maternity leave can cause considerable inconvenience for colleagues. Replacements may not be available during the weeks of absence. Where the woman is a specialist it may not be possible for colleagues to replace her or for a suitably qualified replacement to be found. As one woman put it: one may not be indispensable but one is not interchangeable. In some cases, the woman arranges her pregnancies so that maternity leave comes during university vacations anyway or reorganises the year's timetable so as to give her classes without interruption: but in many instances some disorganisation or inconvenience results from maternity leave.

Attitudes towards maternity provisions varied. A few had found colleagues unsympathetic to the problems which pregnancy imposed — and this reaction came from female as well as male colleagues. Yet one married woman with four children of her own considered that some of her women colleagues exaggerated the maternity leave requirement and insisted on taking the maximum amount of leave even when this was unhelpful to the work of their department. It seemed to her also that some such women indulged themselves in excessive absenteeism and showed lack of enthusiasm for their university work on the pretext of having to attend to family responsibilities.

Prejudice against women

Answers to the question about possible prejudice against women in university teaching varied considerably. Certainly there was no indication of general prejudice on the part of students, though one respondent observed that students coming from countries where the status of women is lower may find it difficult to adapt to meeting women in positions of authority in the university. There was consensus that the atmosphere in the university is more liberal than that to be found in industry and commerce where inequalities of pay were noted and women had difficulties in reaching positions of authority. Two or three women commented on the belief common among employers that women are more often absent from work and employers' use of this belief to give women lower pay and lower positions. One instanced the extreme difficulty that had been found in placing a highly qualified young woman with a firm which could use her skills in computer science: she was amused at the anomalous reaction of a firm which was persuaded to employ her temporarily: once they had overcome their initial resistance and got to know her work they were keen to keep her, since she was excellent at the job.

Within the university women often said that in their own department or faculty there was no prejudice against women. It was sometimes suggested that other faculties might retain prejudices: but women now in those faculties — natural sciences, law, medicine which were suggested by outsiders — did not find prejudice there, though some prejudice had been noted in the past by young female medical students. Further, some of the group maintained that they had never encountered prejudice against women in their own personal experience. They substantiated this view by referring to appointments made within their own department and the policy of certain professors in recruiting women teachers in the department — even if this policy had not led to equal numbers of men and women staff in the department. As we have seen, there was even some questioning as to whether women are in a minority. (Yet in one university studied the proportions were one woman out of 14 at 1st class professor level, 6 out of 26 at second professorial level, 23 out of 75 at maître-assistant level and 15 out of 37 at assistant level.) This strange misperception had been noticed by one eminent woman who recalled that when she was about to enter the Sorbonne in the 50s one of the few women already there asked her if she did not think there were perhaps quite enough women already in the place. (Similar misperceptions were noticed concerning the proportion of women who are married and coping with university work: some women said that relatively few married women were able to cope, they themselves being unmarried: yet in one university, at professorial level (both ranks), 6 out of 7 women were married, 18 out of 23 at maître-assistant level and 12 out of 15 at assistant level. Similarly, women may have the impression of equal numbers of male and female students at mastership levels: counting sometimes surprises them by revealing a greater number of males.)

Nevertheless the facts of their own appointment must have reinforced for women an impression of absence of prejudice. Apart from those entering the Ecole Normale Supérieure de Jeunes Filles, all had entered departments where the head was a man: their appointment was approved by men and in many cases they were positively encouraged by male professors to seek or to take up an appointment. The number of women in positions of authority is not yet great enough to enable a 'female line of succession' to be established. Mostly the research work done by the women had been directed by men, though some women now have experience of heading a research team and being in a position to encourage — as many explicitly are doing — young women to seek higher academic qualifications. Thus it is not surprising that mostly the women say they themselves have not encountered prejudice: though one did emphasise the importance of the 'patron's' voice in getting promotion: one felt that her promotion had been delayed through the fact that she was a married woman with children: one had not been appointed earlier to a post in her university because at that time in the past there was prejudice against women.

Yet even if prejudice had not been personally encountered women generally did not deny that prejudice against women exists in universities. Frequently it was suggested that among the 'old guard', the professors appointed many years ago, there is a belief that women are not really suited to university studies and certainly not to high teaching posts in universities. The university has been 'le fief des hommes' ('a male preserve'). Such prejudices might affect the decisions made when applicants for posts were being considered: but in cases when a woman is not appointed it is impossible to know whether prejudice has entered into the decision or not, since outsiders have no knowledge of the 'dossier' (records) submitted by applicants. Some prejudice had been noted in committees where the challenging of a male president's view by a woman seemed to be particularly resented. On a few occasions it seemed as if it simply did not occur to men to nominate women for various posts. One woman entering a department noted for its progressive views had found that, initially at least, male colleagues seemed to resent to some extent her superior status: two others had encountered such a reaction as directors of departments: one who had in fact been encouraged to come to the university by a male colleague found that when she was in post he apparently resented her position. More generally it was noted that the learned Academies are still almost exclusively male: there are few women in the Collège de France: only recently have women been getting places in the Grandes Ecoles and been appointed to the major state administrations.

An index of the belief that some prejudices still remain is to be found in the statement made spontaneously by many of the group: to be appointed to a post, a woman has to be better than a man — the estimates of how much better varied from 'twice as good', 'have done twice as much research' to 'a bit better' or 'ten times better'. Once appointed, however, women were accepted: or rather, once their competence had been shown, they were accepted on equal terms. But to gain this acceptance there had to be some special effort, not only in the quantity and quality of research or publication, but possibly on the personal level too. In leadership roles, one woman thought women tend to be less authoritarian than men: they have nevertheless to see that their authority is accepted and this requires some role-playing on the part of the woman.

One of the group noted the consequences of this situation in which women have — allegedly — to be better than men to be appointed. Mediocre men have a chance of getting to top positions in universities: but women who do get there have to be good. Hence, sometimes, men experience a certain fear of their women colleagues, of women who are indeed distinctively good and are, in many cases, imposing personalities.

Yet women who are successful are not necessarily feminist in their outlook. More than once it was suggested that women who succeed in university teaching assimilate to men, adopt their way of behaving and their standards of judgment so that eventually they end by being rather anti-feminist in their outlook. This form of assimilation was viewed as regrettable. But one successful woman did comment that while there was prejudice against women, to some extent, some women were themselves to blame because of their failure to work as competently as their male colleagues, their readiness to absent themselves and to avoid some work on the excuse of domestic commitments. Some women were seen as over-reacting to any anti-feminist remarks: more than one member of the group thought the ability to laugh off any such comments was worth having — and she herself possessed it. For some of the group, women's lack of advancement was due not so much to prejudice as to lack of determination on the part of women themselves.

Prejudice of course can be found not only in public life. Parents and families may also have stereotyped views of the appropriate role for a woman. In the main the women interviewed had come from families where such prejudices did not exist though some had had mothers with traditional views and, as we have seen, families not opposed to higher education for women still had — fathers especially, perhaps — decided views as to the kind of career which was suitable for females. One woman noted also that her father, an industrialist, had very stereotyped ideas about women employees.

The dominant impression was that universities may, in the past, have entertained some prejudices against women but such prejudices are dying out with the older generation of male professors. At present universities are more liberal than the rest of society. Women are seen as having equal chances in competitive examinations: the evaluation of research and qualifications is probably fair — it was noted in various cases there simply were fewer female than male applicants for a post. The (then) Minister for Universities was cited as having bemoaned the fact that in the 'vivier' (stock-pool) from which appointments to official committees and similar bodies could be made, there were very few women. Where prejudice exists, it may be implicit and even unconscious — men, perhaps, do not want women crowding them. It was not regarded as a major factor in determining the minority situation of women in university teaching or at professorial levels. Few women felt that they themselves had suffered from such prejudice.

Attitudes towards the feminist movement were similarly affected by personal experiences. As various women pointed out, one should not speak of 'the' feminist movement since there have been, and are, a number of such movements in France: it is indeed possibly a weakness that their energies, within a feminist trend, may have been dissipated by 'des querelles de clocher' ('parish pump disputes'). Reactions to feminist movements seemed to fall into three categories.

1) Some women were enthusiastic participants or had been so. They joined in meetings, writing, teaching certain courses related to women's rights. Similar enthusiasms were noted among female students in some Paris university departments. In Paris were some women who were very well-known in feminist circles and highly active in one or other movement. One organisation mentioned was the international organisation CEFRES — Centre Européen Féminin de Recherche sur l'Evolution de la Société — whose aims are to improve communication between societies and between the sexes by disseminating information, by research through working groups, by education and by the establishment of an institute to ensure these activities. Founded in 1977 CEFRES has consultative status within the Council of Europe.

2) A larger group was that of women who expressed some sympathy for feminist movements but were not themselves members of such movements and would not take an active part in furthering such activities. The amount of sympathy for feminism varied from those who admitted to feeling guilty about not being more active — one said that at least she defended feminist activities in social discussions with friends, at dinner parties, etc. — to those who felt that they personally had no reason to engage in work for the rights of women but that they recognised that the reforms which feminists were trying to introduce were worthwhile. Equal pay for women — in occupations outside the universities — was admitted to be something that should be introduced. There was also generally approval for feminist work in promoting legislation about abortion (though it was noted that in France the period during which 'voluntary interruption of pregnancy'

can be carried out is shorter than in Britain, ten weeks being the limit for termination.) Yet one or two had reservations about abortion: one stressed that in dealing with both contraception (which she approved of) and abortion (about which she was 'réticente') feminists did not always take psychological factors sufficiently into account. Quite a number of women, while expressing some support for feminism thought that at times the feminist organisations made themselves laughable by exaggerated claims. One objected to the 'absolutism' of claims that women are the same as men in all ways. 'Je suis femme' and I like being a woman, she said. Men and women are different: it is silly to claim otherwise. Many deplored the wish of some feminist groups to erect barriers against men which might be as unreasonable as the barriers set up by men against women. If society is to be improved, there should not be exclusive, hostile separations.

3) Extreme views and claims were negatively evaluated by the small minority who actively dislike feminist organisations: this group found such organisations unnecessary and unreasonable.

Further points were made concerning prejudices affecting women. Some of the group objected to being used as symbols for propaganda purposes because they were women who had been successful in their careers or extra-mural activities. One who was outstanding in mountain sports disliked the way in which feminist groups tried to use her: she certainly did not want to restrict competition in such activities — or participation in them — to one-sex groups. Others, women in particular, were trade union members in self-defence. (Thus another factor comes into the making of appointments. Much may depend on the political convictions not only of a department but of the central body of the university or of the members of central committees evaluating suitability for appointment. A candidate, either male or female, whose political views are in tune with the immediate university environment may be looked upon with less favour by a group in another university or central committee whose political orientation is different.)

Career prospects are thus influenced not only by possibly anti-feminist prejudices but by other prejudices or deeply held opinions. There are, too, other aspects which may awaken prejudices. One unmarried woman thought that attitudes towards married women are more favourable than those towards the unmarried: the married woman has a definite status, the authorities feel they 'know where they are': but the young unmarried woman may be seen as a potential threat to settled relationships within the department — or indeed, from the point of view of conservative elders, potentially immoral. Unfavourable interpretations may also be made of the life-style of the older unmarried woman. But this was not a view widely expressed.

Relationships between teachers and students may also be differently interpreted for men and women. Friendships or liaisons between male university teachers and female students are not regarded as matters for official disapproval: but, one woman suggested, such relationships between female teachers and male students would evoke adverse reactions. It seemed to her too that this kind of relationship was more likely to develop in arts than in science departments: the claims of laboratory work in science keep teachers more fully occupied: arts male teachers, with a limited number of teaching hours, have more time to become bored and are more likely to fill the vacuum with interests in female students. But this view may well be idiosyncratic.

In general then, though a minority actively supported feminist activities and felt strong commitments to them, the majority were sympathetic but gave only passive support. Evaluation of feminist organisations did have positive aspects and one woman suggested that in France such organisations concentrate sensibly on major issues instead of on the trivialities reported of some American groups.

Perceptions of differences between male and female characteristics

Most but not all women agreed that there are some differences perceptible in the attitudes and beliefs of males and females though the origin of such differences is unclear: the majority pointed out the very strong effects of social conditioning of girls to adopt allegedly feminine roles and feminine traits.

The causes of differences may therefore be the result of pressures in the family and society rather than innate factors. But, whatever the cause, many women noted differences in the styles adopted by men and women in public meetings and in leadership situations. Women were seen as less aggressive; as having to force themselves, on occasion, to express their views strongly in order to have them recognised in discussions where men were in the majority: as having to adopt a different style of language on some such occasions. At the same time, women who had occupied leadership positions thought that women could be more effective than men in dealing with difficult interpersonal relationships, in sorting out administrative squabbles, partly because of an ability to be more generally understanding and less inflexible about their own position than men, partly because of lesser personal involvement and a refusal to tangle with heated disputants.

Some three or four women suggested that women have less self-confidence than men because of social conditioning. But generally it was not believed that lack of self-confidence could lead to failure to publish or to apply for positions. Two women admitted that they disliked writing scientific reports but this they saw as a personal reaction, not necessarily characteristic of their sex. Another disliked speaking in meetings of university committees though she had no problem in talking to student groups. This too seemed a personal rather than a general reaction. There were thus relatively few examples of feelings of handicap because of distinctively female traits: and many of the women had in fact published extensively and had no problem at all about seeking publication or offering their work for public scrutiny.

Changes in the minority situation of women in university teaching

While it was agreed that more women are now teaching in universities than formerly it was not anticipated that equal proportions of men and women teachers or professors would be found in the near future. Some years would elapse before women now at assistant level could write their theses and qualify for professorial appointments. But two or three women suggested that university teaching is no longer so attractive to men: it is enjoying or beginning to enjoy less public prestige: much higher salaries can be earned by men with similar qualifications outside the universities. Hence women, making lesser demands for pay and prestige, may encounter less competition from men when they apply for posts. One young woman asserted that a man would have to be remarkably highly motivated to enter university teaching at the present time.

But the major reasons given for the absence of women at the higher levels of university teaching and in university teaching generally did not suggest that there would be a radical change in the situation soon. Overwhelmingly, the reason most often mentioned was the effect of children on a woman's career. While it was evident from the example of many women interviewed that a woman can successfully combine a family — even a family of three or four children — and a university career, the family factor was frequently instanced as the major drawback to academic advancement.

Closely allied to this reason was the matter of writing the thèse d'état. Certainly the importance attached to this factor varied according to the discipline. It was in Arts, the area in which women are most likely to be found, that the problem was greatest, the requirements of the traditional thesis involving a period of concentrated work for some ten years. Not only was there the question of the amount of time required, the nature of the work itself was substantially criticised. Women did not like the idea of being committed to one particular area over so long a period of time: interests could change, new ideas for research present themselves: or the research interests of some women were not in areas which could be satisfactorily dealt with by the traditional forms of thesis — e.g. clinical psychology. The researcher with an interdisciplinary approach may find it difficult to obtain the necessary sponsor-supervisor and may be sent from one department to another, under the pretext that the proposed thesis does not 'belong' to the departments approached. Thus thesis requirements may be seen as hampering the creative development of researchers rather than enhancing it. Since too there is the tradition of not publishing during the period of preparation of the thesis — so as not to 'déflorer la thèse' ('deflower the thesis') — there could be a long period with no publication record. Further there was the new factor that in present circumstances successful completion of a thesis does not ensure appointment at a higher level. Both women and men with a completed thesis may remain at maître-assistant level.

Some women mentioned that the state doctorate can now be obtained by a 'thèse sur travaux', that is, by a work incorporating a number of the writer's existing publications. But while this is technically an equivalent qualification it is not recognised as having the same validity for appointment to higher posts. Informally, it may be regarded as more appropriate to those nearing retirement age and keen to have a respectable title.

The higher education agrégation as it exists in other subject areas of law, politics, economics and management studies, does not seem to be regarded as such a significant barrier: nor does the secondary education agrégation seem to be regarded as problematic, especially for those approaching it through the ENS. Certainly the higher education agrégation which follows on a doctoral study is viewed as a very demanding test: in some ways, it is less under the individual's control than a thèse d'état which, after all, can be done in the individual's own time, at the individual's own pace, whereas the agrégation demands concentrated thought on specific examination days, full preparedness to cope with questions and to remain constantly up to date with the subject up to the time of examination. (Though one must recognise that the final 'soutenance' (defence) of a thesis also leaves the candidate open to possibly hostile and certainly searching questions by experts in the field.) Certainly the agrégation was not cited as a barrier to women's progress; though the possibility of being sent to a post in some unsatisfactory location was indicated as potentially a deterrent to some women.

The 1983 reform of higher education may thus be a means of removing, through the abolition of the state doctorate, something that women have seen as a barrier to advancing in their career. Yet it posed clear conditions for appointment. It remains to be seen whether a new 'habilitation' process, if introduced, will be more objective or more or less demanding.

The mobility problem is clearly important in women's careers too though the group interviewed consisted of women who had, on the whole, managed to find an appointment in the same place as their husbands. Even so, there were some reports of very strenuous experiences of commuting over a period of years — e.g. from Paris to Bordeaux, from Grenoble to Clermont-Ferrand. A few with this experience did recognise that it can put a considerable strain on a marriage in addition to the strain of constant travelling for the individual. Mobility questions can well affect the French university woman teacher's decisions about applying for posts.

Yet, as has been evident, the care of the house and of children can be coped with. Women interviewed had managed to find suitable domestic help. If both partners have a good income, such domestic provision can be paid for without too much difficulty. They had also benefited by an acceptant attitude on the part of husbands: though some had accepted that they must maintain a high level of domestic comfort since that was what their husband expected and was accustomed to. But the sheer interest in being with children, particularly in the early days was recognised by various members of the group: while they had, in most cases, managed to satisfy both this interest and the demands of work outside the home, they could see that other women might well opt to look after their children and they were familiar with examples of women who had given up university work to do so.

Other causes of the minority situation may lie, finally, in the attitudes of women themselves towards their careers. In a good many cases, it takes a considerable length of time to achieve top positions. There are other interests for the woman: not only domestic interests but social, sporting, political activities to attract her. Given these and the demands of research, publication, teaching, administration, thesis-writing, some women — as a number of the group remarked — simply get tired: they give up. It was widely admitted that to be a successful university teacher and to cope with family demands (or other relationships) demands a very high standard of self-discipline and organisation: as one highly successful young woman remarked, one has no 'personal time', every hour is earmarked for teaching, research or family. Health also affects or is affected by this demanding life-style. It is indeed rather remarkable that so many women in fact accept and thrive upon such an exacting way of life: though one must recognise the great strength of motivation coming from interest in their subject. This interest is a highly important factor.

Motivation, however, seems to be reinforced in rather few cases by the desire to make a success from the career point of view. As some pointed out, women in present-day society, do not have quite the same pressure as men to be the breadwinner. Women can offer themselves the luxury of staying at home: and one very eminent woman said that at times she could envy such women. Few, if any, seem motivated by the feeling that they must establish female potential in a male-dominated world. They simply go ahead with work which interests them and which they feel they can do well.

Thus the lack of large numbers of women at professorial level seems explicable. Fewer women write theses, fewer are eligible for appointment. Fewer women have been appointed at the lower levels of university teaching. Some women may be inhibited from seeking to go further by consideration of how placement might interrupt the family life they cherish. Some are simply contented with the level at which they find themselves.

It became clear in interviewing in France as in the other countries that there are distinguishable types of women. We noted earlier the different career patterns that could be traced. But it is also noticeable that there are some women, the highly distinguished scholars, who have from an early age been keen to study and carry out research in their subject: they have published their work and acquired a reputation. There are others who are keen to influence events in their university or community: who have driving force and energy and enthusiasm which leads them to top administrative positions.

Others, of whom some have entered university teaching almost by accident, have done or are doing some useful research but are also keenly interested in teaching (there is not an inevitable dichotomy between teaching and research but individual interests may lean to one side or the other). They do not aspire to positions of authority: they want to continue work at their present level of maître-assistant or chef de travaux because this combines happily with other aspects of their life, possibly the care of their family, and they find it satisfying. So they will not write thèses d'état nor apply for professorships.

Developments in university teaching in France

At the time of the investigation, governmental measures seemed to be bearing hard down on the universities. In particular the areas where women are most involved, the Arts, education, the social sciences, had been subjected to cuts in resources and in state validation of courses offered. Reductions in the number of posts available could reintroduce discrimination against female candidates: the argument, with some evidence to support it, that women less often produce thèses d'état, could be advanced as a reason for appointing male rather than female candidates. Such arguments could persist even with new reforms of the structure.

The coming to power of the Mitterand government in 1981 seemed to reduce the pressure on the universities: the disappearance of the separate Ministry for Higher Education could however be regarded as an ambivalent move, possibly to be interpreted as bringing the universities back into more centralised control. The 1983 reform provisions while allegedly maintaining university autonomy yet indicate greater control of teaching performance, additional teaching duties and limited-term validations of qualifications. The new provisions once formulated and enforced by law will of course affect both men and women teachers (teachers-researchers) in universities. But there is no mention in the statement of general objectives, of a need to ensure equality for women in higher education, either as students or staff. Perhaps it is assumed that this has been achieved or can be left to take care of itself. Careful attention is given to stating the (democratic) nature of the new CSU committees — but will women be well represented on them?

In sympathising with all teachers in higher education in France as to the turmoil which far-reaching reforms, however well-intentioned, must cause, one must wait with special interest to see how the new conditions will affect women who are or who could be university teachers.

Notes:

1. J. Minot: *L'Enseignement Universitaire,* (Ministère de l'Education — Ministère des Universités, 1979), p.54. Unesco Statistical Yearbooks, passim.
2. Ministère de l'Education, Service des Etudes Informatiques et Statistiques: 'Statistiques des Examens du Baccalauréat d'Enseignement Général, du Baccalauréat de Technicien et du Baccalauréat Expérimental, Session 1980 — Résultats Définitifs' (Paris, 1981), Note 81-05, p.3.
3. Ibid.
4. Ministère de l'Education, Service des Etudes Informatiques et Statistiques: 'Année 1979-80: Effectifs Post-Baccalauréat' (Paris, 1981) summary table.
5. Le Monde de l'Education: 'Treize ans de résultats à Paris: la palme aux lycées de filles' (mars, 1983), pp.22-24.
6. Joël-Yves Plouvin: *Le régime juridique des universités depuis la Loi d'Orientation* (Economica, Paris, 1980).
7. M. Cordier: 'La situation des femmes dans les cadres professoraux de l'Université', (Diplômées, déc. 1979), 11, pp.70-85.
8. Ministère de l'Education, Service des Etudes Informatiques et Statistiques: 'Les Principales Caractéristiques des Enseignants en Fonction dans les Etablissements d'Enseignement Supérieur, Année 1978-79' (Paris, 1979), Note 79-34, p.2.
9. F. Euvrard: 'Travail des Femmes et Revenu Familial', (*Informations Sociales,* mar. 1980), pp.54-60.
10. R. Kelsall, A. Poole, A. Kuhn: *Six Years After* (Higher Education Research Unit, Dept. of Sociological Studies, Sheffield University, 1970), p.83-4.
11. K. Starke: *Junge Partner: Tatsachen über Liebesbeziehungen im Jugendalter,* (Urania Verlag, Leipzig-Jena- Berlin, 1980), pp.182-3.

Chapter Four

'A Woman Has To Choose'

The situation of women now teaching in universities in West Germany must be seen as deriving from an educational history shared with East Germany until the years following the Second World War. Germany has some of the longest established universities of Europe: but in Germany as in other European countries university education was, almost without exception, for men only until the growing demand of women for admission to this territory in the latter part of the nineteenth century. The delights of traditional student life, the student songs, the student societies and even the distinctive principles of Lern- und Lehrfreiheit (the freedom to study and to teach — in universities) have been part of the heritage of German men rather than German women: though one should also note that this heritage has been mainly transferred to males of relatively well-to-do families. Germany, again like other European countries, has shown a predominance of middle-class family backgrounds among its university students.

Entry to university study in the nineteenth century was complicated by women's uncertain position with regard to matriculation requirements. The Abitur was recognised as the certificate giving matriculation qualification: but women might not have this certificate. If not matriculated students they might, nevertheless, be admitted as 'Hörer', listeners to lectures, a favour which gave them access to knowledge, certainly, but not to subsequent professional qualifications. The attitudes of universities varied considerably and, in some instances, it was affected by the government of the state in which the university found itself: the Minister for Education might declare that decisions to admit women to lectures were to be made by the Minister rather than by the university authority or individual teachers.

This matter of state governments remains of importance in West German education today. There are 11 states constituting the Federal German Republic and each has its own Ministry of Education. While there is coordination at federal level and, since 1969, a Federal Ministry of Education, decisions on legislation affecting education are made in the Parliament of each state: even when agreement as to a policy has been reached at federal level there can still be delays in implementation and differences in interpretation at state level, according to the views of the political party in control of the state in question. Thus the Federal Law concerning Higher Education which was passed in 1975 was still being worked out by individual states some four years later.

But intervention of central government has in the past also affected the decisions of individual universities and the fate of individual students. The earliest

German woman graduate, Dr. Dorothea Erxleben, was admitted to study at the University of Halle (now in East Germany) by a special dispensation of Frederick the Great — a dispensation which had, incidentally, to be given twice since the first permission in 1741 was not used, the lady having decided first to get married: only after having four children, and after the death of her husband, did she pursue her university plans and in 1754 achieve the doctoral qualification. As Professor Lotte Adolphs points out in her report of this interesting case,[1] Dorothea Erxleben herself analysed clearly the difficulties which lie in the way of women who want to study and some of these are still highly relevant today. She recognised the problem of combining household duties and study: and though she did not accept that the two are necessarily incompatible, Dr. Erxleben's own experience would seem to demonstrate the interruption, or at least, slowing down of academic advancement which a family may cause. She did however suggest that while women may recognise the value of study they also see it as a heavy burden and prefer other occupations to the exertions that study demands: they may lack persistence and fail to study consistently when the time is ripe. From a later point of view we might note another circumstance of considerable importance, the role which her father played in Dorothea Erxleben's studies. He himself was a medical doctor and instructed his daughter in philosophy and medicine. He also provided a preface to her book encouraging women to study — and, incidentally, assured readers that the book was her work alone. The value of the right family background is thus, as Professor Adolphs points out, of considerable importance.

But such instances of learned women have been uncommon. It was not until the nineteenth century that a concerted demand for women's place in universities grew in strength: and it is possibly significant that some of the strongest motivation seems to have been in the desire of women to study medicine. Intermittently, various German universities gave permission for women to attend lectures, subject, on occasion, to the agreement of the individual lecturers.[2] (Heidelberg appears to have been the earliest in allowing such admissions in 1864.) Only in 1896 was the situation regularised and women made able officially to become matriculated students of universities. And it was not until 1920 that women were admitted to university teaching.

Once entrance was conceded, progress in the admission of women students to universities would appear to have been rather similar to that in the United Kingdom, apart from the effects of the Nazi regime in the '30s when the role allocated to women did not emphasise higher learning and when entry to university was hedged about with some additional restrictions. (The *total* number of university students fell during this period from 121,000 to 56,000.)[3] But when Hans Anger carried out a survey of *Problems of the German university* in 1954-55,[4] the proportion of women among university students was 21%. But, as he pointed out, the proportion of women among university teachers was remarkably low, not only absolutely but in comparison with other Western European countries at the time. In making such comparisons however one has to bear in mind which people are counted as university teachers. If in West Germany only those in 'established' posts are taken into account, this will produce unfavourable comparisons with countries like the UK in which lecturers are, as holders of tenured posts, taken into the reckoning. In the German situation only those of higher ranks are classed as Hochschullehrer — university teachers. Even so, when Anger made his survey the percentage of women among established professors was 0.6 (there was no 'ausserordentliche' professor). Among supernumerary professors, Dozents and Privatdozents, women's percentage rose to 2.9. But among the 'nichthabilitiert' wissentschaftliche Assistenten (non-qualified academic assistants), the percentage was 11.0.[5]

Anger, whose point of view seems generously liberal on the matter of women's participation in universities, notes that various findings pointed to the effect of not only a university attitude towards women but of a general social-political attitude; this attitude was conservative-traditionalist and rejected the presence of women in the academic world. To some extent, it was associated with the attitudes of the members of traditional student organisations or 'corporations'; such societies were favourably viewed by members of the physical science, medical and catholic-theological faculties who had a negative or sceptical attitude to women students or women teachers. Anger found that when the performance of male and female students was discussed, the majority opinion was that no perceptible difference in achievement was evident: but in many cases this statement was followed by comments indicating that women achieved their good results through 'bee-like' diligence whereas men were qualitatively superior in the range and depth of their thinking. There was a widespread tendency to assume that women should follow the stereotyped roles of wife and mother and that they were neither physically nor mentally fit for the role of university teacher. Attitudes to women students showed the following distribution:[6]

positive	4%
conditionally positive	15%
conditionally negative	40%
definitely rejecting	24%
uncertain	17%

And to women university teachers:[7]

positive	2%
conditionally positive	9%
negative, with reservations	40%
definitely rejecting	39%
uncertain	10%

Not surprisingly, 89% of a group of Dozents found the reason for the minority situation of women among the teaching staff as being due to defects in women themselves: 32% of Professors did recognise the possibility of the influence of some prejudice against women in the university faculties or in society generally: yet even here only 8% attributed a really important role to prejudice while 24% thought that it might be playing a certain subsidiary role.

The distribution of reasons which attributed the minority situation to characteristics of women themselves was this:[8]

Lack of intellectual or productive-creative abilities	54%
The career of university teacher is incompatible with the constitution, biological destiny or natural aspirations of a woman	37%
Lack of physical strength and 'robustness'	16%
Lack of teaching effectiveness, ability to convince, authority	9%
Lack of persistence, strength of will and self-confidence	8%

The conclusion reached by Anger was that the existence of a general stereotype of the role of women in society generally determined attitudes towards women in the universities. Those respondents who specifically referred to their own experiences with women students or university teachers were likely to give positive evaluations of women in universities: those respondents who claimed to have no such experiences were universally negative in their view. But there was no correlation between the frequency of women students in the respondents' faculties and the favourable or unfavourable evaluation: the willingness of the individual to make such contacts seemed more important than the possibility of making such contacts. A good point of language use is also made by Anger: those who referred to 'women' or 'the nature of women' only in the collective sense — as if women were one entity — never showed a positively favourable attitude to women.

In general there was a hostile attitude to women as university teachers and to a certain extent to women as university students. Such attitudes could obviously affect the numbers of women proceeding to university teaching in a system where at that time initial entry as assistant depended largely on professorial decisions. Thus the analysis of what university teachers perceived as the *motivation* of male and female students is interesting,[9] even if the number in this sub-group of respondents was small (51).

	Students	
	Female	**Male**
Irrelevant motives, including 'marriage market'	40	9
Family tradition	10	13
Vocational preparation, clear vocational aim	9	25
Idealistic motives	9	5
Subject interests	6	5
Attempt to achieve social status	0	22
Economic-materialistic reasons	0	22

It could be argued that there is a tendency to attribute to women students the more idealistic motives: men students are perceived as having a definite down-to-earth motivation. But since nearly half the women are thought to be attending for 'irrelevant' motives, the interpretation of their behaviour can scarcely be said to be favourable.

Such were the attitudes in a sample of German universities in the mid-1950s. Many people currently in the system are likely to have been affected by these attitudes, possibly as students: in a few instances, some of the older generation of university teachers may still be influencing events. But during the 1950s the number of university students was increasing:[10] it doubled during that decade and in subsequent decades, especially in the late 60s and the 70s, it increased dramatically: between 1960-61 and 1977-78 it tripled, to reach a total of 900,000 students in 1977-78. Women too shared in this expansion, their numbers showing the same upward curve as those of the men's numbers; from some 60,000 in 1960, women students reached approx. 280,000 in 1977-78. The women students' participation had by 1977 arrived at 43.8% of those entering higher education institutions,[11] though it must be noted that a large part of this total is reached by the inclusion of Pedagogical Institutions of Higher Education where women were 73.7% of the entrants. The percentage of women in universities only was, according to the Unesco Statistical Handbook, 36% in 1979. The position therefore of women students has considerably improved even if it is not yet good. This change is naturally dependent on the progression of girls through the kind of secondary education which leads to the Abitur, the leaving certificate of the German Gymnasium, which gives right of entry to university (though this right of entry has been much restricted in recent years by the imposition of a limitation of numbers on entry to various faculties of the universities, the much reviled 'numerus clausus'. Hence it is nowadays not simply a matter of achieving an Abitur but of achieving it with high enough marks to ensure entry to the chosen course of study in what is now a highly competitive situation. In fact disappointed students have challenged the right of the universities to refuse entry to 'qualified' students, holding an Abitur, and the court decision has been that such students do indeed have a right of entry: nevertheless the universities' decision to refuse entry is upheld. (In any case the percentage of women students in Gymnasien (the academic secondary schools) rose from 41.3 in 1965 to 48.4 in 1976 — i.e. practically equal access to full secondary education had been achieved by the mid-70s.[12]

The large percentage of women entering teacher education does serve to alert us to the problem of sex bias in choice of subjects at university. Here the situation in West Germany is similar to that in other Western countries. According to figures issued by the Federal Ministry in 1978,[13] in higher education in 1975-76, the percentage of women studying social sciences or social work was 64: in Art History and Art it was 61: in Pharmacy 50: in Psychology 48: in Medicine 29: in Law 25: in Chemistry 20: in Mathematics 16. Figures for one state in particular,[14] North-Rhine-Westphalia for 1978-79 show the percentage of women students in Humanities (Geisteswissenschaften) as 52: in Languages 65: in Law 26: in Economics 20: in Social-Political sciences 37 and in Social Work 65. In Natural Sciences, the percentage was 35: in Medicine 32, and in Dentistry 21. Engineering in general showed 8% of women students but in this was included Architecture with 37% of women students. Art/Music showed 55%, Sport 42. The overall percentage of women students in this fairly typical West German state was in fact 36 — though it should be noted that women in 1978-79 formed 40% of *new* entrants to universities.

Not only the choice of subject is important. The qualification aimed at can differ within a subject area. Thus in the state cited,[15] 42% of women in the Humanities aimed at teaching qualifications, 46% aimed at the qualification of Diplom or Magister, the ordinary first level qualifications. In Languages, 79% aimed at teaching and in Natural Sciencs 58%. In Social-Political Sciences and Social Work, percentages of women intending to teach were 39 and 41. It may be the case that career intentions of women are changing in some faculties. Although the majority of those studying Natural Sciences intend to become teachers, there has been a fall from 70% in this category five years earlier to the figure of 58% quoted for 1978-79. Similarly in Economics there had been a fall to only 11% intending to teach. (In the West German system, those intending to teach take the First State Examination at the end of their university studies. This requires preparation in a combination of subjects recognised as appropriate for a given level of school teaching. Students not intending to enter school teaching present themselves for examination for the University Diploma, which is roughly equivalent to a first degree in the UK system, or for the newer first degree of Magister. After a two-year probationary period of work in schools, intending teachers have to take the Second State Examination.)

To some extent the choice of subjects is likely to depend on the secondary school attended. Although the Abitur is the general entrance qualification, the secondary schools have been differentiated by emphasis on specialisation in subject areas: thus, for example, in 1980, of students entering the University of Bochum[16] 6.77% came from classical languages Gymnasien, 32.7% from modern language Gymnasien, 21.90% from maths-science Gymnasien and 3.27% from economics and social science Gymnasien. (The remainder had a variety of qualifications, including evening Gymnasien and higher technical school qualifications.) But within these percentages there were variations according to sex. Women were 14.4% of those from classical schools, 41.9% of those from modern language schools and 42.3% of those from economics and social science schools: they were only 11.9% of those from maths-science schools. The total numbers from economics and social science schools were small. So far as numerical strengths are concerned, the modern language Gymnasien were obviously those from which women students were most likely to proceed to university. The reasons for this would have had to be investigated further in schools themselves, in their entry and option policies. It is also possible that the entry to Bochum which has a distinctively applied science strength might differ from that of more traditional universities. But in thinking about the circumstances of entry to university one must recall the intense competition which now rages round gaining the Abitur with sufficiently high marks to be accepted. Since the total average grade point may make a vital difference in deciding whether the candidate secures a place in the faculty of his or her choice, pupils engage in highly complicated calculations as to which selection of basic and specialist courses is likely to give the best grade point prospects. Pupils may well opt for courses in which they are strong rather than for courses which particularly interest them — or may even by-pass courses which would be highly relevant to their future university studies. Given the traditional sex biases in secondary education, the present Abitur is likely to reinforce them rather than reduce them. A 'reform' of the Abitur which has left somewhat greater freedom to pupils to choose courses instead of following the formerly prescribed 'class' course may also lead to more choice on sex bias lines and reduce the broadening effect which the former compulsory inclusion of various subjects might have had.

Nevertheless, the increased proportion of women among university students and their increasing representation among new entrants to universities each year indicate improvement in the position of women. As in other countries, the question arises whether the growth in female student levels is matched by improvement in the representation of women among university teaching staffs: and if not, why not.

Career structure of university teaching

In West Germany also the profession is in the process of changing and has already undergone considerable modification since the 1960s. Most notably, it has been changed by the Federal Hochschulrahmengesetz (the higher education framework law) of 1975 and the subsequent implementation and interpretation of this Law and accompanying laws about grades of employment in higher education by the individual Länder. Thus in different Länder there remain differences caused by varying interpretations and modifications of the former structures within the individual Land. Uniformity has not yet been achieved.

In the past, the Professor, the Ordinarius, holder of an established Chair, was clearly at the head of the hierarchy and enjoyed what has been described as godlike authority within his (very seldom her) department. Below this level came the Extraordinarius (the ausserordentlicher Professor) who usually represented a rather narrower, specialist field than the Ordinarius: e.g. while there might be an established Chair of Surgery, the ausserordentlicher Professor could be an expert in surgery of some specified part of the body. The Extraordinarius was usually on a waiting list for appointment at a higher level but some did remain at this level for their entire career. Nowadays, both types are designated simply Professor but the former Extraordinarius would now be a C3 Professor (which, oddly enough, is better than being a C1 or C2 Professor but less good than C4 level, that of the former Ordinarius). (The C scale indicates rank and salary.)

Below these levels came that of the Privatdozent or Dozent who would, like the above mentioned professors, have achieved 'Habilitation' — recognition by a university of qualification through a major thesis, a work carried out after achieving the initial Doctorate (or 'Promotion'). This doctorate normally followed on a first degree (Diploma, Staatsexamen) though some students might proceed straight to the Promotion without a first degree. (Nowadays however it would be expected that a Diploma or MA would first be taken.) The Privatdozent would be paid simply for the teaching given in his or her specialty. In earlier times, this employment would possibly be on a part-time basis but in more modern times, such people have normally had another full-time paid position. The Privatdozent, like the ausserordentlicher professor, was normally awaiting a call to a Chair.

At a rather similar level, possibly after a year or so as Privatdozent, was the ausserplanmässige Professor (supernumerary professor), an individual not holding an established Chair of the university but being paid for out of departmental funds, having qualifications similar to those of the established professors (i.e. habilitiert) but still waiting for a call or nomination to a Chair in another university. Such people were not as specialised as the 'ausserordentlich' professors but could cover the whole field. Another appointment at this level is that of Honorarprofessor (honorary professor), someone employed elsewhere but invited to do some teaching in his or her special subject in the university.

Since the reforms the title of Professor applies to people holding different ranks and not necessarily appointed to Chairs. As we have noted, the designations C4 to C2 have replaced the former designations of H4, H3, H2 relating to professors. Privatdozenten and Dozenten have been assimilated to one or other of the professorial ranks but in various universities wars are still raging as to which members of non-professorial staff should be promoted or assimilated to professorial ranks C2 and C3, thus acquiring both the title and the lower teaching load of professors. In some universities however the title and post of Dozent may be retained, within the faculty of Medicine, for people who have attained Habilitation and are going to move, probably, to Chairs elsewhere.

Another relatively senior post has been that of Akademischer Rat (academic counsellor). This position began to emerge in the 1950s and especially with the expansion of universities in the 1960s. It required experience of work in a university and the initial qualification of the Doctorate. For assistants for whom no jobs at professorial level were likely to be available it offered an established position and the much valued tenure; and, within the grade, promotion to the rank of Oberrat followed normally after a few years. A further distinctive difference between the position of Akademischer Rat and that of Assistent was that the assistant was under the authority of a Professor and appointed to be subordinate to that authority whereas the Akademischer Rat was appointed to the institution and was subject to its authority rather than that of a professor. This post, for which one cannot find a British equivalent, still exists in various German universities but is in process of being phased out in the wake of the reforms. The Akademischer Rat's teaching duties are at least 12 hours per week (some rise to 18) whereas the professor's teaching load is 8 hours: hence the desire for promotion to professorial level.

At the lowest level of the hierarchy came and come the assistants. The wissenschaftliche Assistent (academic assistant) was appointed largely at the professor's discretion in former times but more recently the posts have normally been advertised and applicants' qualifications scrutinised by the competent authorities — the policy of 'openness' popular in the years following the 1968 disturbances reinforced this system. But the reforms introduced by the government at federal level have eliminated this lowest rank. The former assistantships' functions have been allocated to two types of post. There has been created a new category of Hochschulassistent (higher education assistant) who, according to the old traditions, will still work towards gaining Habilitation (the doctorate is an initial qualification for appointment) and take part in teaching but will not be a Hilfsarbeiter (personal assistant) for the professor. The intention is that Hochschulassistent posts should be restricted in number, made available in consideration not only of the potential of individuals to achieve Habilitation, but in consideration of the probable prospects for appointments to Chairs. What seems to be intended is a more rigorous selection for a strictly limited number of posts. The greater part of the service and teaching given by assistants in the past will be taken over by the other (already existing) category of wissenschaftliche Angestellten (academic employees) of whom the great majority are appointed for a fixed number of years but with the possibility of renewed appointment. These Angestellten are not established civil servants as the professorial ranks are (that is, they are not Beamten): the professorial ranks (Hochschullehrer) have a permanent appointment and life tenure. The Angestellten do not have this guaranteed tenure on first appointment. Yet they cannot be dismissed unless their post ceases and after 15 years in post they acquire tenure. (If they had been in post for 15 years and the post ceased to exist they would have to be re-deployed: but such cases are likely to be very rare.)

The West German government has thus been attempting to restructure the university teaching profession (and other institutions of higher education and their staff structures are included in the reform). There is interesting evidence of concern to ensure a succeeding generation to occupy the top academic posts: whether the system will operate successfully remains to be seen. It must inevitably pose problems of deciding what selection techniques are to be used in appointment to posts where academic success must be confidently expected. From the women's point of view there would certainly seem to be danger in traditional beliefs that a male Hochschulassistent will be more likely than a female to follow the route to Habilitation and a Chair. (In Frankfurt there were 28 male Hochschulassistenten and no females at the time of the enquiry.) The position of the Angestellten also remains rather uncertain. Most of them must now already have the doctorate qualification. The extent to which they engage equally in research and teaching, or with a bias towards one or the other, seems still to depend considerably on conditions within individual departments and subject areas. The distinction between Beamter and Angestellter is however common in the German labour market and is well understood in various public service occupations. Thus the distinctions regarding tenure fit into an already existing framework: they are not new, since university teachers having tenure have been clearly distinguished in the past from those having 'temporary' appointments as assistants or Angestellten. Consequently the expectation of almost automatic early acquisition of life tenure which has characterised British university teachers in the past is not a consideration affecting German academics' reactions to the new structures though many feel strongly about the reduction in assistantships and the more limited career prospects set before the Angestellten.

Mention should be made of what could be regarded as the first step into university teaching, appointments as part-time wissenschaftliche Hilfskraft (academic helper): at this level people are appointed by a professor or other senior person to help in research or in tutorial teaching of students. The higher education general law in fact provided that states could introduce the category of Tutor, appointed in this way, to support and guide students in their learning activities. This is not a tutorship in the sense of an appointment — as in British universities — to give pastoral care to students. It would perhaps more nearly correspond to postgraduates' appointments for small group teaching or demonstrating. But in practice the system of Tutoren, though existing in some universities, does not seem likely to become widespread.

Another temporary form of appointment for which no clear equivalent can be found in British terms is that of the school teacher seconded to the university service — Studienrat (secondary school teacher, usually from the Gymnasium) im Hochschuldienst. Very rarely a Lehrer (from the Hauptschule or secondary modern school equivalent) might be appointed. The purpose of such secondments, which arise from the responsibility universities have accepted for teacher education, is to provide students with instruction in methods of teaching the subjects they are studying. Normally the secondment is for a two-year period but it could be renewed for another two years, the teacher thereafter returning to school work. Some such people, during the period of expansion, were promoted — especially in teacher training institutions of higher education — to the rank of Studien-professor (a rank no longer existing) and some, by this route, have become C3 professors at the present time.

The situation in the West German universities is thus in a state of change, the change occurring at different rates according to the policies of the various Länder and universities. Former ranks still exist as the holders of these positions remain in universities and not all of them have been assimilated to the new structure as yet. But one must note that women have appeared and still do appear most frequently in what is described as the Mittelbau, the intermediate ranks in which tenure of posts is likely to be for limited periods. Thus many women have limited prospects of promotion and are likely after a defined number of years to move out of university work. Of course, men who are teaching at these levels similarly may be likely to leave university teaching.

It is also to be recognised that under the former system's strict definition of the rank of Hochschullehrer (teacher in an institution of higher education) only professors and Privatdozenten of universities would deserve this title. And the position of the Privatdozent may be anomalous in that some of them have been assistants, have become 'habilitiert' but have found no suitable post; hence, though they may teach at least two hours a week in a university, they could not live on the payment for this and may therefore be regarded almost as unemployed university teachers. At any rate, under the stricter old definition in one of the universities visited the number of women to be interviewed as 'university teachers' would have been nine. But naturally, other ranks also were regarded as essential to the survey and women working at the bewildering variety of levels just described were interviewed.

The Group Interviewed

The two universities visited for interview purposes were Bochum and Frankfurt, the former in North-Rhine-Westphalia, the latter in Hessen. The former state had in 1979-80 37% women among students in higher education, the latter a percentage of 35. The two universities chosen are large, by British standards, Bochum having 25,053 students in 1979-80 and Frankfurt 23,027. Frankfurt may be regarded as an 'old' and traditional university though in common with others of its kind it has changed its faculty structure into a combination of subject departments. Bochum, founded in 1964, was 'intended to unite the scholarly disciplines of the traditional university and those of the college of technology. Ten years of experience cast doubt though on whether hopes of bringing the arts and sciences into contact at all levels of the university can be realised'.[17] It is unusual in combining Engineering studies with the other more traditional groups of Humanities, Natural Sciences and Medicine. It has also made a special effort to provide accommodation for students in hostels or residences on its custom-built campus or in the neighbourhod. At the same time it has been described as 'the last of the old universities' rather than a typically 'new' university. Possibly because of its applied science weighting, its percentage of women students in 1979-80 was only 32 whereas that of Frankfurt at the time was 42. Bochum too has one of the highest percentages of working-class students — about 20% and (in West Germany as in Britain) working-class girls are less likely to attend university. It may be too that the 'image' of Bochum appeals less to women. But it seemed probable that taking one long-established university and one new university would give a fair impression of trends for teaching staff even if, since they are in different states, the two universities have rather different staff structures and regulations.

Yet the proportion of women at different levels on the staff of the two universities studied did vary to some extent. In Bochum,[18] of the various professorial staff, there were 9 women out of a total of 442 (2%)., At Honorarprofessor level there were 40 men and no women. At the ausserplanmässige professor, Dozent/Privatdozent levels there were 4 women in a total of 150 (2.67%). Among the wissenschaftliche Mitarbeiter (including Assistenten and Angestellten) there were 115 women out of a total of 1128, i.e. 10.19%. Overall, women were 7.27% of the teaching staff but the distribution varied according to faculty, with a relatively high representation of women professors in Philology, Philosophy and Pedagogy, equivalent to some 8.14%, while in other faculties the percentage of women professors was less than 1%. In many departments too, women appeared only at the level of wissenschaftliche Mitarbeiter: in theology there were only 2, but none in Catholic theology; in physics and astronomy 4; in economics 5; in geology none.

The Frankfurt situation was more difficult to define since the names of those at wissenschaftliche Arbeiter level were not printed in the calendar.[18] But among emeritus professors there were 6 women, a percentage of 6.45%: among professors, 38 women in a total of 631, i.e. 6.02%: at the level of ausserplanmässige professor, Dozent/Privatdozent were 11 women in 138 (7.97%) and among honorary professors 4 out of 176 (2.27%). The overall percentage of women staff at Frankfurt worked out at 5.68% but it must be remembered that this does not include the lower levels where one would expect to find a larger proportion of women. Again, the different subject areas in Frankfurt showed differences in the proportions of women: in philology, old and new, in psychology and education, women were relatively well represented at professorial level, giving 16.32%: but in other areas the total of women professors gave a percentage of only 2.89%. Again, there were apparently no females in geology. Physics had one woman at emeritus professor level but otherwise no women. Informatik and Economics similarly showed no female names on staff though the total staff here was admittedly not numerous.

Thus there was some difference in the representation of women in the two universities though the total percentage of women in both is small. It is perhaps notable that the older university is apparently the more liberal in employing women (both universities were about the same size) but it does have the reputation of being a fairly progressive university while Bochum, though 'new' is, as we have noted, reputed to be in many ways very traditional and orientated more to 'masculine' subjects. (Yet figures produced by a women's movement in Bochum[20] suggested that other institutions of higher education in the state of North-Rhine-Westphalia were not more liberal in appointing women to top professorial posts: e.g. Dortmund had 1% ordentliche professors, Essen 2%.)

The publication by the two universities of their Vorlesungs-und-Personenverzeichnis (list of courses and staff) made the process of finding women for interview rather easier. In reading these lists an attempt was made (i) to get in touch with all women professors — this was very easy in Bochum, though unhappily one of the small group could not be contacted in time (ii) to obtain a good balance of different subject areas and (iii) to include a fair representation of women teaching at assistant level. In the last instance, one of the easiest ways of making contact was to ask one of the women in a senior position to effect an introduction to a woman assistant in the department. To some extent it was again a matter of chance whether the woman in question was there to answer her telephone at the time when a contact was attempted. In no case did a woman refuse to be interviewed, though in one instance it was not possible to find a time convenient for a meeting. One woman responded to the request with 'We-ell, if I must' but this discouraging tone was not at all maintained when the professor in question was interviewed — her attitude, she explained, arose simply from the fact that there are so many demands on one's time. But another woman professor made it clear at the beginning of our talk that she would not have received me if I had been a colleague within the university: she disliked the agitation for feminist causes which some young colleagues were responsible for at the time and regarded the discussion of feminist issues as misguided. Nevertheless she proved most cooperative and illuminating in an extensive interview. The admirable language skills of these women must be recognised. Some did prefer to talk in German but it was clear that in most, if not all, cases they could very well have coped with talking in English — occasionally, a mixture of the languages was used. No one seemed to object to notes being taken though at one or two points a few women said that they did not think the matters under discussion should be recorded: these points tended to relate to the social status or occupation of their husbands.

Again, it was evident that the universities offer their staff a variety of rooms and that women react individually to the accommodation they are offered. Some, in the modern and austere — and somewhat cramped — rooms of new buildings had apparently resigned themselves to unlovely and unadorned surroundings. But the majority had imprinted their own personality by posters, table-covers or pictures. Some, especially in older buildings, had charming rooms; book-lined walls providing a particularly attractive and dignified environment. Other women chose to be interviewed in their normal work-place, a science lab. Few women in this German group seemed to have the problem of sharing a room — possibly the relatively high rank of the majority affected this as well as the new buildings — so the tactful disappearance of colleagues was not frequently required.

The distribution of the posts held by the 49 women interviewed in these two West German universities was this:

Professors	30	(of these 11 were C4, 3 were C3 and one C2 — the precise ranking of the others was not given)
Dozentin	1	
Akademische Rätin	3	
Wiss.Angestellte	5	
Wiss.Assistentin	10	

Subject grouping was as follows:

Humanities	Languages, philology	9
	Psychology	6
	Education	6
	Philosophy	1
	East Asian Studies	1
	History	2
	Geography	2
Economics	3	
Law	2	
Social Sciences	2	
Medicine	7	
Natural Sciences	7	
Applied Sciences	1	

And age grouping:

25-29	3	45-49	6
30-34	8	50-54	4
35-39	9	55-59	7
40-44	9	60-65	3

If anything, the group is rather older than the British group but corresponding quite closely to the French group, at least in the over-50 categories. Again, the majority are in the traditionally female subjects of languages and humanities. This corresponds to the general distribution of women in the universities visited.

It is also characteristic of a group which had achieved — in most instances — tenure in the university profession that the majority had the doctorate qualification: only six were still working for it, these being the younger members of the group who as yet had obtained only Diplom qualifications. But at the higher qualification levels differences become evident. 19 of the women had taken the Habilitation in the traditional way by the presentation of a thesis. But 14 had been 'habilitated' in alternative ways: in two cases, women appointed as professors had achieved this appointment in years when the formal Habilitation was not required. (In Hessen, for most of the 70s Habilitation was not required and, indeed, had become almost a taboo topic. But more recently it had again become essential though the new federal law refers to qualification by Habilitation 'or equivalent work'.) Those who had not gone through the traditional thesis presentation had in most cases been appointed because of publications which were judged to be equivalent. Four other women were, as assistants, working towards Habilitation with, they thought, reasonable hope of completion in the near future. One of these would, if successful, be the first woman to achieve habilitation in her subject area in the university. She had been assured that the fact of being a woman would not be any handicap to her in this candidacy.

In some ways, seven who had decided against attempting Habilitation are more noteworthy. These women had decided that if they were to have a reasonable social life, to enjoy the companionship of their husbands or friends, they could not embark on a traditional Habilitation work. One, admittedly, expressed her intentions rather vaguely — 'for the time being' she had no intention of taking Habilitation: but at her age level it would obviously be unwise to postpone further work for this qualification if she seriously wanted to have it eventually. Another said that there would be special problems about Habilitation in her subject area in the university where both she and her husband was employed: and in any case she had left it too late. But in the majority of cases the woman had clearly decided that to embark on a further demanding piece of research and writing was not worthwhile: she was happily established teaching her subject and she was content to remain at her present level. 'It is a job' said one, 'I do it well: but it's not everything.' Comments in this respect did tend to suggest two categories in the group interviewed, those primarily involved in research and devoted to it and those moderately interested in research.

It is also to be noted that those who had decided not to attempt the Habilitation did regard it as a major hurdle. One woman also pointed out that in her subject area publications would not be regarded as providing an equivalent to the traditional thesis. Yet quite a large number of others in the group had been able to achieve habilitation in this way. Granted, some of these women had written books which had been acclaimed as excellent — at an outstanding level which might differentiate them from publications simply of moderate academic respectability. But it did seem possible that women were not always aware of the alternative routes. It may also be relevant that the alternative validation tends to be in the 'women's subjects': it is in areas of the humanities — literature especially, history, education and psychology — that this route is possible. The woman making a career in the more traditionally male routes may find that there is less flexibility about recognising other proofs of excellence.

The time of entry to university teaching was also an important factor. The expansion of student numbers in the late 60s and 70s brought a need for greater numbers of qualified teachers. Thus people who had not gone through the traditional Habilitation procedures but who could produce other evidence of high ability and experience were appointed to posts. Formerly rigid procedures were relaxed at this time. But, as we have noted, this expansion has led to a bottleneck at present and in the immediate future: numbers of students are stabilised and may even be reduced, so new appointments are improbable: those members of staff appointed to Chairs in expansionist times are still in post.

Some further observations concerning qualifications seem of importance.

(i) The amount of time required to obtain them varied considerably. In some cases the doctorate was a matter of one year's study following on the first qualification: in others, the doctorate took some 5 years. Similarly, even the Habilitation could be obtained in one or two years of study by some fortunate candidates — but they pointed out that they had already gathered a great deal of material in the years before they formally registered. Others took the more traditional 6 to 8 years to arrive at Habilitation.

(ii) It was pointed out that Habilitation must avoid what is described as 'incest'. The candidate is habilitiert in his or her own university, normally then becoming a Dozent, Privatdozent or ausserplanmässige Professor. But the appointment as full professor must then be in another university. Anyone already a Professor in a university, having been accepted on other qualifications, finds it extremely difficult to achieve a formal qualification of Habilitation in that university. (It can, in exceptional cases, be done.)

(iii) The procedure of Habilitation is in itself of considerable importance. Normally a thesis is presented by the candidate: it is judged by external assessors: it is read by the faculty of the subject area: the candidate formally presents the thesis and is subjected to questioning by members of the faculty. Opinions differed as to the efficacy of faculty members' interventions on these occasions: once or twice it was suggested that the questioning was based on ignorance or on prejudice in certain cases but other respondents said that, in their experience, the questioning was fair and just.

(iv) A side effect of decisions to try or not to try for Habilitation had been perceived by a few women. The attitude of male colleagues became more friendly when a decision not to try to be habilitated was announced — a potential competitor was thus removed from the list.

Marriage and family circumstances

The marital status of those interviewed was:

Single	19
Married	25
Divorced	3
Widowed	2

The percentage of unmarried women, 39 (38.77) corresponds closely to the percentage of 40 in the British group and is also greater than the French group's percentage of 28. Seven of the 'single' women said that they were living with a Freund (the interpretation of this word has notably altered since the days when the simple translation of 'friend' sufficed). In some cases this alliance has continued for many years and in one, at least, the relationship continued in spite of geographical separation. One of these couples had a five-year-old daughter and the man had elected to stay at home to care for their child. In other cases, however, it seemed that if the couple were to decide to begin a family, they would probably get married. One of the younger married women in fact had recently married after cohabiting for a number of years and was about to have a child. Various women mentioned that cohabiting is also a way of life for women students and there is no disadvantage in this if one is applying for a job. One woman indeed thought that this background might be reassuring to a selection committee who might consider that a woman with this kind of relationship would be less likely to be an ambitious, domineering career woman. It is not possible to know how many of the other unmarried women may have had a similar relationship: some may have felt that this was an aspect of their private life not relevant to the investigation. The women who mentioned having a Freund did so spontaneously: supplementary information as to his occupation and attitude to household tasks was then requested as for husbands of the married women in the group.

The family situation of the group is shown in the following table:

No children	12
One child	9
Two children	4
Three children	3

In addition, there was the one unmarried woman with one child. Another woman cohabiting with a man who had not obtained a divorce from his previous marriage was responsible for the care of his three children. Of the married women included in the above table one was in fact caring for her husband's daughter by a previous marriage.

It is evident that only a minority of the group interviewed had responsibility for the care of a child or children. The proportion of childless marriages is rather higher than in the British group and considerably higher than in the French group. Of course there remains the possibility that some couples might yet begin a family: but the size of families, granted that incompleteness may affect all groups studied, does seem relatively small: the 'only child' is the most frequent pattern and there are no 'large' families.

The impression given by the figures is reinforced by comments made during the interviews. Repeatedly, women asserted that to have a career as a university teacher a woman must give up the idea of having children — 'man muss darauf verzichten'. The word 'verzichten' — 'renounce' 'give up the idea' — kept recurring when this topic of children and a university career was raised. The common view was that a woman must choose whether she wants to have a 'normal' family life, with children, or have an academic career. 24 women who were single or married without children indicated that the combination of children and career did not seem possible to them. Various aspects of the problem were pointed out. Children, quite simply, are likely to suffer if the mother cannot give them her full attention. If she has to be at the university all day, as may be necessary in natural science areas, for example, then someone has to look after them, especially while they are young and not yet going to school. Here two difficulties would arise; (a) being able to find and pay for a suitable person to look after the children: (b) entrusting so much influence over the children to a stranger. Indeed in two cases the unwillingness to leave the children to be influenced by someone else extended to what is otherwise a widely accepted situation — having the children looked after by the woman's own mother: but, as one woman put it: 'I would not want my children brought up according to my mother's ideas.' And the other pointed out that 'If a woman has children she wants to bring them up in her own way.'

Women holding that there was incompatibility between children and university work did recognise that some women fulfilled the dual role. But women in this situation were regarded with some uncertainty, by both married and unmarried women colleagues: there was questioning as to whether the children suffered and whether the mother was being unfair to them. This attitude was obviously found in society outside the school also: one of the women who was successfully combining university teaching and family responsibilities was amused that when she went to a Parents' Day at her daughter's Gymnasium she was complimented by a teacher because her daughter was NOT a child who had problems due to a mother out at work — since her daughter was a good pupil the teacher had assumed that she could not have a working mother. Another young woman, teaching in a university outside the group studied, recalled how persistently a male colleague kept enquiring after the health of her child, his attitude indicating more than normal friendly interest, almost a conviction that something must be going seriously wrong with the child.

Even where some possibility of having children looked after was recognised, discrimination was made between the teaching and research aspects of university work. It was conceded that the woman with children could perhaps cope with teaching. But, it was argued, to do research a woman must have her mind clear, be able to think creatively as well as devote long hours to her research. If there are children, concern about them may well keep her from creative thinking. The simple presence of children may keep her from writing at home so that the only time when she can possibly get on with such work is late at night when the children are asleep. A further complication, noted by one woman with two children, is attendance at conferences abroad or even at other places in Germany: it is particularly difficult for a mother to absent herself for conferences and yet this failure to attend may be prejudicial to her prospects of advancement as well as to progress in her work.

The majority view seemed to be that if a woman had children she ought to give up work, at least for the years when the children were young: two of the married women said that if they had had children they would have resigned their post: and two of the younger unmarried women said they would give up university work if they began a family. At the same time it was recognised that to be out of university work for a period even of a few years would be a serious handicap to a university career: especially in science subjects, it was pointed out, the woman would lose touch in a way which would make it difficult to catch up again: being out of university teaching would certainly mean loss of practical experience — e.g. in medical skills — which a refresher course for returners could not fully compensate for. The possibility of part-time work was mentioned occasionally but the main implication was that while it might be agreeable to women it was not likely to be accepted as constituting university experience of a successful kind. Yet one young woman, unmarried, did suggest that if she gave up her job to have children she could continue to work on a freelance basis from her home and thus maintain her professional status. Another thought that, if qualified, she could get a Lehrauftrag — appointment to do some part-time university teaching — which would be compatible with family responsibilities for a few years and keep her place in the academic profession.

Occasionally it was suggested that not only children but marriage was incompatible with a university career. A husband might not understand his wife's preoccupation with research, the long hours spent at work or absences for conference attendance. Certainly comprehension on the part of the husband was needed. One woman commented that university women teachers do not manage to keep their marriages going: most of them divorce or separate after 8 or 10 years. (Yet the divorce rate in the sample interviewed was not noticeably high.)

On the other side there are the women who evidently are successful in combining marriage, children and career.

Among these women a few with young children suggested that the universities or other authorities really ought to provide some child-care facilities. Nothing of this kind seemed to be available to them. They had to make private arrangements to find someone to look after the child — occasionally the woman's mother was at home and could help in this way but such help seemed to have been more readily available for the older women of the group. One woman had solved the problem temporarily at least by bringing her daughter into the university to play quietly in her room on the one day of the week when she could not make arrangements to have the child cared for at home: but she regarded this as very much a short-term solution until she could find, as she had done in her previous place of employment, someone to look after the child during her absences.

The situation seemed easier when the husband was also a teacher. If he taught in university it was possible to arrange the hours so that either husband or wife would be at home to look after the child at mid-day or after school — though this timetabling depended greatly on the subject areas in which the couple were employed. In certain disciplines at least, university teaching was recognised as having advantages over other occupations because hours can be arranged to suit the teacher's convenience to a considerable extent. If the husband taught in a Gymnasium he could be home by 2 or 3 p.m. so that the wife could organise her teaching and other duties in the university for late afternoon or for the evening.

It emerged from such discussions that importance is still given to having the family together for the mid-day meal. Some women emphasised the advantage of the German school system which does not expect young children to spend their afternoons in school. They pointed out the value for the cohesiveness of the family if in fact all meet together at this meal time. The school meals system of the UK and the long school day which the UK system imposes on children at school seemed to these German women undesirable even if they may lessen the problem of family care.

Some women in fact had not had to face the worst of the dual role because they had embarked on a university career only after their children were finished with school life or were at least old enough to be left to their own devices during the day. But in the case of a woman who had acquired qualifications and entered university teaching only after her children had reached the ages of 15-16, prospects of making a permanent career in the university seemed distinctly unpromising. To begin an Assistantship over the age of 40 is unorthodox and puts the candidate at a considerable disadvantage in the competition for permanent posts — unless, of course, in the case of outstanding ability and research work.

Certainly those women who were combining looking after children with their university work found the situation demanding. One indeed said that if she had realised just how much is needed in caring for children she would not have had the nerve to apply for her present position: but she had made the application while her children were still very young indeed.

Both husband's attitude and husband's career were emphasised in the discussions of this topic. As in other groups, women's husbands were usually of similar academic background to themselves. Occasionally the husband's professional standing meant that the woman had additional responsibilities and work in coping with the social occasions which his position entailed. Such a problem is perhaps more likely to arise if the woman marries a man considerably older than herself: in such cases, social obligations are likely to be imposed on her while she is still at an early stage in her own career — her work, even apart from any problem of looking after children, is likely to be slowed down in this way. If the couple marry while both are still relatively young, with their way to make, this social aspect is less likely to be important. While, as we have noted, a few women in the French group indicated their feeling of responsibility for providing satisfactorily for the social engagements which their husbands' occupation made appropriate, in West Germany the obligation seemed to arise particularly when the woman was the wife of a Professor: there was, perhaps, some indication of the higher social standing which a Professor may still enjoy in West Germany and possibly of a stronger sense of formal social conventions.

If both partners are in university teaching there is of course the problem of finding suitable posts for both in the same university; a problem exacerbated if both work in the same subject area. In the group interviewed, five had husbands teaching in the same university and three had husbands teaching in another university. In most cases the husband was at a higher level than the wife in the university hierarchy, but not always. In one case the woman had realised that this problem of being in the same subject area would arise and she had deliberately chosen to specialise in a different branch of the subject from her husband. Now, however, he had been appointed to a professorship in a university where her specialism was not taught; she could possibly have been appointed in another university but she thought that commuting would be too tiring physically and also too disturbing of their married life: so she had accepted remaining in a lower position than her qualifications deserved. In some cases, husband and wife had accepted being appointed in different cities and one or other commuted or both travelled to an intermediate place of residence. Inevitably this imposed at least some physical strain: but since in some subjects the university teacher may have to put in an appearance only on certain days of the week, the commuting problem was not regarded as a major hindrance. One woman certainly recalled extensive commuting in the days of her youth with obvious conviction that it had been well worth while.

Husbands working outside the university also were involved in this mobility problem. In some instances it was noted that the husband had moved from university teaching back into industry or an equivalent professional occupation while the wife continued in university work: this, possibly, was a sign of poor economic prospects in university teaching at present. One husband's good position in a law firm made the wife feel that it would be impracticable for them to move to another city. Another woman's husband was a television producer who would be willing to move with her if her new position was in a centre where he could find appropriate employment: but not all university centres would necessarily offer this: yet the woman was in a position where she would have to make a move within a few years' time. One husband in the education service had followed his wife in three moves as she achieved better posts: but now they had reached a point where it would be very difficult for him to move again to an equally good position in his own career structure: so her future mobility was considerably constricted.

Not only the married women had met with this question of mobility. One woman had refused an invitation to a professorial post at a higher level in another university because she did not want to leave the place in which her friends were — whether this decision was based on one friend in particular was not revealed. Personal relationships had brought another to her present place of employment without any clear prospect of a job: she had had to fill in with other work for a period of some months before she managed to find a university post. But another had been quite clear that she could not remain in the same place as her Freund because she would have been very unhappy at the lack of progress in her career: so she had moved.

Thus where husbands' careers allow for some flexibility, some husbands have proved willing to move to advance their wives' careers: these may be, as their wives considered, rather exceptionally understanding husbands. In other cases personal factors restrict mobility. But marriage may now have unforeseen effects on both partners' careers. An interesting variant of the situation was the case of a young woman professor whose husband was also in university work: he was in a limited-term post and the couple were apprehensive that when it came to the moment of re-appointment the committee might consider that as he had a wife who was obviously in a good position he was therefore less suitable for re-appointment — in times of restricted employment opportunities — than a man who was the breadwinner for a family.

Altogether, the problems arising out of marriage and a family were in many ways similar to those noted in the other countries. There were examples of women who were managing to combine family and university responsibilities with apparent effectiveness and success. Even so, they had obviously to be prepared to meet among their colleagues, both female and male, some questioning — spoken or unspoken — as to whether they were perhaps being unfair to their children. But there was also this attitude among some of the unmarried or as yet childless women that a woman should give up full-time career responsibilities at least while her children are young. One unmarried woman said this is just how society is: when children arrive, someone has to tend them — usually the woman: someone has to earn money — usually the man. In some instances, women had dealt with the conflict of interests by opting against having children or against marrying. Yet various women reported that they had known women — friends or acquaintances — who had given up their university career on marriage or on the arrival of children and they believed that in such cases the woman quite frequently regretted her choice later and remained somewhat envious of women who had maintained a university career. But not only the role conflict had kept some of the women in the group interviewed from having children: some had been unable to do so because of health reasons or by the particular circumstances of their marriage.

As has been noted, there was criticism of the lack of facilities for child-care other than by private provision. This point was one on which a number of the women felt that action should be taken by university authorities. Perhaps, with increasing awareness of demands for women's rights, some such change will be made.

137

Attitudes towards discrimination against women

Opinion on feminist issues was sharply divided within the group but so far as the personal experience of the women in question was concerned, the attitude of colleagues within the university was generally reported as friendly and cooperative. Where a woman was the only female in a department she appeared to find nothing awkward or peculiar about this situation: indeed it was likely that she would forget there was any sex difference. Similarly, on committees or similar bodies being the only woman did not lead to any feelings of being out of things or less regarded than other members of the committee.

It was commonly recognised that the attitude within the university towards women was much more liberal than outside though differences were also to be found between universities, some being much more likely to appoint women members of staff than others. Certainly some women reported instances of strong anti-feminist prejudices in the world outside the university. One young woman who had applied for a number of different positions in industry had been dismayed by the overt discrimination she encountered: whatever her qualifications some firms were simply not going to appoint a woman to posts of a good level. In social life, strong anti-feminist attitudes had been experienced: a woman attending a function without her husband had been slightingly treated — to appear at such a function without a suitable male escort indicated that the woman was inferior or at least odd. The wife of a male professor was regarded as having much greater social prestige than a woman who was a professor in her own right.

Within the university, even generally liberal views were subject to some discrepancies: but different women had different experiences of the consistency of liberal views. Some senior women affirmed that if a woman works hard and shows by her performance how good she is, then she will be treated completely fairly and receive the promotion and recognition due to her work. But one who had served on an appointing committee had heard critical comment on women applicants — 'Women wanting to be professors'. And when a woman applied whose husband worked in the same field, there was a question as to who had really written her publications. Other women believed that in order to succeed a woman must be rather better than a man — twelve expressed this view in a variety of ways. Another woman commented that she had always felt she was rather better than her male colleagues. Such beliefs may of course have further consequences: one woman remarked that sometimes males seemed to be rather afraid of the successful woman or women in their departments: 'We are a pretty terrifying lot!'

Two additional comments on the situation should be noted. Although it was quite often stated that once a woman has done good work and been appointed to a high position and established herself in it, she is fully accepted, one woman had first discovered anti-feminist prejudice in the university only when she was appointed as a professor and became involved in the power struggle at that level. Secondly, as more than one of the group pointed out, women in high positions are not necessarily in favour of other women's advancement: the anti-feminist prejudices of the successful woman professor can, in some instances, be as strong as the prejudices of male academics against women.

Yet it was evident in the comments of many of the women that much also depends on the attitude of the woman herself. The ability to take jokes against women and not to read too much into them was thought to be of value: 'If you look for prejudice, you find it — better not to bother!' Women, it was suggested, needed at times to show themselves more aggressive, to blow their own trumpet more. They need to stand up for their rights, in ensuring they get fair contracts, for example, not a 'gentleman's agreement'. They need to fight (bewerben) for posts. In dealing with men on committees, women have to resist being browbeaten or even treated in a kindly patriarchal way as if they were children. Instances of successful behaviour of this kind were quoted though one woman claimed that on one occasion only the intervention of a male colleague had saved her from physical attack when she was maintaining her right to be a member of an examining board: a senior male colleague found this claim totally objectionable, apparently because she was a woman, and completely lost his temper. But this did seem to be an isolated incident.

Attitudes towards feminist movements

In Bochum there had recently been established a group concerned with women's rights in higher education and in general. Consequently there was interest in such developments and awareness of them. Some of those interviewed were strongly in favour of the group or active in it. At the other extreme there were five or six who felt strongly hostile to it. One, as has been noted, would have refused an interview to a colleague studying the position of women. The view of the critics of the movement seemed to be that it arose among bitter women who were dissatisfied with their own personal circumstances and not thinking clearly enough about the issues — for example, not considering the burden that is laid on men by their obligation to provide for the family. Some women opposing the movement proclaimed themselves to be in fact feminists: but in their opinion the way to cope with the situation was the way they had chosen, to concentrate on getting on in their own particular circumstances, working hard and successfully there. Some women, it was said, were unreasonable in wanting to have everything — husband, children, home and university Chair: some had found by experience that a woman cannot have all these at once.

An intermediate group thought there was some justification in the demands made by the movement: for example, there should be better child-care facilities and part-time teaching jobs. But they did not regard the movement as the best way of achieving improvements. One expressed dislike for women who 'harangue' — but perhaps, she said, she has assimilated male norms.

The Bochum group[21] had collected statistics of the distribution of posts at top professorial levels in North-Rhine Westphalia, showing the typical under-representation of women. It had also provided in the University a Frauenraum (room for women) where women could meet to discuss problems of women's working life and other circumstances — a provision that had been the object of some mockery on the part of men. Its door posters on rape on the university campus were certainly dramatic. But there was resentment that mockery rather than an attempt to understand the problems was the reaction to the situation.

Another reason for viewing the women's movement with restrained enthusiasm was that those involved in it were thought to be also politically radical or of a political orientation not shared by some of the other women teachers. (This was a political orientation other than the 'political' activity of some of the women within the university, as representatives of assistants or Dozents: such activity was for the well-being and conditions of appointment of all those at their level in the university hierarchy rather than a feminist activity for the well-being of women only.)

Yet there were instances of strong support for the movement. One young woman found she was only now beginning to be aware of women's problems: perhaps women had accommodated too much to men's values: a society organised by women might perhaps be better than the present society.

The supporters of the women's movement did feel that a useful beginning had been made and that better conditions might result, as well as greater solidarity among women. There was some uncertainty however about the best mechanisms for advancing women: a quota system had been proposed as a solution to the under-representation of women in high positions but it was felt that women might not wish to be appointed on such conditions. Insisting on making appointments from the small number of qualified women candidates might further seem ridiculous since it would not reflect the balance of males and females among the candidates.

In Frankfurt, some women had — or claimed to have — no knowledge of a women's movement in the university. Others referred to attempts which had been made to organise seminars, though these attempts had been generally unsuccessful. There were certainly some feminist posters encouraging women students to take an interest especially in female candidates for appointment to a Chair; and interest in feminist matters among female students had been noted by some of the women teachers. Such interests were likely to be found among both students and staff in Social Science departments.

In Frankfurt too there were differences in response to the idea of women's groups. Where such groups were attempting to exclude men, such discrimination met with disapproval among some of the women interviewed. One woman considered that in the past there might have been value in women's organisations but today they seemed to show some hysteria in their approach: women getting together, as some of her colleagues did, 'to say they hate men' would get nowhere. And she disliked the idea of 'token' women's appointments. Another similarly felt that the movement was taking the wrong approach in that it was making men feel nervous and apprehensive (why this should be undesirable was not explained). Resentment had also been aroused by a questionnaire on women's work circulated by a central organisation. It was asserted that the questions here were loaded so that the answers must imply that women were being unfairly treated: at least one respondent had refused to complete the questionnaire for this reason. And again, one woman who had personally found it tactically advantageous not to dispute with men but simply to listen to them and then do what she thought best herself thought that women's movements possibly were endangering women's interest by the hostility which they were arousing in some men.

Other women took a more neutral or a more favourable view. One, for instance, said she had a bad conscience about not being militant; yet as she herself had not experienced prejudice, she did not feel personally committed. Others similarly felt a general interest in equal rights for women but did not engage in feminist activities. One who disclaimed knowledge of the existence of any such group in the university, felt that it could serve a useful purpose if it dealt with specific problems, e.g. nursery facilities, which men would not understand.

One comment was distinctive. It was that so-called emancipated women are not really so: it is rather that they have become like men. Women should do things differently from men because they are naturally different; they need to develop their own special characteristics and derive maximum benefit from these; they need to develop not only their logical power but also their emotional powers. Natural differences tend to be shown in the work methods the two sexes develop, though mature women tend to approach men's more economical attitude towards work: younger women students emphasise the importance of a good social atmosphere in the working group. Some women are unwisely opposed to all men: they are immature concerning the position of women and become self-pitying instead of recognising the advantages women have. Recognition of these natural differences is evident in the ways in which different societies treat sex differences, for example in the variety of social evaluations learned by girls with regard to menstruation.

Reasons for the minority position of women in university teaching

There was a very clear consensus as to the reasons for women's minority situation in university teaching generally and at the higher levels of the university structure. Typically, it was said, women are brought up in a family situation where the girl is expected to marry and have children. Her parents expect this of her: but even if the parents are liberal in their outlook and do not let this influence the girl's education, the outside world maintains this expectation. Whether through this socialisation process or by some innate trends, young women accept this goal and so they give up their university studies if they marry or they give up their work when they have their first child. As we have seen, even among women who are in university teaching there is a strong feeling that the mother should be there to look after the child, especially in the early years. So the young woman is motivated not to seek her fulfilment in academic pursuits but in the traditional role of wife and mother.

In addition to the strong attractions of the domestic role — and it was recognised by various women that the family is not simply a load to carry, it is also something which gives support to a woman — there is the matter of the amount of work required to achieve academic qualifications. On the whole, the doctorate

(Promotion), though requiring serious concentration, did not seem to present grave obstacles: it did require a certain amount of staying power. But the Habilitation which was normally thought necessary for access to professorships was regarded as requiring major efforts: it would demand some sacrifice of social life and possibly — if the woman was married — sacrifice of family life with husband or children. From the point of view of some women, the Habilitation is simply not worth the sacrifices entailed, especially in present times when there is no guarantee that it will, as in the past, lead almost automatically to top positions.

These then were the major reasons commonly and confidently adduced for the minority situation of women in university teaching. Women do not complete their studies: they do not go on to the doctorate: they do not attempt Habilitation. Consequently there are few women eligible for nomination to professorships.

There is some difference of opinion, however, as to attitudes which would encourage women students to progress into higher studies. Many of the women interviewed owed their academic progress to the encouragement given by senior male professors to be ambitious and to gain higher qualifications. Yet the invitation to take assistantships has been more likely to go to male students than to females. While a professor may think that a woman is a pleasant and likeable assistant he does not see her as a future professor: a young male assistant is more likely to be seen in this role. Hence attitudes — possibly unconsciously held by the professors in question — may affect the earlier stages of women's careers in university teaching.

At higher levels of appointment many women felt that although they could not prove that prejudice worked against women yet men were likely to have better chances of nomination. Here too came the assertions that a woman has to be better than a man to get a post. Some women had subsequently had comments of a nominating committee reported to them. Three, for example, had learned that members of the committee had questioned whether a woman would be strong enough to control groups of students: a woman would not be able to shout at them: disciplinary troubles might develop if a woman was asked to teach certain groups. (Such attitudes, it may be recalled, were noted by Anger in his earlier research.[22]) In fact, the women whose competence had seemed doubtful to the appointing authorities had had no experience of such problems: but apparently such concerns had seemed plausible, especially, perhaps, at the times of student rebelliousness in the late 60s.

A further question had been as to whether a woman's husband would come to live in the same town, if she were to get the post. A woman who was questioned on this point was certain that the same question would not have been asked of a man: he would not have been asked to say whether his wife would be willing to move with him. One woman had been questioned as to whether the illness of her mother — who helped in looking after her children — would prevent her from carrying out her duties efficiently; the question was particularly galling since she had *once* been prevented by a sudden illness of her mother from attending a meeting.

Again, as one woman put it, appointing committees might deliberate: 'What age is this woman? Under 40? Then she can't have published much of value yet. Over 40? Oh, that's a dangerous age in women . . .'

Again it must be noted that the great majority of women said that they had not met any experience of prejudice. But some had encountered these comments which may be significant.

Those interviewed had managed to survive. Moreover, many of them were in senior posts and had thus successfully surmounted any prejudices there might be. But from their comments can be seen why the socially approved course of retiring to be a simple housewife will be chosen by many women.

Additional factors

There is the factor of housework, for instance. But domestic work can apparently be coped with reasonably well if the woman is single. Many say that they have a satisfactory routine for coping with it: some even enjoy housework as a balancing activity: and they have usually only a limited amount of housework to do. One however commented that single men may live with their mothers and so avoid housework: a single woman in such a situation would still have to do some.

Those with a Freund also do not seem to find housework a problem generally: in many cases the man takes his share — one woman indeed reported that a former relationship had not led to living together because the man would have been too involved in academic work to take his fair share of practical chores. One woman reported that she and her friend had automatically assumed responsibility for certain tasks: their arrangement might seem sex-biased, since she saw to the laundry and he to washing the car, but it simply had suited them, without discussion, to work this way: they shared cooking though he was a rather better cook than she was — she preferred to use convenience foods.

Husbands occasionally were reported as sharing with housework. One married woman without children commented that neither she nor her husband was houseproud. Another pointed out that since they had quite a small flat — four rooms only — they shared housework and could cope with it easily. But such sharing was less common among the older couples. One woman, married without children, reported that she did the housework at the weekend since it would be trying for her husband if, when he came home after a tiring day at work, she was rushing around trying to do the housework in the evening.

Where there were children, the situation was different. Those women who had children all had some kind of domestic help, at least while their children were young. In three or four cases the woman's mother had also helped in caring for the children. One noted, however, that though an au pair girl may be useful in looking after children, she cannot help with housework at the same time: so in this case the woman herself had still had to deal with housework.

By general agreement, domestic help is expensive. Opinions differed as to the level of salary or salaries at which one can reasonably expect to pay for domestic assistance. The older married women seemed not to have had great difficulties of this kind: the problem of expense was more often cited by the younger women. Long-term benefits of the wife's continuing employment did not seem to be taken into account: what the couple could afford at the present time was the dominant consideration.

Domestic expenses could on occasion acquire an unexpected prominence. Thus one couple who had moved house were now finding that the cost of their new home took almost the whole of one salary — a matter of serious concern since the husband's post was not tenured.

Domestic considerations may thus be one element in deciding whether a woman continues with university work and whether she advances to higher qualifications. A comparison was made of the situation of the man writing a Habilitation thesis, protected from interruption from children and provided with material comforts by an understanding wife and that of the woman who is simultaneously trying to deal with household tasks and child-care.

Psychological characteristics

It was not clearly established whether the minority position of women could be ascribed to sex-linked psychological characteristics. Some of the most eminent women interviewed remarked that to succeed in university work one must have self-discipline, the capacity to work hard, determination. Too many women, they thought, lacked the persistence (Ausdauer) which is essential to success.

Such women certainly did not feel that they themselves lacked self-confidence: nor did they think that other women lacked this confidence. But others did assert that social conditioning encourages women to be less confident about their abilities. Further, in order to make a career, one must have a certain lack of sensitivity: a cold-bloodedness (Kaltschnäuzigkeit): women may be too sensitive and lack this ruthlessness in competition: they 'lack elbows'. Diffidence too may cause women to speak less than men in committees.

Few differences were suggested in male and female methods of work or approaches to study. A good social atmosphere in the working group was cited as something valued by young female students rather than by more mature females or by men. Differences in student attitudes in some subject areas might be due to differential recruitment. One woman teacher had noticed that initially women students talked as readily as men but that later they tended to let the men do the talking: this seemed to her a kind of social conditioning by attitudes prevalent in the university as well as in society outside. Yet it could be that women were also affected by their minority situation in a subject like economics. Men who studied German language might be rather poorer academically because those obtaining the highest school marks in the subject had used those high marks to secure entry to the prestigious faculties like Medicine. Psychology is an area much chosen by women: men opting for this area may be more 'feminine' in personality than the average male student — though this also might depend on the aspect of psychology they opted to study, males preferring — it was said — the more experimental, behaviourist approach and females the areas concerned with emotions and personality. Thus, within individual subject areas, some differences in male and female characteristics might appear to be present but if allowance was made for the factors determining choice of study, these differences could not be thought absolute. (Differences in choice of subject area are of course interesting in themselves, even if much affected by social and school factors.)

Generally, while personality factors were occasionally mentioned — most notably, perhaps, the unwillingness of females to enter into competitive situations and defend their own interests in the fight for promotion — there did not seem to be a clear opinion that such factors materially affected the career progress of the women. It was however suggested that too few young women study natural sciences because they seem 'difficult': hence a scarcity of women in university teaching in these areas.

Conclusions

We return then to the matter of family responsibilities as the major reason given for women's situation in the university teaching profession in West Germany. This reason seems to have been all the more strongly supported as the social background apparently stresses more strongly than that of the other countries the essential nature of the mother's care for the children. There seems to be evidence that a number of university women teachers themselves share this view. The long process of writing a Habilitation thesis also comes at a time when a woman is likely to have young children. In the German situation it would thus appear that the woman's better policy with regard to family planning would be to acquire qualification first and then have children. As various women pointed out, once the woman has reached a higher post, it is much easier to organise her timetable so as to accommodate domestic as well as academic responsibilities. But this must mean postponement of child-bearing until the early thirties. The alternative solution, having a child while still at the student stage, or before embarking on university teaching, was found in some cases. But it did seem to bring problems if the woman was to avoid letting too much time go by: the child or children must be born while the woman is still in her early twenties if qualifications are not going to be acquired too late to allow for the accumulation of publications and appointment to higher levels. One young woman who had her child during her first studies at university was an example of this pattern but even in her case employment prospects seemed limited and the new structure of assistantships made rising to professorial status rather improbable.

One should note also that not all the junior women wanted the administrative responsibilities that professorial status brings. One was repelled by what she perceived of a professor's work load. Some who had been involved as representatives of their department or teaching level in university committees were not attracted by the in-fighting which occurred on certain occasions. They would rather be involved in research and teaching than in these power struggles. At the same time, some did serve as directors of their institutes and took their full share of administrative responsibilities. The majority however seemed to do this more out of a feeling of duty than out of an enjoyment of this kind of work. The occasional woman who admitted cheerfully that she is a 'bossy' type and so revels in such encounters was exceptional. Most seemed uninterested in engaging in the manoeuvres of inter-departmental negotiations, concerned though they may be for the well-being of their own department or category. The positions of Akademische Rätin, under the old structure, or Angestellte, with reasonable security of tenure, give much more time and opportunity to enjoy both academic life and social life and so attracted some women.

Such attitudes perhaps accord well with the observation that in relatively few cases did women see a path towards university teaching posts clearly from the beginning of their working life. Two or three had had such career prospects in mind. But for the majority it had been a matter of discovering an interest in research, an aptitude for it — and then accepting openings as these occurred. This devotion to the subject of study was obviously very strong in many women. One, for example, had been willing to accept all kinds of part-time employment and initially a post as part-time librarian while her Institute built itself up. Other women had simply been pursuing the research which interested them and had found it a happy coincidence that some university department had wanted to have someone with their specialism at the particular time when they were ready to be appointed. Others had set out in one branch of study and moved to another; or moved from non-university work into university teaching. There is little impression of much advance planning for the career of many of the women interviewed: often, the career seems simply to have happened.

It was also noticeable at the lower levels of appointment that women are by no means certain that they will stay in university teaching: partly this is a reflection of the job situation but it is also a reflection of their evaluation of work in a university. One woman, for example, felt that she should perhaps move out of university teaching back to applied work in her discipline when she reached the age of 40. Another young woman in applied science knew that she must acquire practical experience outside the university: whether she would then try to return to the academic world was not something on which she was decided. Yet, given their great enthusiasm for their subject, for many of these women the important consideration is to be able to continue their research — pressures of teaching and administration are at times deplored because they impede progress here. Where women say that they are glad they made the choice to stay in university life (even if the choice was between family and career) it seems to be because they value principally the opportunity to contribute to the development of their chosen subject.

Notes:

1. L. Adolphs: *Die Beteiligung der Frau an der Wissenschaft,* (Walter Braun Verlag, Duisburg, 1981), pp.9-17.
2. R. Drucker: 'Zur Vorgeschichte der Frauenstudiums an der Universität Leipzig: Aktenbericht', in *Vom Mittelalter zur Neuzeit,* ed. H. Kretschmer (Rütten und Loening, Berlin, 1956), pp.278-90.
3. Arbeitsgruppe am Max-Planck-Institut für Bildungsforschung: *Das Bildungswesen in der Bundesrepublik Deutschland* (Rowohlt, 1979), p.213.
4. H. Anger: *Probleme der deutschen Universität* (J.C.B. Mohr (Paul Siebeck), Tübingen, 1960).
5. Ibid., p.452.
6. Ibid. p.478.
7. Ibid., p.489.
8. Ibid., p.491.
9. Ibid., p.461.
10. Arbeitsgruppe am Max-Planck-Institut für Bildungsforschung, op.cit., p.218, p.220.
11. Bundesminister für Bildung und Wissenschaft: *Statistisches Material zur Bildungssituation von Mädchen und Frauen* (Bonn, 1978), 11A3-2860-4.
12. Ibid.
13. Ibid.
14. Minister für Wissenshaft und Forschung des Landes Nordrhein-Westfalen: *Handbuch Hochschulen in Nordrhein-Westfalen* (Düsseldorf, 1979), p.392.
15. Ibid., p.392, 6.1.4.
16. Ruhr-Universit1at Bochum: *Personal-und Vorlesungsverzeichnis* (Wintersemester 1980/81), p.564.
17. C. Führ: Education and Teaching in the Federal Republic of Germany (Inter Nationes, Bonn-Bad Godesberg, 1979).
18. Bochum: *Personal-und Vorlesungsverzeichnis, passion.*
19. Johann Wolfgang Goethe-Universitat, Frankfurt am Main: *Vorlesungs- und Personenverzerichnis für das Sommersemester 1981.*
20. Kontaktfrau J. de Jong: 'Memorandum und Dokumentation zur Situation von Wissenschaftlerinnen an den Hochschulen von NRW und Vorschläge zu ihrer Verbesserung' (Ruhr-Universität Bochum, Juni, 1980).
21. Ibid.
22. H. Anger, op.cit., p.491.

Chapter Five

University Women Teachers in a Socialist Society

East Germany and West Germany share a common educational history and common traditions of university life. Although the two systems have been separate since the years following the Second World War it is evident that some thirty years is unlikely to be enough to wipe out all influences of that common heritage. Changes in structure of the educational system are obvious. What is more difficult to discover and document is the extent of change in attitudes and in the perception and actuality of career structures for women in the developing socialist society of the German Democratic Republic. Given the new system of schooling, the new structure of the labour market, the new governmental policies, has the situation of women in universities been totally transformed? Does it offer a sharp contrast with that of women in West German universities and with that of women in universities in other countries?

The situation of women has certainly received governmental attention and has been included in governmental policy statements. Thus at the Xth Assembly of the SED (Socialist Unity Party of Germany) in Berlin in 1981 the President of the Republic referred[1] to the policy of promoting equal rights for women and girls: 'the really great advances in the vocational and social work of women, their growing share in responsible functions of the state and the economy, as well as the still rising birth rate, show that in our Republic a high level of equal rights and conditions in which these rights can be used in daily life has been reached. What the women and girls of today really bring to the social progress of our country is much more than diligence and skilful hands. It is vocational and political knowledge and competence, courage and confidence in their own abilities and strengths . . . it is now very important that the leadership of our party, of firms and of the women's organisations but also the state and economic leadership organisations use well those social and individual values created with equal rights in order to make still more effective women's will to contribute to the further formation of the developed socialist society'.

The school system has undergone radical changes during the thirty years of the DDR's educational policies. Initially, it experienced the most radical purge of school teachers to be carried out in any European system: some 85% of existing teachers were dismissed from teaching because of their proven or alleged Nazi sympathies; the teaching staff was built up by the introduction of Neulehrer (new teachers), young people and older with some relevant knowledge and with strong commitment to the new state, who were prepared by short introductory courses and further qualified by in-service training. The school system itself moved from a basic primary school of eight years, common to all, followed by differentiated upper secondary schools, to a common polytechnical school of ten years, followed by entry at the close of class 10 into vocational training, or to three years of vocational training combined with academic study to gain the Abitur, the leaving certificate which qualifies for entry into higher education, or — for a selected minority — progress into classes 11 and 12 in the extended upper school to obtain the Abitur. The system is coeducational and the curriculum, despite some internal differentiation from class 8, the same for all pupils. Thus it can be argued that girls receive precisely the same education in school as boys and this should materially affect their subsequent careers and occupations or subjects of study in higher education. Indeed the system would almost seem to show some favouritism towards girls:[2] the percentage of girls in classes 11 and 12 in 1979-80 was 53.5 and 52.8: but the disproportion is possibly insignificant. Certainly entry to vocational training[3] seems to show some reduction of traditional sex barriers to various occupations: thus in 1979, females were 80.6% of apprentices in the chemical industry, 48.7% in agriculture, forestry, fisheries and 21.2% in electronics — though admittedly they were more in line with sex-stereotyping in their 92.2% percentage in textiles.

The system of higher education has also undergone radical changes in the thirty years of the Democratic Republic. Teaching staff were, like school staff, denazified: new staff were appointed. One early development, in the 50s, was the creation of workers' faculties in the universities to enable those who had earlier not been able to have full secondary education to make good deficiencies in their education and achieve university qualification. These provisions were phased out as the ordinary school reforms took hold but a further development was of evening and correspondence courses provided by universities so that those already at work can improve their qualifications. Entry to universities was also affected by reforms seeking to bring about a proportionate representation of the different social classes among university students: thus priority was given to children of workers and peasants in university entrance and, at school, in access to classes 11 and 12 leading directly to the Abitur and entry to higher education. These moves were claimed to be highly effective in raising the percentage of working class students.

An important development was the increase in the 1950s and 1960s in the number of institutions of higher education with specific vocational orientations (technische Universitäten and Hochschulen). And in more recent reforms, the number of places in higher education is determined by the foreseen needs of the economy so that graduates are assured of employment in their specialist field: a small percentage is allowed for 'wastage'. University courses have been standardised so that the number of hours to be spent in each of the many components is fixed and common to all students on the course. Marxism-Leninism, Russian and sport are common to all courses. A further reform has been the introduction, for certain groups of studies, of a requirement for preliminary practical experience of one or two years before entering higher education: but this requirement has fluctuated in recent years. In many courses, however, a period of practical work is built into the higher education programme.

Higher education has thus become clearly vocational though not — it would be maintained — narrowly so. It is not always possible to obtain separate figures for those entering universities and those entering other institutions of higher education. The DDR has 6 universities, 18 technological Hochschulen or universities and a number of pedagogical colleges, colleges of Art, Music, etc.[4] Statistics normally refer to these collectively. Thus we find that[5] in 1979 women students were 53.97% of new entrants to higher education and 50.84% of those completing qualifications in higher education (at first qualification level). This shows a distinct advance from 1965 when the respective percentages were 33.9 and 36.1%. It may be noted that women still seem to be less strongly represented in the category of those studying by correspondence: in 1979 they were only 26% of new entrants and 27.7% of those completing: similarly they are less well represented in evening students: but as those are less important groups of students in higher education and since numbers in these groups have been falling, the important consideration is this apparent equality in entry to higher education.

One might also note the strong majority of females in those studying at the lower level of technical colleges (Fachschulen): there, in 1979, they were 71.3% of the total:[6] but this seems due to the dominance at this level of educational and nursing studies where women are, characteristically and traditionally, strongly represented. The percentages of women students in medical and health studies in technical colleges was 97.8: in educational studies (including, for example, preparation of kindergarten teachers), 84.8: and — though the absolute numbers of students were smaller here — 90.0% in literature and language studies.

Choice of subject areas by women in higher education shows some similarities with the traditional sex-stereotyped patterns but at the same time some departures from traditional expectations. In 1979 the percentages of women students in subjects of higher education were as follows:[7]

maths/physical sciences	45.4
technology	27.0
medicine	57.1
agriculture	47.9
social sciences	57.5
philosophy, history, law	33.2
culture, art, sport	36.8
literature and languages	70.9
education	74.1

Women continue to be strongly represented in languages and literature, in educational studies and social sciences. But at the same time one must note their presence in technology and agriculture and their near equal or more than equal presence in maths and physical sciences and in medicine. The relatively low proportion of women in cultural studies, art and sport is however something which one would not traditionally expect.

It should be recalled that as the proportions of those engaged in the various branches of study in higher education are determined according to the needs of the national economy the distributions among subjects may differ from those found in other countries. In 1977-78 the percentages of those entering higher education in different areas of study were:[8]

Maths/Natural sciences	5.3
Technology	30.5
Medicine	7.7
Agriculture	5.4
Social sciences	15.8
Philosophy, history, law	6.5
Culture, Art, sport	1.9
Literature, Languages	1.6
Art	1.9
Education	23.1
Theology	0.3

These percentages correspond nearly to the percentages of those actually engaged in studying the subjects in 1977, with slight increases in Technology and Education in the figures for new entrants — from 29.2 and 22.1 respectively. It will be noted that girls are in a minority in the most popular branch of studies but they are strongly represented in the next most popular branch, Education.

A comparison may be made with the distribution of undergraduate students in the different subject areas in the United Kingdom in 1981-82, university students only:[9]

	Total percent	Percentage of Women
Education	1.5	61
Medicine, Dentistry, Health	11.1	41
Engineering, Technology	14.6	6
Agric., Forestry, Vet. Science	2.0	37
Biol. & Phys.Science	23.4	30
Admin., Business Studies	23.6	40
Architecture & other Prof.,Voc.	1.7	32
Lang., Lit. area studies	13.0	66
Arts other than langs.	9.1	38

A major difference is of course that Education students in the UK are largely taught in non-university institutions. But despite the problems caused by different systems of classifications some differences in emphasis are obvious.

What one cannot decide from the DDR figures is whether the school system is gradually eroding the traditional differences between boys' subjects and girls' subjects: or whether the bias still evident is due to a real preference found, on average, in one sex rather than the other: or whether social factors and employment prospects are contributing to choices in areas of study. (It might possibly be relevant to numbers entering university and opting for different studies to note that military service gives males the possibility of opting for a double period of service which can provide specialist training in technical skills: thus some males, after military service, might opt to enter directly the skilled occupation for which they have been prepared rather than go on to a period of penurious living as a university student.)

But at postgraduate level, the equality of women seems not yet to have been achieved. In a system which seems closely related to the past German traditions East Germany has two types of postgraduate qualification, Promotion A and Promotion B. The first — the doctorate under the old system — gives the right to the title of doctor in a specified branch of learning — e.g. Dr. rer.nat. It is achieved by the writing of a thesis showing research in depth in the chosen field. The second, Promotion B, gives the right to the title of doctor of science (Dr.Sc.), a wider title, and is achieved by a second thesis and evidence of competence in directing a research project and inter-disciplinary knowledge: the candidate should also have some experience of academic work abroad. In many ways, Promotion B resembles the Habilitation. And in practice, it is regarded as the qualification for a 'call' to a Chair or to the position of Dozent. (It is true that people may be appointed to such positions without B, as occurred, for instance, during the years of rapid expansion of the higher educational system and as may still occur when those appointed come directly from the exercise of their profession in practical life.) The percentage of women[10] among those achieving Promotion A in 1979 was 27.1: and at Promotion B level, 9.3. These figures admittedly represent a considerable increase over the position at the beginning of the decade: the respective percentages were 11.9 and 4.4 in 1971. But they show that there is still some distance to go before equality is achieved at this level: and they have obvious implications for the proportion of women to be appointed at higher levels within the universities.

As for the structure of university teaching itself, there are some similarities and some differences when the West and East German systems are compared. In the East as in the West, entry is at the assistant level. Assistantships may be for a limited term or 'unlimited' (unbefristet) — i.e. they may be held with security of tenure or with limited tenure. But for the newcomer to university teaching normally a limited term assistantship will be given, the expectation being that during this time the assistant will write the thesis for Promotion A. Five years has been regarded as the appropriate time for such writing but various circumstances — e.g. heavy teaching commitments or the birth of children — could lead to a longer period being given. As yet, there has been no clear rule about sending away people who fail to complete the first doctorate within a recognised period of time but suggestions have been made that this procedure will be followed in future. The way to the A doctorate may be easier if the candidate has an Aspirantur, that is a scholarship which requires only a small amount of teaching and leaves the candidate free to concentrate mainly on the research: a three-year period would be regarded as the norm here though for an 'ausserplanmässige' Aspirantur — a supernumerary Aspirantur — a four-year period may be the norm. After success in the first Promotion, the entrant may continue as a tenured assistant and after a number of years become an Oberassistent (Higher Assistant). The next stage to aspire to is that of a Dozentur, a post which is recognised as being of genuine Hochschullehrer level: it has tenure, as do some assistantships and higher assistantships, but it has higher salary and sickness benefits and considerably greater prestige. It may be regarded as the stage of waiting for a call to a Chair though by no means all Dozents will reach that higher level. To reach these levels of Dozent or Professor, Promotion B is, as we have noted, almost always required and it involves not only the writing of a more important thesis but the qualities to be expected in the head of a research group and normally six months' experience in a foreign country. (The USSR is the most probable place of such experience but other countries are also acceptable, according to subject areas: in modern languages, for example, six months in the USA could be the qualification.)

Promotion B is thus an important stage in the career of a university teacher. But by no means all university teachers — men or women — aspire to it. There has been considerable unease on the part of state and university authorities about the failure to produce more people qualified at this level just as there has been unease about the long period of time which characteristically elapses between Promotion A and Promotion B. Analyses in one university in recent times[11] have found that for 35% of those achieving Promotion B, up to 8 years elapsed between A and B: for 26%, 8 to 10 years: for 19%, 11 to 13 years: for 15%, 14 to 16 years: and for 5%, over 16 years. To achieve this higher level of qualification a two-sided decision has to be made: the candidate decides to work for it but decisions have to be made by his or her Sektion (department) as to whether some reduction of teaching load can be given. Thus an Aspirantur at this level also is a valued opportunity to get on with the necessary research work. Given too the emphasis on collective research projects there is the greater need and opportunity for the aspiring university teacher to rely on the goodwill and cooperation of colleagues in the department. But for men as well as for women there may be some considerations which make it seem not worth while to strive for Promotion B. To some it may seem to be socially more commendable to join in a piece of cooperative research than to sit writing a thesis for personal satisfaction. Or commitment to teaching and administrative duties may prevent the expenditure of time and energy required for the thesis at the advanced B level.

The initial entry to university teaching is normally on the invitation of the department in question. As early as the second year of study at university a student may be approached with an offer of a research contract when qualified: and departments are urged to be on the look-out for students who seem likely to be promising members of the Nachwuchs — the academic succession. It is possible, of course, for a keen student to ask for an Aspirantur in his or her department: but much of the entry does seem to be sponsored by the teachers who know the student's work. The department continues to play an important part in the career prospects of the individual for, as has just been indicated, lightening of the teaching load to facilitate research work is dependent on the collective view of colleagues and the decision of the Director of the department. Hence there is the possibility of regulating — at least negatively — the numbers of those aspiring to the higher ranks of university teaching. But the situation has changed in one respect in recent years in that whereas normally promotion took place within the university and movement from one university to another was uncommon, now advertisements of Chairs and Dozentships appear in *Das Hochschulwesen,* the higher education journal, indicating the possibilities of such inter-university mobility. Such advertisements indicate, as advertisements would in Britain, the aspect of the subject which is considered important for the post and the experience considered important, e.g. in teaching similar courses or in work in industry or applied research. The candidates are to provide a curriculum vitae and statements as to academic qualifications, publications and other achievements. Applications are sent to the Rector of the institution concerned.

Information as to the exact proportion of women in university teaching and at the different levels of university teaching proved impossible to obtain. Various attempts were made, culminating in an assurance from high officials in the Ministry of Education that the exact statistics were not available. Consequently all that can be done is to give estimates derived from people's impressions in the universities visited — the Humboldt University of Berlin and the University of Leipzig. An estimate so produced is that at Assistent level percentages of men and women are about equal though in different subject areas percentages of women may range from 10 to 60 per cent. At Oberassistent level, the estimate was about 25%: at Dozentin level, 21%: at professorial level 12-13%. Overall it was estimated that there are about 38% of women on teaching staffs, rising perhaps to 42% in medicine and falling to about 36% in Hochschulen generally. But the impressions and estimates of the percentages of women varied from one subject area to another. In the natural sciences it was recognised that the percentage of women was relatively small: in Education there was the impression that at least an equal proportion of women was to be found among the staff, if indeed not a majority of women: naturally, in the area of pre-school education, there was a majority of women. Yet it also seemed that the salience of women affected estimates. When actual counts were made within a department it was sometimes discovered that although the informant had believed women to be in the majority in fact there was an equal number of men in the department or even a slight majority of men.

The groups interviewed

The Humboldt University of Berlin seemed an obviously good choice to be visited since it is a highly important and prestigious university and one which prides itself on its progressive policies, especially where the advancement of women is concerned. The University of Leipzig had the attraction of being associated with the University of Leeds in a cultural interchange. It is also one of the ancient universities, dating its foundation from the fifteenth century, in 1409: it was given the title of the Karl-Marx University of Leipzig in 1953.

Preliminary arrangements for the visits had not sufficiently clearly indicated that individual interviews would be sought for. Consequently, to help the researcher, some last-minute arrangements had to be made, resulting in some group interviews with three, four or even, on one occasion, six women to supplement the individual interviews. Obviously it would have been more satisfactory to have more time with each woman individually: and note-taking in the group situation is decidely more strenuous. But later analysis of notes showed that in fact the basic questions were satisfactorily dealt with in the group situation. Women in the group — like academic women everywhere — were not likely to adopt a conforming attitude: they were ready to disagree with each other as to answers being proposed. And the information provided made good sense. What was lost was the chance to discuss in a leisurely way the woman's own research interests and personal experience: on various occasions it was a matter for regret that there was not more time available to continue the discussion on a one-to-one basis as was possible in the cases where women were interviewed individually. But at the same time, there was evident in the DDR universities as in other universities visited a very friendly and cooperative attitude on the part of those interviewed. There was no lack of helpfulness and considerable interest in the eventual outcome of the enquiries was expressed.

One should note here that in both universities there was a committee for the advancement of women, a committee which has the responsibility of looking carefully at the present status of women members of staff and planning how their progress can best be achieved. In the Humboldt University there had been for some years a list showing the developments planned for the various women staff and a yearly check to see whether the intended progress had been made with research dissertations.

In Leipzig 23 women were interviewed, including two who were teaching in other institutions of higher education, a College of Art and a Pedagogical Institute — given the emphasis on the unity of higher education in the DDR it seemed helpful to include such representatives of women at this level: in fact their experience did not seem to differ from that of the university staff. In Berlin 24 women were interviewed mainly in group situations. There was perhaps less variation in the type of place of interview in East Germany, many taking place in the formal reception rooms of the older university buildings: some in fairly typical offices, again in older buildings: and some in the more modern rooms of the new skyscraper tower of Leipzig., But one was in the office adjoining a museum of Egyptian Art and Antiquities and one in the University archives office.

The age distribution was as follows:

25-29	6	45-49	7
30-34	2	50-54	9
35-39	9	55-59	1
40-44	12	60-64	1

It may be noted that in East Germany the retirement age for women in universities is 60 though after retirement professors and others may continue to engage in some teaching and research in the department. The concentration of the group in the middle age ranges may be characteristic of 'survivors', those who have managed to stay in university teaching: but at least some young women at the Assistent or Aspirant stage were included to discover the characteristics of newcomers to the profession and their attitude towards their future career.

Only one woman of foreign nationality was included in the group, a Hungarian married to a German.

Marital status was as follows:

Single	6
Married	34
Separated, divorced	4
Widowed	3

While of course one cannot be sure that this distribution is representative of the situation among university women teachers generally in the DDR, it is interesting that the percentage of married women (87%) coincides with that for the population in general. The percentage separated or divorced (8.7%) is slightly higher than for the population as a whole (6%)[12] but the numbers are too small to be reliable.

Of the married women 4 had no children. The family sizes of the others were:

One child	15
Two children	13
Three children	9
Four children	1

In the one-child families, one child was adopted and another was the child of an unmarried mother. The question of family size is one which has received much publicity and official attention in the DDR. Much emphasis too is laid on child-care provisions and maternity leave. These are questions to be returned to later.

Occupational levels were:

Assistentin/ Aspirantin	13
Oberassistentin	13
Dozentin	13
Professor	8

Clearly this distribution does not represent that found in the profession generally; there are obviously much greater numbers of women asssistants and Aspirants than Dozents. An effort was made in fact to provide interviews with as large a number of women in responsible positions as possible, including women serving as leaders of Sektions.

The distribution of women students, as we have noted, to some extent follows traditional lines by showing large concentrations in languages and in Education but smaller numbers in applied sciences. Medicine does attract large numbers of women both at student and staff level but it proved difficult to include in the sample women teaching in this faculty since their work apparently made it more difficult to find times at which they could come along to a group meeting, the more so as they also were normally working in buildings some distance away from the university buildings in which most interviews were carried out. Consequently the subject distribution of the sample is not as representative as might have been hoped. The large weighting on the side of Education is due — as it was in other universities visited in other countries — to the fact that I was the guest of Education departments and it was therefore easier for arrangements to be made to meet members of such departments. It can be remarked that Education included a number of special interests — comparative education, history of education, further education and pre-school education, for example.

The subject distribution of those interviewed was this:

Education	18	Economics	1
Humanities		Psychology	1
Foreign Languages	6	Geography	1
History	5	Maths	1
Philosophy	3	Medicine	2
Art History	1	Biology	2
Egyptology	1	Biometrics	1
Near Eastern Studies	1	Vet. Science	1
German Literature	1	Food Production	1

Possibly the most noticeable effect of having so many representatives of Education was that my initial statement that in most countries women are in a minority in university teaching met with questioning. In that subject area women certainly did not have the impression of being in a minority, though in fact numbers seemed to be about equal when men and women staff were counted: at assistant level however there was a deliberate policy of giving priority to women. Here it was stated that if it were a case of two applicants having equal opportunities, one a man, the other a woman, preference would be given to the *woman*. At the same time many people interviewed in this subject mentioned the very serious concern being felt at the increasing feminisation of school teaching. This concern related to the practical difficulties of schools if many teachers are women who take maternity leave or are kept away from work by their child's illness: but it also included psychological considerations of the lack of male models for boys during their school career. Discipline difficulties in schools were also mentioned as possibly related to the feminisation of the teaching profession. Rather similarly there was reference to problems of feminisation in Medicine, where maternity leave may produce staffing difficulties: one woman interviewed said that formerly there was a 60:40 ratio in favour of women among students admitted to Medicine: it had now been modified to a 50:50 ratio.

Career patterns

As in other groups, there seemed in many cases to have been no initial intention to become a university teacher: some indeed were still uncertain as to whether they would remain in university teaching or, on the completion of their Aspirantur, return to work outside the university. One indeed would willingly have made this return to practical work a few years ago but had been urged to remain in her present line of activity.

Naturally, many of those engaged in the faculty of Education had arrived there through longer or shorter periods of school teaching. But two had in fact come into school teaching in a fairly dramatic way by being in the group of Neulehrer, those rapidly enrolled to go into schools and fill the gap left by the purge of the former generation of teachers in the 1950s. In such cases, willingness to be of service to the community seemed to have been the determining motivation: and the initial lack of professional training had been made good by various in-service and full-time courses of study at a later point. Four women had in fact left full-time day schooling after class 8, i.e. at age 14, and had come through evening studies, technical college studies and other means to eventual qualification and university graduation. Two of these had benefited from the special faculties set up in universities in the period 1953-59 to enable those who had not completed full secondary schooling (or even, in some cases, full elementary schooling) to bring themselves up to university standards and achieve a university qualification.

Another who had found her specialism almost, one might say, by accident, had been completing her secondary school studies at a time when there was a recognised need for many more qualified people in agriculture. Directors of schools had been urged to look out for suitable people who could undertake such studies. She was from a village background and the head of her school had urged her to take this course. She did so — and found that she had never regretted the decision.

As in other groups, there were some who had initially wished to go in for Medicine but had eventually specialised in some other subject. One of the four who specially mentioned this childhood ambition had in fact stayed in an allied field, that of Biology. One who had wanted to study medicine — though her mother thought that domestic science would be a more suitable choice — had been given a place to study it but at the same time a new institute in communication studies was opening in her university and she seemed a particularly promising recruit (having shown journalistic ability during her school time) so she opted for that line of study instead, the more willingly as it enabled her to stay in the same university as her Freund. Another had found that the opening available for her was in training as a child nurse and from this she had in due course advanced to specialising in pre-school education. One who had never really wanted to teach and would have preferred Medicine, for example, was strongly urged by her university teachers to go into teaching and in fact did so. But on the other side, one woman who had originally become a nurse moved from that career into Medicine: yet she had been, she claimed, anxious to be a doctor rather than a university teacher and her interest still lay on the practical side.

It is also of interest that on occasion women referred to the influence of their section or teachers as having determined certain career decisions. In more than one case it was a former university teacher who proposed coming into the university as assistant and undertaking research work. One woman reported that when she was first asked by her professor to begin specialising in her present subject area she was by no means enthusiastic: her interests, she felt, did not really lie in that direction: yet she did not feel that she could refuse the professor's invitation so she entered that line of study — and became strongly enthusiastic and successful in it.

In other instances, the section was indicated as the reason for proceeding to a higher qualification at a point when the woman herself felt she had reached her ceiling. One woman, for example, was asked by her section to go ahead and take the B level qualification so that she could be appointed to a Chair though she herself was contented with the point she had reached: but she did take the qualification and was duly appointed to a Chair. In another case, the section had advised staying on in university work rather than going back into school teaching even though the woman herself felt she was rather old to embark on an academic career.

The social demands of the times did not always work to the individual's satisfaction. One woman going through school in the 1950s, at a time when there was considerable emphasis on trying to achieve equality in the proportions of worker and peasant children reaching higher education, found that her family background — her parents were middle-class, Angestellten — meant that she could not proceed in full-time secondary education and had to leave school and take her further academic qualifications by attendance at technical school.

There were, on the other hand, some whose careers had followed a more direct path. A mathematician had loved mathematics from an early age. Some, though not many, had followed the direct path of qualification, with A and B coming in fairly rapid sequence after their initial qualification. Two had studied abroad, in Leningrad. Others had similarly completed periods of study in other countries, a procedure which, as we shall see, does involve problems for married women with children.

Only a few had experience of teaching in other universities though many had experience in teaching in other departments or branches of higher education. Some had intermediate periods in administration, partly of social work, intertwined with their academic teaching. Many had had extensive periods of work outside the university, in television, in animal husbandry, and of course in teaching — at further education level as well as in schools.

Reasons given for the minority situation of women

While some doubt was expressed in some subject areas as to whether women actually are in a minority at the lower levels of university teaching in the DDR, there was general and ready acceptance of the statement that women are a minority among university professors.

Some of the respondents pointed out that this minority situation among professors is the view one arrives at by taking a cross-section at the present time. If the situation is studied with regard to age groups it may appear that in future there will be greater if not complete equality between the sexes at the different levels of the hierarchy. At professorial level, it was pointed out, many Chairs are at present held by people appointed in the expansion period of the 1950s: these are mainly men since at that time the policy of the advancement of women was not fully in operation. As Chairs become vacant and are filled again it is to be expected that the proportion of women professors will increase.

This argument seems to have some validity and it could be expected that in the DDR, as in other countries, there will be some improvement over the next ten to twenty years — this view that it is largely a matter of history and that future conditions will be better, with more women at the top levels, is one which was expressed in almost all the countries visited. Yet it does depend on the progress of the young women who are at present reasonably numerous in the lower ranks of the profession. It depends on whether they are as decided as men about staying in the profession, attempting to gain higher qualifications: or whether they find the attraction of practical work outside the universities stronger than men do: or — we keep coming back to it — whether the demands of family and social life reduce their numbers effectively. Certainly in the DDR group it was evident that some of the assistants interviewed were likely to opt for a return to work outside the university in the fairly near future: by no means all of them were committed to going on to write dissertation B and attempt to reach higher positions.

A further 'objective' response to the question about minority status was that sex bias in choice of subjects means that there are fewer women available for nomination to Chairs in some subject areas. If these subjects have large numbers of promoted posts, the representation of women is inevitably affected by this sex bias.

Most frequently the answer to the question about the minority status of women in university teaching was that the weight of family responsibilities and the care of children prevent women from advancement in university work. This reason was given by 34 of the women interviewed.

Many aspects of family cares and responsibilites were mentioned. Women, it was pointed out, still do more of the organising and planning of the household even when husbands may contribute to coping with household chores. Although husbands are becoming more skilled in looking after small children, it is still customarily the woman who stays at home if the child is ill — though legally the husband has the right to absent himself from work for this reason. If a man did take the days off he is entitled to for this purpose, he would certainly be asked, said one woman: 'And where is your wife? What is she doing?' Two or three of the women suggested that in any case it is to the mother that children turn when they are feeling ill: they did not know whether this was due to a biological factor or simply the result of having been more often cared for by the mother. Thus the woman has a considerable load of work which a man would not have. As one woman put it: the man gets up in the morning, has his coffee and goes off to work. The woman rises, gets the children their breakfast, takes them to the kindergarten and plans what the family are going to eat in the evening: then she gets on with her work outside the home.

While there is said to be some tendency for husbands to be more involved with child-care and housework than formerly — one kindergarten expert noted that nowadays it may be as often the father as the mother who brings the children along in the morning and collects them later — it would seem that equality has not been achieved. Research carried out earlier,[13] in 1972, would support this view: it showed an interesting difference between men and women's perception of the situation: in response to the following questions, a group of 1007 men and 992 women gave the percentages of answers shown:

		Men	Women
Is there a division of daily housework duties in your family?	Yes	44	35
	Partly	42	45
	No	14	20
Does the wife, even though out at work, do most of the housework?	Yes	46	64
	Couldn't say so without qualification	35	21
	No	19	15
Who looks after your children if they are ill?	Myself	3	78
	My spouse	64	1
	Sometimes one, sometimes the other	28	17
	Other people	4	4
	No one	1	0

And as to general responsibility,[14] these were the percentage replies to the question — in your family who brings up the children?

	Men	Women
I do	1	8
My spouse	4	1
I, more than my spouse	4	32
My spouse more than me	28	2
Both of us equally	63	57

There is even official recognition of working women's greater responsibilities in that married women are given a day off each month to cope with domestic tasks: similar concessions are made if there are children under 18 living with the woman: if she has living with her relatives in need of special care, as certified by a doctor: if she is above the age of 40.

It was noted by various women however that domestic work has become considerably easier to cope with in recent years as the availability of running water in the home, washing machines, dry cleaning and convenience foods has become greater. Even so, there do remain problems of queues in certain shops: and the difficulties caused when some services — e.g. domestic repairs — are provided by shops which open only at specific hours on certain days. But as some women said, it is not necessary to be houseproud: some university teachers certainly feel they have 'modified' their standards of housekeeping.

Pregnancy and child-bearing

It was often pointed out that having children slows a woman down in her professional advancement. She may succeed in writing thesis A but then she has children: and by the time she is ready to write thesis B, there may be a question in her mind as to whether it is worth the effort. One woman suggested that thesis B should be written at the age of 35 but this is rather early for a woman with children: yet if this qualification is not obtained by that age, the prospects of getting a Dozent appointment or a Chair may appear so remote as to make writing B seem irrelevant.

Age limits do offer a complicated picture when the prospects of men and women are concerned. The differential ages of retirement — women at 60, men at 65 — might seem in some ways to disadvantage women for although they can enjoy the benefits of early retirement (with possibilities of continuing to do some teaching and some research — and professors retire on full salary) yet their effective working life may be affected by child-bearing in the early years and then they have a smaller number of years available in the subsequent period. The women interviewed however did not seem to regard early retirement as a relevant factor. And the situation is also complicated by differences in estimates as to the age at which a call to a Chair may be expected: some held that by 40 it should have been achieved: others thought that appointment at the age of 50 was still possible. In fact an authoritative statement was that 43 was the average age of nomination to a Chair: but this was regarded officially as rather too old to be satisfactory. Exceptional people are certainly appointed younger: one instance given was that of a man appointed at age 29.

Other factors too may operate to the advantage of women. It was calculated that a man might do a three year period of military service after school, thus reaching age 21: then he might have to undertake a two-year period of practical work (a pre-requisite for entry to some subject areas): then four years of university study, bringing him to the age of 27: experience in university or practical work plus three years for thesis A and three years for thesis B would bring him to about 35 before qualification. Women would not have the three years of military service (admittedly men are not compelled to opt for the double period but there are, as we have seen, advantages in doing so). Yet this absence of military service was regarded by some teachers as a disadvantage for women in that women students tended to be more conforming, docile — more like school-children — in their approach to university work: men with the service experience tackled university work in a more independent and mature way and might have more practical experience in their field.

The age at which the first child is born is a topic of considerable interest and importance, especially in discussions in the DDR. Most of the women in the group were of a rather older generation which had not been affected by the present debates and provisions for maternity leaves. The emphasis currently was on having children between the ages of 20 and 23: two or three of the women interviewed referred to themselves as having been 'elderly primates' in having their first child about age 26. Research reported by K. Starke in 1980[15] showed that 42% of females and 38% of males in a group of young workers thought that 20-21 was the best age for having the first child: 32% of both males and females thought 22-23 the best age: 8% approved 24-25 and 6% favoured ages 18-19. Thus there are indications that the first child should be born during a woman's university studies and in fact there has been reported a considerable increase in the number of women students having children during this time. In the group interviewed it had been exceptional to have a child before completing the first university or other qualification. The present trend of public opinion in the DDR would thus seem to favour the life pattern for a woman of combining child-bearing with the first qualification, then proceeding to work and further academic qualification while the children proceed through kindergarten and school. Figures for natality rates in 1978[16] do indeed show 21-22 as the ages at which the greatest numbers of women had children, closely followed by 23-24, 19 and 25. (The desired family size, as indicated by research among young people,[17] appears to be overwhelmingly that of 2 children, 68-70 percent of the population studied opting for this.)

This situation is naturally closely linked to the provision of facilities for child-care. In university residences for students, there have been introduced 'baby étages', floors on which there is provision for washing, changing the baby and generally looking after it. Within the residences young couples may have a room for themselves and their child. The provision of creches for the population generally has increased dramatically with recent times[18] so that in 1980 there was provision for 60% of children in the relevant age groups (up to 3 years of age): and some creches are Wochenkrippen, keeping the child all week, the parents looking after it at weekends only. At kindergarten level,[19] the coverage is still nearer to 100%: in 1979 it was 92.3%. For some cases, there is also provision of 'weekly' kindergartens from which the children return to parents' care only at the weekends. In addition, for children of primary school age, there is full provision of the Schulhort, the system by which children are cared for in schools during the afternoons (the teaching in the schools occurs during the mornings: afternoons are left for extra-curricular activities, of various kinds, or the child is expected to work at home): at the school they are supervised by special staff, they do homework and various activities are organised for them. Thus if parents choose this, there is a system to care for primary school children when both parents are out at work.

Again it is interesting to see what research[20] found about opinions on child care in 1972, though with increased and improved provision since then, opinions may have changed.

		Men	Women	(N 797) Working Women	(N 195) Women not at work
The wife should interrupt her work outside the home until the children are three years old	Agree	38	35	33	45
	Agree with reservations	15	13	12	20
	Disagree Partly	25	26	26	19
	Disagree	22	26	29	16

There was a variety of opinions in the group interviewed as to whether it is really advantageous for female students to have children while still engaged in first level studies at university. Some commented that this can be the ideal time to begin a family since the woman student is given every encouragement to complete her studies in the normal number of years; arrangements are made — often through the assistance of fellow-students — to help her to keep up with course work and take examinations. Thus, it is said, she can complete her first qualification, have a child or even two children and be ready to enter working life and go ahead with her career without having to interrupt that career for pregnancy. In this way she can avoid the kind of situation one of the group had in fact found herself in, beginning her teaching career in September of one year and going off for maternity leave in December of the same year. Another woman who had combined study and child-bearing remarked that she had made it a point of honour to complete her course as well as her fellow-students, in the normal time. And a really outstanding case of one student was reported: she had had two children during her years of study, was pregnant with her third child as she completed the course and yet she had had top marks all the way through. It was emphasised that in such circumstances the woman has a feeling of security: she is likely to find a place in a creche for her child while she is at university (though one young student-mother interviewed had not been able to do this and had had to place the child with relations and see it at weekends only): both fellow-students and teaching staff are ready to support the student who is combining two roles.

But some women queried whether the young student fully realises what the care of a baby entails and whether it is really so easy to cope with a young child in one room and to study at the same time. Something of course must depend on the husband and his contribution to caring for the child: but some senior women felt that the young woman research student, in times past, entering on her research appointment unencumbered by a child and not intending to have a child immediately, was able to devote herself much more effectively to her research. It was also suggested that the young woman may not realise how much effort a doctorate entails: 'they think it is just a matter of doing their homework'.

But if a woman does not have her child while a student, what are the prospects when she starts a family after working life has begun? The state has encouraged and facilitated having children by successive increases in the amount of maternity leave given. For a first child, a woman is entitled to 26 weeks of maternity leave with pay: for a second or subsequent child she is entitled to the Baby Year, a year off work with a guaranteed return to her post after that time and with payment up to 75-80% of normal pay during that time. Most of the women in the sample had had their children before the present level of provision had been reached: few had had absences as long as these. But one woman had elected to stay at home till her youngest child (she had three children) had reached the age of three: she felt that the children needed a mother's care until then and creches did not seem to her to offer an acceptable alternative. Her view was however hotly disputed by a woman specialising in pre-school education who pointed out the vast amount of work which has been done recently to develop good educational programmes in creches and good training for the workers in them. Another young woman remarked that when she was at home with her child she could not give the child as much attention as a creche or kindergarten worker could — she had housework to do at the same time: and this seemed to be a point made by education authorities. As another woman pointed out, much depends on the health and personality of the child: some children adapt rapidly to creche conditions, others may really require to be cared for at home during the first years. And of course the mother's own health is another relevant consideration.

One woman had in fact recently had a 'baby year' and had found that during it she was somewhat bored at home: she also found some difficulty in settling back into a smooth working routine in her department — though her department leader said that she had made an excellent come-back. But a year out of the university can mean a year's absence from a research project. For those specialising in natural sciences or applied sciences it can mean there is no opportunity to engage in further work during that time though it was agreed that specialists in the humanities can engage in useful reading during their absence — as can scientists too, but with more limited usefulness. There is thus a danger of failing to keep up with the work going on in the department and failing to keep up with advances in the subject during the year. Colleagues too may have to do extra work — even with extra pay — to cover the gap. Thus opinions about the baby year are ambivalent, for various reasons. Another possible danger in the baby year was voiced. Some women fear that it may give too much ease and security to young women: some students, it was suggested, work it out that they can have various periods of time at home, at public expense, enjoying themselves caring for babies. The fact that their husband may be working very hard to provide for the family does not worry them.

Some other general points about too much security were made incidentally. It can, a few women remarked, have its drawbacks for both men and women. One would not wish to inflict difficulties deliberately but the older generation had gained in character by having to struggle: having things easier may not be entirely good for the young.

At any rate there are certainly inducements to have more than one child and to have children while still young. Young couples marrying can receive a loan to help them to begin their married life, to set up a household: a reduction in the repayment due is made on the birth of the first child, and for subsequent children, so that three children can practically wipe out the loan.

Although most of the women had not benefited by the provisions for baby years and full maternity leave they had not found difficulty in obtaining places for their children in kindergartens and creches, even before the provision of such places had reached its present high levels: teachers are in a privileged category on lists of those seeking such places for their children.

Some of the women too had found that grandmothers were a great help in looking after children. But it was recognised that this is increasingly less common, as more and more grandmothers are themselves out at work. More than one woman who had been helped by her own mother recognised that now when her daughter wanted similar help with a baby she herself was simply not available — she is busy with her own career. More generally, as the level of qualification for women working in industry improves, women are less likely to be willing to stay off work to look after grandchildren: in earlier times, when the grandmother was an unqualified worker, absenteeism for such purposes was more probable. (Interestingly enough, there was no suggestion that grandfather — even in those days of liberated men helping in the home and with child-care — should play some part in looking after grandchildren. And yet, life histories reported in Maxine Wander's popular book[21] *Guten Morgen, Du Schöne* showed how important a figure grandfather had been in the lives of the women she interviewed.)

167

The possibility of obtaining domestic help was non-existent. One young woman did mention that in the past female students had sometimes been willing to look after children as a means of supplementing their grant income: but this source of supply seemed now to have dried up. 'Unskilled' child-care or domestic work simply would not offer attractive prospects in the present state of the employment market.

Nor is it only the problem of being there to look after young children that is important. The attitudes of the children themselves have to be taken into account. Teaching in the university is not, as women repeatedly pointed out, an 8-hour-day occupation. Research especially may involve work in the evenings and at the weekend. Children may sometimes resent this pre-occupation of their mothers. One woman noted that although she had tried to give her daughter all possible attention, her daughter had complained at one point: 'You're never *there* when I want you!' and another woman had been met by the comment 'I know you have important work to do but other parents have more time for their children'. Yet it was also suggested that university women give more time to their children than other mothers do. Other women remarked that the understanding and support of their children were essential to them in continuing with their academic career. And a few noted the problem of having a divided mind, thinking of the children while at work and of work while at home. Another woman remarked on her good fortune in being able to manage with little sleep and so do much work late at night.

Another point made by various women should of course also be kept in mind. A family is not simply a burden: children are rewarding. The contact with children is a source of pleasure — as we have seen, one woman opted to stay at home for some years, to enjoy this family life: another recalled that when her mother reported what a toddler had said or done during the day she felt that being out at work was depriving her of some very real pleasures. At the same time there were also women who pointed to the advantages of flexibility of university work which allowed them more freedom in attending to their families. Yet the timing of departmental meetings can detract from this flexibility. One or two women commented on the awkwardness of departmental or professional meetings which go on late in the afternoon and suggested that there is a distinct difference in the attitudes of men and women in such circumstances, the women being anxious to conclude the business at a reasonable time, the men being untroubled by thoughts of what still has to be done that evening.

Husbands

Twelve women spontaneously mentioned the support given by their husband, not only in material help with housework but also in interest in their work and discussion of it. It was generally agreed that the husband's attitude makes a great difference to a woman's progress in an academic career.

This attitude seems likely to be all the more helpful if the husband himself is in the same occupation or in a related occupation. It seemed as though these university women teachers tended to have husbands who were also graduates and in a professional occupation. In 23 cases the husband was also an academic (Wissenschaftler) and in two was in a medical post, as surgeon or Oberartz. In five of these cases the husband was in the same branch of academic work as the wife. Two husbands were school teachers. Other husbands were in engineering, three described as Diplomingenieur, two as Bauingenieur (constructional engineers) and one Bergbauingenieur (mining engineer) which the wife said gave an unusual combination of interests in their marriage. Another was in aeronautical engineering. Two were officers. One husband was simply described as being in a non-academic occupation. One was described as a Handwerker (craftsman) and his wife found him admirably useful about the house, and most supportive of her career. While information on husbands' occupation was not complete — and while of course the sample may not be fully representative — there did seem to be a pattern of similar levels of qualification. Cases in which the husband's level of qualification was markedly lower than the wife's were in a small minority and indeed one woman pointed out that women generally have husbands with equal or superior qualifications. In one case where both were in academic life but the wife had the higher qualification and position, questions had been asked, apparently, as to whether the husband resented this situation: but he did not do so and the marriage was going smoothly in spite of this inequality. In another case where the wife had the higher qualification — Promotion A — it was assumed by acquaintances, she said, that the qualifications were the other way round. One woman however remarked that her daughter was having some domestic problems because she was wanting to study for a higher qualification: this use of her time — sitting studying in the evenings — was leading to quarrels with her non-academic husband: but the mother hoped that the husband could be led gradually to try to improve *his* qualifications and thus could gain insight into his wife's aspirations.

In another case, the fact that the husband already occupied a prominent position within the same department seemed to the wife a reason for *not* attempting to work for higher qualification herself. The social duties associated with her husband's position were another reason for not devoting her leisure to further research — though her own age level seemed also to be a factor influencing her decision, since she felt that she had passed the age when striving for promotion was appropriate.

The husband's attitude could be important too when it was necessary for the wife to study abroad — as we have seen, such study is considered important in determining suitability for appointment to a Chair. A few women had been able to leave their children in the husband's care on such occasions: but one at least felt that although her husband would be willing to look after the children during her absence she herself would not be willing to be separated from them for as long as six months: she would therefore try to make up the necessary qualification by shorter periods abroad.

The mobility question was not one which seemed notably to have affected the academic progress of the married women in the group though one woman had not accepted a call to another university since, she said, it would have involved tiring commuting — her husband could not move his appointment. But she now had an equivalent post in her own university so the decision had not caused problems. To some extent, the lesser amount of movement between universities in the DDR system might mean a more stable domestic situation than in other countries. Problems of mobility would be more likely to occur in the earliest years of a marriage when the young graduate would have to go to whatever post called for her services: but even then attempts are made to appoint husband and wife to the same area — indeed the argument of being about to be married to someone in a certain place may be invoked when posts are being allocated at the end of the first period of university study and the graduate is particularly anxious to get to a given area — or to avoid being posted to certain others.

It might incidentally be noted that there was some comment on the advantages to husbands of having non-working wives and it was noted that a number of men in top university postions have this advantage. The one man at such a level who did have a 'working' wife was said to be more sensitive than other men to the need to end meetings at a reasonable hour.

Attitudes

A number of individual comments suggested that women's own attitudes may be related to the minority situation of women at the top levels of university teaching. Some 18 of those interviewed spontaneously referred to attitudes as playing a noteworthy role in women's careers but there was no clear trend in the references made.

Two women suggested that although society is trying to give women equality with men, some women still tend to take the traditional view of women, that is, they see themselves as fit to occupy only the second rank. This acceptance of the traditional stereotype means that women may lack self-confidence and will not try to achieve high positions.

In fact one or two women noted occasions on which they had been uncertain of their own ability to succeed, not in academic work but in administrative positions: but whether this was due to some lingering prejudice or to simple individual differences in personality could not be determined.

Women were occasionally said to be more sensitive than men: to be less keen to be leaders: and not be able — or willing — to 'use their elbows' as effectively as men. Men, it was suggested, have a clearer perception of where they are going. They are also more self-protective when it comes to taking on additional administrative tasks in a department: they query, on such occasions, how this is going to affect their research whereas women would accept the tasks without such questioning. Women, it was said, are more interested in pleasing others.

It was also suggested that women sometimes feel that they have to prove they are as good as men and therefore must produce very outstanding work. But when members of the group were asked specifically if a woman had to be better than a man in order to achieve promotion there was not a general feeling that this was so. One or two considered that yes, the woman does have to be better. Two interpreted the statement in an unexpected way: since a woman has to cope with so many other things as well as her academic work then in fact, given the width of her activities, she *is* decidedly better than a man. But the majority view was that promotion depends on performance in academic work and that no sex bias would affect decisions about promotion.

Was there then no belief in the existence of prejudices against women? This matter was dealt with in a variety of comments. Some women did feel that — especially in certain faculties like that of natural sciences — there lingers something of old beliefs about women's inferior capacities: but they apparently did not think this would affect a woman's chance of promotion. It was also stated that even if men have such prejudices they would not venture to assert them openly. (This, of course, would not prevent prejudice from being operative.) But it was felt that prejudice had been there in the 50s and 60s. In medicine particularly women were seen as of inferior calibre: a professor might like to see a pretty woman about the department but would not regard her as a potential successor. There was then some belief in the effectiveness of official policies stating equal rights for women though in practice opinions in the group seemed to be fairly equally divided between those believing that prejudice does not exist and those believing that in fact it does still linger in some areas. It might be, for example, that a woman's performance would be more carefully scrutinised than that of a man: one 'might be taken for silver not gold'.

In one field of study, however, some prejudice was thought to be operative: this was the field of Fine Arts where women are very rarely appointed as professors in the Arts themselves. It was suggested that there is still a belief that women cannot be as effective in creative work as men: hence appointments to posts reflect — or are thought to reflect — real differences in ability. The world of the fine arts seemed to be rather anti-feminist, not in the individual cases but with regard to female competence as a whole. Exceptions might be found: but one woman pointed out that historically the members of craftsmen's guilds had only exceptionally allowed women to learn and practise their crafts: a woman could enter only if she had some family connection with an established craftsman — if, for example, a widow took over her husband's business or a daughter was allowed to learn her father's skill. But when there was any likelihood of a general move by females to enter the protected craft then the guild closed ranks and prevented this break with tradition.

Although there is the official recognition of equality between the sexes, the group differed to some extent in their attitudes towards women's organisations. Some were actively involved, holding official positions in such organisations. Others felt that it was preferable to concentrate on activity within their own field: by making good progress in their own university section they could encourage younger women to make progress in academic life and build up their confidence in their academic competence. But no one would have accepted being thought of as an 'Emanze' — the stereotype of the woman who has become entirely masculine and aggressive in the assertion of equality. Indeed three or four of those interviewed pointed out that a woman must remain a woman: that is, she should continue to have feminine charms and feminine qualities. Such feminine qualities were, it was suggested by these women, likely to lead to greater success as an administrator: a woman could be more effective than a man in interaction with colleagues because she behaved in a womanly way.

Questions of differences between the sexes in attitudes to work were occasionally raised. On the whole, there was little assertion that male and female students had different attitudes to work. Some did suggest that women students are in fact more diligent than males. The other difference that was mentioned was more a matter of maturity than a genuine sex difference. As we have noted, some women thought that girls coming to university at an earlier age than their male counterparts were likely to be more docile: older women, especially with the responsibility of a child, worked in the same directed, rational way as men though one woman suggested that after having a child the woman student tended to turn her attention to the child and away from her studies and another, unkindly, that some unmarried students were more interested in the search for a husband than in their work.

So far as ambition was concerned, most of the group did not think that there was a sex difference: women were as ambitious as men. Nor was there any perception of sex differences with regard to publication. Publication presented no special problems for women.

At the same time, there were not many among the group interviewed who showed ambition to become a professor or even Dozent — though of course some had already reached these levels. Of the others, some pointed out that they worked mainly because they enjoyed what they were doing: 'Es macht Spass!' They were not anxious to acquire an administrative load and they felt that their professional self-esteem was amply rewarded by the respect of their colleagues and the consciousness that they were doing good work. In one instance a woman said that she and her husband had agreed that neither would go on to attempt writing a B thesis — both had already the A qualification — but would continue to work within the sphere of their existing qualification. Another woman pointed out that she wanted to enjoy life: she and her husband went sailing at the weekends, for instance: a good social existence was not compatible with devotion to further intensive research. In addition there was of course the age factor: it was generally felt that after the age of 40 — which many of the group had reached — writing dissertation B would come too late. Thus there seemed to be a widespread readiness to be content to remain at the point already reached and to work steadily away at teaching and at rather shorter-term research. Some of the younger women interviewed said modestly that they did not think they were qualified for higher appointments: though they conceded that they might be so qualified one day. Others in this younger age group were not certain that they would remain in university teaching: some might return to practical work outside the university and would prefer to do so.

Thus, though there was general agreement that the proportion of women at professorial level should reach greater equality with that of men, there seemed to be little evidence of unsatisfied ambition within the group studied.

But one should perhaps take into account here the system within which they are working. It may be clear that in their own department there is not likely to be an establishment of an additional Chair or Dozentship. Movement to another university is not considered necessarily part of the characteristic academic career and the total number of universities is small. Further it may be that the specialist subject area is not considered to be of sufficient importance to merit the establishment of a higher level post. Possibly the new system of general advertisements of Chairs and Dozentships will gradually lead to greater mobility between universities: the emphasis laid by the government on increasing the numbers of people qualified at the higher levels may also play its part in increasing determination to arrive at those levels. But at the same time one has to bear in mind some comments that suggested university teaching is not necessarily attractive. One woman cited the case of an acquaintance of hers who had just opted not to go on teaching in university because he did not like the prospect of going on for years repeating the same thing to unattractive groups of students. But other members of this particular group disagreed sharply here: some emphasised the enjoyment of human relations in contacts with students and they queried whether school teaching — which had been cited as more rewarding — really was so.

Yet it was also made clear by two or three of the women that they felt they had been given special advantages by the policy of Frauenförderung (advancement of women): they had been given Aspirantur posts to enable them to get on with writing A or B dissertations. The prolongation of an Aspirantur because the woman had a child during that time was regarded as a particularly valuable concession. Many women stressed the importance of the attitude of the collective in which one finds oneself: they appreciated the cooperation and help their colleagues had given. Yet one woman remarked that while it is encouraging to be asked by the Rektor or the appropriate committee what progress one is making with one's research — it does make it clear that other people are interested in what one is doing and how one's career is advancing — yet ultimately finishing the dissertation must depend on the individual's own determination and skill.

Sponsored mobility

From what has been said, it would appear that in the East German university system there is a system of sponsored mobility: official policy can intervene to affect the promotion of the individual or of women in a much more distinctive way than in the other systems studied. Statements as to equal opportunity for women are not necessarily effective — there is evidence in various educational systems that they can co-exist with continuing prejudice and various possibly unintentional biases. But in the East German system the emphasis on departments' responsibility for identifying and encouraging talent among students and staff can clearly work to the advantage of women. The explicit policy of development of the Nachwuchs so that recruitment to university teaching and research can be effective and adequate does make active encouragement more likely than in the other systems where much is left to individual initiative — though one could presumably place on an equal footing the offer of an assistantship or research studentship or, after some practical experience, an Aspirantur, and the offer of a postgraduate scholarship or an assistantship in other systems.

It should also be kept in mind that in the East German system, selection of future recruits may be made more reliable by the requirement of practical work in a relevant occupation before entering certain subjects of study and by the inclusion of practical work within the course programme. There is however the other aspect of recruitment, that university courses in the DDR are closely related to the economy's requirements for specialists of different kinds. Thus the intake into a given field of study is gauged according to the estimates of need four or five years hence. Similarly too the needs for teachers within different subject areas can be estimated. Further the guarantee of employment on satisfactory completion of the university course may mean that students think in terms of future work outside the university: it is probably the exceptional student who will form aspirations about continuing to a career in research and university teaching.

This need to develop young people's interests in Wissenschaft, the academic study of their subject, was emphasised by some of the women interviewed. While some young women will have this approach, others may be more interested in practical work or in their family. But the most crucial point for the development of sponsorship was seen by women as that where decisions are made to go on writing thesis B. It was recognised by women who had done it — and by others who had decided not to attempt it — that writing this thesis is indeed a demanding and time-consuming task; an 'Ochsentour' — hard slog, was one description of it. Women who have found it difficult enough to cope with family and other commitments to write thesis A may very well feel that that is enough. Yet thesis B could be satisfying when the writer felt that the research had been really useful: as one woman put it, she knew that her work was not simply sitting on the shelf, it was being used. There are however different approaches to thesis B. It would seem that in the past there has principally been encouragement of the development of an original idea by the candidate, the fostering of a new approach, however vaguely it might be defined in the first instance. But increasingly the tendency is for the research for thesis B to be part of a wider research project in the section: the research topic may thus be allocated to the candidate. Obviously such developments facilitate sponsored mobility: candidates can be helped on their way by the allocation of a promising part of a general project. The acquiring of further qualifications then is a matter in which decision-making can be helped or even determined by a collective view in the department as well as by the willingness of the leader of the section to advance the career of a junior member of staff. The allocation of an Aspirantur is the formal expression of this decision and, as various women testified from experience, it can make a considerable difference to the ease with which the higher qualification is obtained.

The existence of the committees for the advancement of women within individual universities must also be looked upon as very deliberate sponsorship. As one woman pointed out, this movement can be interpreted as showing that there *is* discrimination — in favour of women. While again the existence of a list of women members of staff and an outline plan for the development of their careers does not necessarily ensure the fulfilment of that plan — as one woman pointed out, we noted earlier, it still comes down to the individual's own effort and as others commented, it is ultimately a matter of individual self-discipline — yet it does enhance women's awareness of their situation and what is needed if they are to achieve advancement.

In the group interviewed, as in other countries, there was nevertheless a considerable proportion of women who had not consciously set out to make a career in university teaching. Many of them had come into the system relatively late, after experience of practical work: this was, of course, particularly the case in those working in branches of education. Few of them had set out to be university teachers — as we have seen, one had found even her progress to university rather difficult because she was at school during the fifties when the official policy was to give priority in upper secondary and higher education to the children of workers and peasants: her parents were too middle-class (Angestellten) to allow her to proceed directly to those levels of education: so she had come by a roundabout way of technical college qualifications. Some had, as we have noted, specialised eventually in subjects which were not their first choice but rather accidentally taken up. Others had clearly entered the profession through the encouragement of teachers who had recognised their abilities and encouraged them to take posts which otherwise they would not have thought themselves entitled to. But some, among the younger women particularly, had been invited to assistantships after qualifying at the first level and were now writing thesis A or B and feeling part of the group of women whose university careers were being officially encouraged.

There are thus provisions in the higher education system of the German Democratic Republic which could easily determine the percentage level of women in university teaching and as holders of university Chairs. (One assumes, in saying this, that enough women would be found willing to accept the sponsorship and tackle the admittedly demanding tasks required to gain B qualification — not only the thesis but the acceptance of leadership responsibility and the inclusion of foreign study.) Naturally much must depend on the intentions to expand or contract or maintain at steady state the supply of posts. The indications are that some expansion is still considered appropriate: but the expansion will not necessarily be in areas where large numbers of women are studying: there might then be some problems in finding sufficient women or in discriminating very obviously in favour of women in a subject dominated by male students.

A further complication to a manpower planning approach is, paradoxically in some ways, the generosity of maternity leave benefits and time off for looking after children. As we have seen, the policy is to encourage natality and to encourage having children while the woman is still young. But the consequences for the staffing of schools and hospitals or clinics have already caused some concern and, allegedly, have led to some kind of restriction on having a majority of female students in Medicine. Thus the encouragement of women to have children may make them less desirable employees from some points of view: and certainly it may mean that the young women are pre-occupied with family cares at a time when they should be beginning preparation for higher academic qualifications.

Even apart from government policy and planning there is the question of women's own attitudes. While the group interviewed were, on the whole, less likely than groups in other countries to think that prejudice against women could affect their career prospects, some did think that prejudice might linger in some quarters: and prejudice might still be accepted by women themselves, affecting their concept of their own role in professional work.

More importantly, the group interviewed agreed with groups in other countries in pointing out the tremendous effect of family responsibilities on the career of the woman university teacher. They noted perhaps more than other groups the difficulties of coping without domestic help — domestic help being largely unobtainable — and, while welcoming the easing of domestic work by more modern aids in recent times, still found it a considerable and time-consuming task. Husbands were, in some cases — as in other countries — willing to take their share of housework and child-care but the main load for these was still seen as falling on women. In one respect certainly the married woman with children is in a more favourable position than those in other countries studied: the extensive provision of creches and kindergartens for children under school age does mean that, if she wants to use this form of assistance, the university woman teacher can count on having it: and the woman university student too can benefit by such welfare provision for her children. For primary school age children there is the Schulhort during working hours.

But the group agreed with other groups in emphasising the attitudes of women towards their family life. For many women the claims of their children — pre-school or older — are an important consideration to put against the demands of work for higher qualification. The quality of family life — and indeed of life in general — is important for them. They have, too, many social responsibilities — work in Parents' Associations, for the youth organisation, the FDJ, or in women's organisations — which also make demands on their leisure. By the time they have brought their children up to an age of relative independence and are ready to concentrate more on acquiring higher qualifications, it may be too late for a university career reaching the highest level of appointments. One woman indeed, reviewing the various possibilities with regard to families, noted the problem of having a child at the beginning of working life: noted that it is not convenient either when one is in working life and concluded that the really appropriate time would seem to be when one has retired! And, some women pointed out, it may be that some women take refuge in the family as offering a more rewarding and less strenuous way of life than that of the career woman. Not all men, it was noted, want to take B qualifications: even fewer women may be attracted by this prospect, especially as much also depends on having an understanding husband. It is perhaps also to be noted that in East Germany at the time of the survey there were no women Rectors of universities — though this is a post to which people are elected. Presumably the number of eligible women was still too small to produce the choice of a woman candidate. Leipzig, however, did have one woman pro-rector.

In East Germany certainly the role of woman as worker outside the house is established: about 87% of those in the appropriate age groups[22] are employed outside the home. No girl nowadays, said one woman, would have as her ambition simply to marry a rich man and stay at home looking after the children: she would expect to have a working career. But whether the next step towards the establishment of women on a footing of equality with men in university teaching can be taken remains a matter of some uncertainty. There are factors which could make it difficult. It would also be helpful in deciding on the prospects of future success if there were precise figures as to the present situation. But against this there is the point made by an eminent educator in the DDR: 'it is not particularly important to know what the exact percentages of women at different levels in university teaching are: we know that the situation is unsatisfactory: what is important is that we are working to make it more satisfactory'.

Notes:

1. Erich Honecker: *Bericht des Zentralkomitees der Sozialistischen Einheitspartei Deutschlands an den X Parteitag der SED* (Dietz Verlag, Berlin, 1981), p.122.
2. Wissenschaftlicher Beirat bei der Akademie der Wissenschaften der DDR unter Leitung von H. Kuhrig, W. Speigner: *Zur gesellschaftlichen Stellung der Frau in der DDR* (Verlag für Frau, Leipzig, 1978), p.197.
3. *Statistishces Jahrbuch der Deutschen Demokratischen Republik, 1980* (Staatsverlag der Deutschen Demokratischen Republik, Berlin (1980), p.295.
4. Ministerium für Hoch- und Fachschulwesen: *Hochschulen und Fachschulen der DDR: Statistischer Überblick* (1980), p.24.
5. *Statistisches Jahrbuch der DDR 1980*, op.cit., p.299.
6. Ibid., p.298.
7. *Hochschulen und Fachschulen der DDR*, op.cit., p.24.
8. Gemeinschaftsarbeit der Akademie der Pädagogischen Wissenschaften *et al: Das Bildungswesen der DDR* (Volk und Wissen, Volkseigener Verlag, Berlin, 1979), p.162.
9. *University Statistics 1981-82* (universities Statistical Record, 1983), vol. 1, p.6, Table E.
10 *Hochschulen und Fachschulen der DDR*, op.cit., p.33.
11. *Das Hochschulwesen*, Zeitschrift für das Hochschulwesen der DDR (VEB Verlag, Berlin, 1982), 9.
12. *Statistisches Jahrbuch 1980*, p.349 and table facing p.400.
13. A. Grandke: 'Zur Entwicklung von Ehe und Familie' in *Zur gesellschaftlichen Stellung der Frau in der DDR*, op.cit., p.245.
14. Ibid., p.235.
15. K. Starke: *Junge Partner: Tatsachen über Liebesbeziehungen im Jugendalter* (Urania Verlag, Leipzig-Jena-Berlin, 1980). p.169.
16. *Statistisches Jahrbuch 1980*, p.370.
17. K. Starke, op.cit., p.165.
18. *Statistisches Jahrbuch 1980*, p.36.
19. Ibid. p.288.
20. A. Grandke, op.cit., p.243.
21. M. Wander: *Guten Morgen, Du Schöne!* (Verlag der Morgen, Berlin, 1977).
22. H. Kuhrig, W. Speigner: 'Glechberechtigung der Frau — Aufgaben und ihre Realisierung in der DDR' in *Zur gesellschaftlichen Stellung der Frau in der DDR*, op.cit., p.51.

Chapter Six

All Things Considered

We have reviewed the situation of women who teach in universities in five countries. Despite differences of language, of countries, of university systems, there are remarkable resemblances among the women studied. They differ according to specialist subject, according to age level, post held and family status, but nationality makes little difference. They have in common their enthusiasm for their work especially. In some ways, the present report must convey a one-sided, partial view of these university teachers for it focuses on selected points and neglects much that they would rather talk about — their research and teaching. It is misleading if the impression is given that they are constantly thinking of the problems of women, alert to instances of prejudice, concerned that they might not achieve promotion. It is an artefact of the enquiry that these points are emphasised. The questions posed were answered but they are not necessarily the questions the women would most like to have discussed.

Yet in the answers given there are also clear resemblances. Certain views recurred with uncanny similarity in different countries and university systems. In all there is a common problem — women form only a minority of those teaching in universities and women are especially under-represented at professorial levels. Yet in all countries there is explicit recognition of equal rights for women and there has been an increase in the proportion of female students in universities. Despite differences in the structure of the systems studied and differences in the methods of appointment and qualifications required, there is remarkable agreement in the answers given by women to the question why this under-representation in university teaching occurs. The most commonly cited reason is women's responsibility in child-bearing and child-rearing. In addition, reasons to do with social attitudes and the attitudes of women themselves towards careers for women were widely offered. Prejudice against women was not totally ruled out as an explanation but it was cited much less often than might have been expected: there are instances where individual women think they have been the victims of prejudice but these are infrequent: there are many instances where women have been greatly helped by male academics. Generally there is agreement that universities are less likely to be prejudiced against women than society outside the universities.

When we consider the findings of the enquiry in greater detail, we recognise that the situation of women is not always different from that of men who teach in universities. Some of the factors affecting women university teachers at present are equally present in the career situation of men. So, initially, some of these general factors in universities are to be considered before we come to the problems indicated as important for women. Women's career problems must be seen in the context of the university situation as a whole.

General factors

Is university teaching in fact a unified profession? It is misleading to assume that it is unified in the sense of offering the same kinds of working conditions and the same kinds of work to all who engage in it. The difference between subject areas and between departments is immense. Life differs for those who have to teach large numbers of students, possibly in an enforcedly impersonal situation, and those who meet only with small groups or who teach on a one-to-one basis. Research varies from the large-scale survey to the meticulously controlled laboratory experiment to the exhaustive analysis of written words. Everyday conditions of work vary for those in cities, for those in smaller towns: for those whose daily experience is of the limited environment of the laboratory and research team to those who daily interact with members of other departments: for those who work on a university campus with some central focus or meeting place to those who work in a hospital or institute remote from other parts of the university. Interaction during the working day may be with a large or small number of people and those people may be colleagues, students or members of society outside the university.

Most importantly, perhaps, there is the difference between what could be described as the applied and the reflective disciplines. In medicine, veterinary science, applied sciences generally there is perception of the immediate effects of knowledge on people and things: there may be positive intervention in the lives of individuals or organisations: university teachers have clinical sessions or consultancies: they receive feed-back on the practical effectiveness of their knowledge. In the social sciences and the arts, such conditions may be lacking. Feed-back may come only from students' reactions to teaching (which are important) or from the reaction of colleagues to written or spoken words. Social scientists may, on occasion, feel frustrated by the conditions which prevent them from putting their theories into practice and experience conflict between the demands of university work and their wish to be involved more effectively in society outside the university. Arts specialists are less likely to suffer such conflict: but they are the more open to charges of remoteness or feelings of alienation. These differences result from the nature of disciplines as well as from interpretations of the duties of the university teacher. They may well be reinforced or made more difficult to handle by official pronouncements, from time to time, on which kinds of study are more beneficial to society in general: but they are intrinsic to the studies. Hence the feelings of university teachers towards the conditions of university life and to colleagues' work in other disciplines vary widely. A practical consequence of differences is that university teachers may have difficulty in judging the quality of the work done by colleagues in other disciplines: decisions about promotion or appointment should therefore be by people competent in the relevant field.

But a further practical consequence of the differences is the possible variation in career structure between those whose career may follow an unbroken sequence within universities and those who may spend some years in work outside. The latter have advantages in some respects in having alternative occupations available when economic factors make life in universities precarious: they may also have superior bargaining powers when seeking appointments in universities. But there may also be advantages of security and of continuity in one type of work for those who enter on a university career while young and remain in it. Different subjects evoke different career patterns. Decisions about tenure — its duration and the age and qualification level at which it is achieved — will have to be taken with regard to the total career structures of possible university teachers: yet subject differences may mean very different structures. It is difficult to see how a short-tenure structure, even if renewable, could be universally applied.

Nevertheless there are sufficient common elements in the work of university teachers of different kinds to make it appropriate to think of the profession as a whole. Apart from their employment by universities (though they differ between countries as to whether they are thus civil servants or not), university teachers do have the functions of transmitting knowledge to the younger generation (or to more mature seekers after knowledge) and of carrying out research in their subject. But there is a haunting question as to whether universities are going to continue as distinct entities or whether their functions are going to be taken over in the relatively near future by other institutions. Medieval universities provided a common framework of knowledge in certain subjects: the tradition has lingered in the requirements for Scottish Ordinary degrees till recent times. But in the modern universities there is no such requirement and even the common background formerly provided by secondary school leaving certificates has been eroded as these too have been awarded on an optional choice of subjects rather than on a common core of studies. The position of universities as providing the highest levels of teaching in their subjects has been challenged by other institutions, particularly institutions of technology. Monotechnics may be increasingly favoured. The need for the actual meeting of teachers and students in universities has been eroded by the development of 'open universities'. The combination of teaching and research no longer seems inevitable. It may be that in studying university teaching we are looking at a profession centred in a dying institution. It is certainly a profession in a state of radical and rapid change.

Further factors common to universities in different countries have been evident in the research reported. One major factor is that of the relative stagnation or positive contraction of university provision in the countries studied, with the possible exception of East Germany. A common background of expansion in the 60s and for part of the 70s relates to a present situation in which governments are seeking to control expenditure on university education and to stabilise the numbers of students in it. It will be recalled that governmental control of student numbers already exists in East Germany where places are adjusted to meet what are believed to be the needs of the economy. Other governments seem to be moving, at different rates, towards systems of manpower planning — for example, France has already produced strong protests among students by determined efforts to exert this kind of control of medical studies. But even without governmental intervention a period of expansion which comes to an end must mean some stagnation in promotion prospects for the newer members of staff. The Chairs have been filled: and, given probabilities that they were filled by relatively young and highly promising people, they remain occupied for some time: no great increases in student numbers justify the creation of new posts. While this situation affects both men and women already in post in universities, it is probably more disadvantageous to women since women's access to university studies and to university teaching has increased only recently. Hence women were less frequently than men in a position to benefit by the good years. It is true that the good years may have resulted in the larger representation of women at the lower levels of university teaching. But they now find themselves, with men at these levels, in a relatively unpromising situation.

Future recruitment

Economic pressures are causing universities to look more thoughtfully at the question of future recruitment, at that body of people described in the German universities as the Nachwuchs — the successors. Governments, having taken steps to reduce the number of posts, nevertheless seem to have some realisation of the need to ensure that there will be qualified people available to fill posts when the present holders retire. The West German system in particular has, by its introduction of the Hochschulassistent type of appointment, tried to link the assurance of successors with the avoidance of an excess of people taking qualifications for posts which will not be available. In the UK the UGC has introduced the 'new blood' exercise, providing a strictly limited number of new posts for people who are under the age of 35 and judged by the university in question to have good research potential. (It will be noted that the stress is on the research component of the work.) In East Germany it is an explicit duty of departments to encourage and offer opportunities for a suitable number of possible future members of departments. But how is recruitment which is more controlled and more highly selective than in the past going to work?

In all the systems studied quite a lot can depend on the impression made by the student during undergraduate years. Such impressions can determine the departmental decision to offer appointments to do limited amounts of teaching or tutorial work: to apply for assistantships or Aspirantur posts coming vacant in the department. Subjective factors can clearly have considerable effect here and it is difficult to see how one could get away from them. It is reasonable that teachers in a department observe the abilities and interests of their students and decide to encourage those who seem to them particularly good: but impressions can be misleading; some students may be overlooked. Possibly, some control of subjective factors can be achieved if even minor posts are advertised in the department and so students are given the opportunity to propose themselves, as happened in one West Germany university, for example, when a woman student proposed herself as assistant in practical laboratory classes for which traditionally men students only had been considered appropriate.

Selection procedures must be more thoughtfully scrutinised in this situation where entry to university teaching is more difficult and more carefully guarded — all governments being concerned to avoid an excessive supply of highly qualified people for whom posts are simply not available. There are factors which might militate particularly against women's recruitment.

There is firstly the factor of simple prejudice. The evidence suggests that this is not likely to be widespread in the universities of today but there does remain the possibility of unconscious prejudice manifesting itself — as has just been suggested — in failure to perceive women as appropriate for initial appointments or for a kind of gradual initiation into the profession. There seem to be two ways of coping with this. One is, as suggested, to ensure that the availability even of minor appointments is made known to both male and female students. The other is consciously to look at the proportions of men and women appointed, even for minor duties, and to relate these to the number of qualified applicants. (The question of positive discrimination in favour of women will be looked at later. It is not here recommended.)

A second difficult question is that of maternity. Where posts are rare and are expected to lead definitely to an established position, there is naturally concern as to whether the person appointed will (a) prove satisfactory (b) continue in the post. Where women are concerned, if they are of child-bearing age, the question must arise as to whether they are likely to have children and to interrupt their work in the university temporarily or permanently. Modern legislation has made the situation better for women in some respects by ruling that they must have a paid period of maternity leave and the right to return to their job. But from the point of view of heads of department in a university the disruption caused by maternity leave may be something they are anxious to avoid. Some of those interviewed spoke from experience — their own or that of others — when they said that this concern could be well founded. Paradoxically too, modern legislation may inhibit asking questions about family plans, since that could be held to be discrimination against women if men would not be asked similar questions: yet the woman, if asked, might well have a reassuring answer to give. There was considerable evidence, in all the countries studied, that most university women teachers are likely to cause the minimum disruption to their departments if they are having children; they are ready to undertake departmental duties even during the time when they are supposedly on leave. They may even show ingenuity in planning the arrival of the baby for a convenient time in the university year. All this is not to suggest that university women teachers should be deprived of the usual safeguards of maternity leave. It is to emphasise the commitment to their department which such women frequently show, a commitment which means that most of them at least will try to avoid as much as possible any inconvenience which might be caused by their pregnancy. The best solution to the problem would seem to be not a speculative avoidance of appointing women because of possible pregnancies but a provision in universities of adequate supply teaching during maternity absences. Granted, not all highly specialised teaching or research can be coped with in this way: but a great deal of work could be covered. It is a false economy to overload colleagues on such occasions just as it is a false economy to overload them on the occasion of study leave or illness affecting either male or female colleagues.

Similarly as to the mobility question: some questions might be raised — and had been put to women in the groups studied — as to whether a married woman would not be able to persuade her husband to move to her place of employment and might therefore neglect her work because she was commuting. Again, this is a matter which can affect both sexes — some husbands are reluctant to move because of their wife's job and some men commute to the family home. And again, there has to be reliance — which, judging by the women studied is well justified — on the university woman teacher's commitment to her job and her determination to do it well. How a couple solve the mobility problem is up to them: and many show great resourcefulness in solving it.

A third relevant factor in recruiting the successors — one which affects women and might be easily overlooked — is that of age. As we have seen, there are many women who come relatively late in life to university teaching, not necessarily because they have been exercising their profession outside the university but because they have discovered, after a period spent in some other occupation and very probably in raising a family, that they are interested in academic work. Such women acquire qualifications at a higher age level than men. Now if, as in the UK, appointments to 'new blood' posts are given an upper limit of 35 women who might first have embarked on higher studies at that age are ruled out. Similarly, in the East German system, it might be held that a woman past a certain age is not really an appropriate person to be given an Aspirantur or specially favourable conditions to work on her B thesis, since she has passed the age at which, on average, professors are appointed. Women themselves are forced by social conventions and folk-lore to be particularly conscious of their advancing years. There are, especially, the stories about the menopause. Such factors had not affected the work of women in the groups studied but they are factors which women have to contend with in public opinion. It is more likely in the case of a woman than of a man that she will be dismissed from consideration for appointment as being 'a bit old', or for higher promotions as 'at that age!' The structure of university teaching careers must be made sufficiently flexible to cope with differences in the ages at which women and men are likely to acquire qualifications. Women, it was remarked by more than one of those interviewed, cannot win where age is concerned: if young they are regarded as probably more interested in their social life than university work — and less likely to have sufficient authority among students and colleagues: if older, then they are past it.

Assessment of qualifications

In all university systems, a major factor for both men and women is the method of appointment. In all, considerable importance is attached to the record of research and publication. But the way in which research achievement is judged does vary from one system to another and the amount of criticism expressed by those within the system also varies.

The UK is the most vague in its statements of what is required and how achievement is assessed. While the Ph.D. may be regarded in some subject areas as an essential, it is not so regarded in all. Whether publications are assessed as to quality or largely on general impressions and quantity depends very much on the appointing committee within the university. This rather haphazard approach may be contrasted with the thoroughness of the Finnish system with its appointment of experts — whose competence can be challenged by candidates — who do have to read the works in question. Finland indeed comes at the extreme of openness about appointments in the five systems studied and is noteworthy in the scope it gives the dissatisfied candidate to request reconsideration. (It is also remarkably generous in its willingness to allow candidates extra time to improve their qualifications.)

The 'big thesis' hurdle

One of the most notable reactions of many women interviewed was dissatisfaction with the need to write a major thesis for appointment to senior positions. Thus in France, the 'thèse d'état' and in West Germany the Habilitation thesis and, to a somewhat lesser extent, the B thesis in East Germany were seen as being not only impediments to promotion but — in the French and West German systems — impediments to realistic and worthwhile research. It has to be kept in mind that in these countries there is a preliminary level of qualification which could be described as a doctorate: judging the levels of scholarship between the British Ph.D. and these continential doctorates is an impossible — and unprofitable — task, the more so as it could not be asserted with confidence that there is a uniform standard of work for the Ph.D. in different British universities and in different subjects. Similarly it must be recognised that in France and Germany also the requirements for the higher qualification do vary according to discipline. The question is, what is the most appropriate criterion of higher level qualifications?

The great complaint in France and West Germany about the requirement for a further major research thesis was that it made too large a claim on the energy and time of the individual over too many years. It was seen as being in some ways a superannuated form of scholarship, tending to pedantry, to exaggerated attention to minutiae and, above all, not likely to be widely read by others — if indeed it were further read at all. Of course allowance has to be made here for possibly prejudiced views of people unwilling to make this particular effort. Yet the complaints seem sufficiently widespread to achieve some credibility. And since in both countries there had been reluctant acceptance of the alternative of awarding the qualification on published works rather than on one weighty thesis, this could be taken as additional evidence that the traditional system needed reform. There had too been years in which the traditional requirement had been waived and people appointed who had not written the thèse d'état or the Habilita-

tion thesis. Yet West Germany seemed to be returning to making the requirement as firm as ever. And in both systems there had lingered also an academic
disdain for the people who had not satisfied the 'normal' requirements.

In France, however, it now seems as if the government proposes to end a system
which has been so much criticised. It is too early to know how the projected
reform of higher education will work out. It is also unclear exactly what system
is to be used in future to judge qualification for appointment to top level posts
in university teaching — some kind of 'habilitation' procedure, possibly relying
on the judgment of experts (who presumably will use published works) seems
to be what is envisaged. Yet if the old burden is removed there will undoubtedly
be many (including those who have successfully written a thèse d'état) who la-
ment this destruction of academic standards.

Two points may be made about the 'big thesis' hurdle. One is that it affects
both men and women university teachers. It can be argued that it has been more
of a problem for married women than for married men since social convention
has accepted that a man could work on his thesis while his wife kept the house
running smoothly around him: while social convention — and husbands and
children — do not envisage similar facilitation for women. There is of course
the possibility of a marriage in which both partners are engaged in such writing:
here they may well encourage each other: but there is still, perhaps, the possibility
that the wife will encourage the husband to get his work done first — and then
feel that it is scarcely worthwhile for her to make life difficult by trying to get
on with her own.

But the other and more interesting point is that these systems of qualification
do not seem materially to affect the proportion of women teaching in universities. France, with the dreaded thèse d'état requirement, still manages to have
a higher proportion of women at top levels than Britain. West Germany, with
its Habilitation thesis, is nearly equivalent to Britain in its representation of
women in university teaching. East Germany, given its sponsored mobility policy,
is perhaps not fairly comparable here: but women in that system also appear
to have achieved better representation than in the UK universities.

What would seem to emerge is that women can cope with whatever qualification system is in operation, even though they may find the qualifying process
hard going — for a variety of reasons other than its intrinsic difficulty. If
anything, they possibly benefit from a clearly defined system. Women in France
were clear as to the importance of the doctorat d'état: women in West Germany
were less clear about the Habilitation, given the fluctuations in official policy
in recent times, but still knew what they had to work for to achieve promotion.
Women in East Germany too were well aware of thesis B and other requirements.
Women in Finland were perfectly clear about the need to have, as well as the
Licentiate and doctorate degrees, a body of publication which could stand up
to scrutiny by experts. In Britain there is on the whole a recognition of the
usefulness of a doctorate and evidence of publications but their essential qualities
are not clearly defined: there does seem to be scope for other adventitious fac-

tors to determine the pattern of a career, particularly personal reference and interviews.

One notes of course that in France, West Germany, East Germany and Finland the thesis plus research is not enough to achieve appointment. There must be some evidence of ability to talk in the formal situation of a demonstration lecture: and/or ability to convince the body of people responsible for the appointment that one is the appropriate person for the job. So personality factors do enter into the appointments system, however much emphasis is put on what appear to be objective factors. At the same time, there is sense in assessing, even if rather inadequately, the probable teaching — or spoken communication — skill of a teacher. There are, too, good arguments for trying to ensure that people are not suitable through 'paper qualifications' only. If evidence of ability in running a research team could be reliably assessed then there would be much to be said for this aspect of the East German criteria. It is important that people should be able to get on reasonably well with students — who perhaps might be given more of a voice in judging teaching competence than most systems at present allow them — and with future colleagues. But of course there are obvious dangers that prejudice may replace honest judgment when personal factors are considered — and it has been noted that this prejudice may attach to such matters as political beliefs (actual or assumed) as well as to sex. The French system of committees of people expert in the subject might possibly reduce some of the irrelevance which can enter into interview situations where some of those interviewing are 'outsiders': the British system has perhaps too much faith in the virtues of a general collection of interviewers. Certainly the possibility of subsequent challenge can do something to safeguard candidates against irrational behaviour on the part of an appointing committee. In Finland this procedure seems to work well, even if it does not speed-up appointing processes. In the UK, awareness that a subsequent case may be brought if discrimination against women has been shown in an interview may reduce at least outward manifestations of prejudice: but this is a very limited form of safeguard and, on the whole, not helpful to male candidates whose need for defence against subjective factors can also be great.

The usefulness of clear definition of criteria for appointment and promotion may be seen in another respect too. Many women in the groups studied had come into university teaching in a somewhat haphazard manner, being invited by someone who knew of them and their qualifications to take up a post that happened to be coming vacant — or even to help in setting up a new course of studies. In such cases, if women are not clearly aware of the qualifications needed to make progress in their new career they may remain in a kind of cul-de-sac, recognised as playing a useful part in the work of the department but prevented by lack of wider or more relevant qualification from upward progress in the hierarchy or from movement to another university. Women may of course choose to settle in such a situation: but in some cases it may take some years before they perceive the consequences of their 'irregular' qualifications or interests and by then they may feel it is too late to improve their situation. Men could be in a similar position but there is perhaps a greater probability that male superiors see the need for them to think about further qualification and advise them accordingly.

Factors specially affecting women in university teaching

The factors so far considered are important for both men and women but there are some which, evidently, are more likely to affect women than men and which have been said to determine the present minority situation of women in university teaching, especially at the higher levels.

i) *Children*

In some countries there has been a past tradition that women who taught in universities remained unwed and childless: it is a tradition possibly linked to a similar tradition concerning women school teachers. But there have always been women who contrived to combine maternity and academic work: and it is evident that in universities today the majority of women teachers are married and many have children; though the proportion of those remaining unmarried may be higher — at least in some countries — than the proportion in the population generally. It would in itself be an interesting study to discover the factors determining the marital status and child-bearing of this group of women. The evidence available in the present investigation is not enough to prove whether in some countries the proportion of married women university teachers is higher than in others: it would appear that marriage is more frequent in France, East Germany and Finland than in the UK and West Germany but one cannot be certain that the samples were representative in this respect. There is evidence to suggest that in the UK there has been, in comparatively recent times, an increase in the proportion of those married. It would seem also that in West Germany there may linger still some attitudes among women themselves which encourage retirement, at least temporarily, from university work when a woman has a child or children, even though many university women teachers there today would reject this attitude.

In this respect university women teachers must be affected by the attitudes of society in general to the working mother and to the proportion of women who are gainfully employed outside the home. In all countries there has been an increase in the participation of women in the labour force but it has been highest, in the countries studied, in East Germany and Finland. (One may recall too that there may be fluctuations in such participation according to age levels: the UK, for example, shows a considerable proportion of women staying at home while their children are in the pre-school years.) The situation in society generally can affect the university woman teacher in two ways, one attitudinal and one practical.

To take first the attitudinal aspect: there may be, in societies where the idea of the working mother is not fully accepted, critical comment from colleagues or other people that the woman is neglecting her children by going out to work while they are young and need her presence in the home. Women in the UK, France and West Germany were aware of such attitudes and had various reactions to them, basically a rejection of the accusation that the children were suffering in any way — indeed sometimes an affirmation that the children were receiving better care and attention than those of non-working mothers. But the awareness of such attitudes in society did make the situation of the woman university teacher harder in these countries. In Finland there seemed to be rather less of such an attitude. In East Germany there was a clear official policy in support of the working mother: on the whole, it is expected that the woman with children will have other employment: though some women still stay at home to care for their children, this would seem rather an exceptional situation — yet there are, as we have noted, provisions for extensive maternity leave during the first year of life of the child.

Thus a woman's happiness in combining the two roles can be threatened by social prejudices against such a combination: and although these prejudices are probably diminishing, they can, in certain areas of society and in certain families, be an important factor for the university woman teacher to cope with.

In addition to outside opinion, however, there is the inevitable conflict of claims on the woman's attention on some occasions: she is divided between the need to concentrate on her academic work and the need to think about a child who is perhaps ill or in some difficulty — or even just longing for the mother's presence. There may too be the simple conflict between interest in the university work and interest in being with young children: some women, more than others, find the company of children a source of continuing pleasure — others find that they enjoy it more in limited amounts. The university woman teacher who has children must therefore have the ability to cope with this division of interests: and be able to resist any feelings of guilt — guilt about failing to be satisfactory in both jobs. It is interesting that in more than one country women referred to the advantages of being 'schizophrenic' in the sense of being able to switch off the other demands on attention and concentrate on the immediate situation. But of course the two sets of claims may recur to attention at the wrong moments: the important feature is the extent to which they can be switched off or postponed as necessary.

To come to the practical aspect: society's expectations determine the provision or lack of provision for child-care services to which the working mother can confide her child during working hours. It was of course pointed out by many women that university work can have the advantage of flexible working hours so that the mother can be at home or attend to the child at various times during the day. But systematic provision of child-care services is undoubtedly important. Here the provision in West Germany and the UK was found to be defective. In France, considerable progress in recent times has meant that more and more working mothers can find places in the écoles maternelles for their children. In Finland the provision of places in day-care centres was not regarded as adequate but state subsidy of child-minders seemed to offer a possible alternative. In East Germany there has been enormous effort to provide fully both at creche and kindergarten levels for children while their mothers are at work: thus the situation of the university woman teacher in that society differs considerably from that in other countries — there is even the additional service of the Schulhort to help to provide for rather older children, during the primary school years.

But of course there is also the alternative of employing women to look after the children — at home or in the woman's home — and perhaps cope with the housework as well. Again, the availability of such assistance varies from country to country according to the economic situation and state of the labour market. Women in the older age groups seemed generally to have had advantages, in that suitable assistance could be found fairly readily when they needed it most and was not ruinously expensive (though naturally the evaluation of cost depended on the joint income of husband and wife and, to some extent, whether one or both of them had already reached a well-paid position). In East Germany such assistance simply did not seem available — but the provision of child-care facilities could at least compensate on that side of the married woman's work. In France, West Germany and the UK it seemed more easy to find than in urban Finland: but younger women were likely to comment on its high cost. (Again, changes in the labour market and rising unemployment could affect this situation also.) But again there are personality factors to be taken into account. Some women were more ready than others to accept that an 'outsider' could be important in their child's life. A few women — in France and Finland — expressed reluctance to employ another woman to cope with domestic tasks which the individual herself did not want to do. Possibly the extreme of opposition to using child-care assistance was seen in the West German young woman who felt that she would not want to hand her child over even to her own mother. Much obviously depends on the personalities of those who are available to help in looking after children: some women had been fortunate in finding someone who was fully acceptable in this respect, others had had to try a number of helpers before arriving at a satisfactory arrangement. In East Germany however it was argued that the trained staff of the kindergarten can provide a more satisfactory learning and play environment than the mother at home could provide.

Generally, in all countries, there was (despite the West German reservation just cited) full recognition of the help that grandmother could give to the working mother. It depended of course on whether she lived nearby. Many women in the past had benefited by such help and some at present. The new problem here is that so many grandmothers today are also out at work and have their own careers. The advancement of women at work does have unforeseen complications.

ii) *Child-bearing*

We have noted that university women teachers have shown in the past, and continue to show, willingness to avoid the disruption of the work of their department when they are pregnant and when a baby arrives. It has also been evident that generous provision of maternity leave and guarantees of return to employment afterwards is an ambivalent provision. While it may seem to encourage the woman in her role as mother, it also raises questions in the minds of those making appointments as to whether a woman in the child-bearing years is a reliable person to appoint. So great may be this consideration that even in East Germany there has been some acceptance of the view that the proportion of women entering medical studies should not be allowed to go beyond the 50:50 ratio because maternity leaves can make the staffing situation difficult.

But for the individual woman there is, in addition to the problems of maternity leaves and child-bearing itself, the question of timing the arrival of children so as to ensure the minimum handicap to progress in the academic world. It should be said that in the past the majority of women have not had this aspect of the situation clearly in mind. For those who had their children early and then came to an academic career the question had not really set itself since at the time of having their family they did not see themselves as engaged on an academic career. Others managed to combine children and career simultaneously, again without much planning, because it so happened that the circumstances of their career fitted well into having a baby and caring for it — in some instances a research commitment during pregnancy and in the months following the birth seemed to have worked out very well. In yet other cases, child-bearing was postponed until after qualifications had been obtained, without conscious intent but because of relatively late ages of marriage.

Nevertheless, given the increased reliability of contraception, it would seem likely that intending mothers would consider which pattern is most helpful. There are clear advantages in having the children while the mother is still young: and there may be social pressures towards having children in the early twenties, as in East Germany — or in other societies where the young woman who has been married for two or three years may find herself questioned as to when she is going to get round to having children. Yet taking some years to concentrate on children — perhaps taking part-time employment or retiring to home life entirely — must mean that other people are meanwhile going ahead to acquire qualifications at the higher levels, are carrying out research and publishing. For many women the pattern of an early period devoted to the home and family followed by a period of return to study has worked: but that has been during a period of expansion and relatively easy access to university posts. It might very well be more difficult in future to make these late entries or to return to university work after time out. And not all young mothers can enjoy the situation of one West German woman and one British whose partners had opted to stay at home and look after the baby.

There is of course the variation on the pattern of early child-bearing which is to work on in the university at the same time. Again, this pattern had been followed and is being followed successfully by some of the women interviewed. But it demands tremendous efforts and great organising power on the part of the woman. Research, it has been said, is almost bound to suffer, even if the woman can keep up successfully with her teaching and routine duties in the university. Interruptions to sleep are noted as having particularly trying effects. Health generally is a dominating factor both for mother and baby. Given good health on both sides — and possibly the capacity here as in other circumstances to manage with very few hours of sleep — the simultaneous development can be made.

The third pattern is that of postponing child-bearing until qualifications have been completed and a secure position in the university hierarchy gained. One woman recalled having received explicit advice to this effect from her professor. But this assumes that qualifications can be obtained within a reasonable time limit and a good post secured. Even so, there may be for the woman — and her husband — the question of whether perhaps the children are being left too late: as has been noted, social pressures may well reinforce anxiety on this score.

There is clearly no ideal answer to the question. But what could be helpful is the awareness of the advantages and disadvantages of the different patterns. The decision taken by individual women will of course not depend simply on such general considerations but also on knowledge of the actual circumstances at home and in the university where they are working or likely to work. The availability of child-care services, the readiness of relations and others to help with child-care, likelihood of finding good domestic help, the husband's employment and his availability to help with the child, departmental commitments and research plans — all these may determine which policy is the most appropriate for the individual: plus of course the woman's own attitude to babies and her preferences for a given family size.

ii) *Husbands*

The importance of the husband's attitudes and readiness to help has already been indicated. It can make a considerable difference to the woman coping with the dual role if her partner is ready to take at least some share of domestic work and is ready to share in looking after the children. There was evidence in all the countries studied of a growing tendency for husbands to share in housework but the development had perhaps gone further in some countries than in others — Finland perhaps was most noteworthy here. Certainly it seemed to be a matter of age-groups, older husbands being less likely to adopt this approach. In child-care too there was evidence of cooperation, even to the extent of rising during the night to tend to a crying child. Similarly too husbands had been willing in some instances to look after children while the wife went abroad or to a conference in some other part of the country — though this form of cooperation did not seem to be universal and some wives felt that they were rather bound to stay near to home until their children were able to look after themselves.

Such factors suggest the need for the married university woman teacher to have a husband who respects her right to develop her career fully. A remarkably high proportion of the women interviewed counted themselves lucky in having found marvellous husbands who showed comprehension of their work and their need to work: who offered them also encouragement to proceed in their research and writing.

In these circumstances it is not surprising that the majority of the married women had husbands who were also graduates and, in many cases, who were also in university work. This assortative mating is of course likely to occur through meeting as university students or, later, through meeting at work or professional conferences. But there is the clear advantage that husbands who have themselves studied — or who are studying for higher degrees also — can comprehend the requirements of academic posts. They can appreciate the point frequently made, that university work is not a 9 to 5 job for five days of the week: it encroaches on evenings and weekends. The non-academic husband might well — as was evident in some cases reported — resent a wife's preoccupation with activities which take her away from family life or which make extensive involvement in social activities and leisure pursuits sometimes difficult. Marrying a husband who does not appreciate these factors may indeed have been one of the reasons for the withdrawal from academic life of women who had begun on a promising academic career: certainly some such instances of former colleagues were reported by the groups interviewed., This is not to say that marriage with a non-academic husband is incompatible with success in university teaching: there were some instances to prove that such marriages can work very well: but they were in a small minority.

One of the major problems for both husband and wife, however, is that of finding posts for them both in the same place. This can be particularly difficult if both are in the same field of studies. In the past, the fashion has been for the wife to move when the husband found a new appointment. But there were instances in Finland, France, West Germany and the UK of husbands moving to suit the wife's job prospects or of couples arriving at some kind of compromise arrangement to give alternate chances of seeking better posts. Even so, there were examples of the more traditional situation where the wife had moved with her husband, sometimes being very lucky in finding a better position for herself in the new place of residence; and also examples of situations in which a wife would find it difficult to go to another university for promotion. Commuting by one or both partners was a solution that some couples had tried. It worked in some cases but in others the sheer fatigue of travelling caused it to be rejected as a possibility or abandoned after some time. According to travel facilities — and the possibilities of compressing work into a limited number of days a week — it can be more or less acceptable as an arrangement: but it did seem, at least for some couples, to impose not only physical strains but psychological strains on the marriage and family. The mobility problem can affect both men and women: the tradition that it mainly handicaps the woman is possibly one that is being eroded.

iv) *Unmarried women*

It is even more difficult to generalise about this group than about the group of married women. Some of those unmarried at the time of the survey may well marry in a few years' time. There may indeed be a tendency for university women teachers to marry at later than average ages and some of the women, in different countries, had married in their forties. There is also to be recalled the difference between the younger generations who may be cohabiting or be involved in a stable relationship with a 'friend' and the older women for whom such a relationship would not have been countenanced in the days of their youth and who have remained single, devoting themselves to their work only.

For those who are cohabiting or involved in a similar relationship, some of the problems of marriage clearly apply. There is the matter of shared housework (one woman had refused to set up house with her friend because it was evident that he would not be ready to take his share of domestic tasks). There is the matter of conflict between work and leisure time pursuits together. There can be the same mobility problem — possibly complicated by rather greater difficulty even now in obtaining a post in the new place for a 'partner'.

The point was made, in more than one country, that for the older unmarried woman there can still be domestic responsibilities in caring for elderly parents or relatives. This can be as demanding a situation as that of caring for a family — it can indeed be more difficult since there is usually no one with whom to share the work and worry. But it is not generally recognised and allowance made for it. And in all countries the tradition that it is the daughter not the son who takes on these responsibilities seems unchanged.

Domestic work in itself appeared to pose no great problem for the single woman. One who most disliked it paid friends' children to relieve her of such tasks: a few employed some domestic assistance for short periods of time. The general reaction seemed to be either to reduce domestic work to the inescapable minimum (according to individual definitions of the minimum) or to enjoy it as a pleasant change from academic work. Gardening and various crafts could similarly be appreciated by some women as almost therapeutic occupations.

But on occasion it was suggested that being a single woman did tend to attract additional duties in the department, the assumption being that one who did not have a husband and family to care for would have extra time on her hands. This assumption was rather resented — especially if there was a married woman colleague who seemed to be having a relatively easy time so far as departmental chores were concerned: but one had the impression that in practice these women accepted their hard-working role. They might complain that they were taken for 'une bonne poire' (muggins) in the department: few suggested that they refused the tasks in question.

Socially, some women felt, there were some disadvantages in being unmarried. The younger unmarried woman could be an object of suspicion to colleagues' wives and a centre of gossip among students. The older unmarried woman could be regarded as rather odd. One woman commented that in West Germany it may even be advantageous to be known to be living with a male friend: it removes the likelihood of being labelled as a dangerously militant career woman. In Finland there was mentioned a kind of embarrassment which might occur in some parts of Britain also, that of going alone into pubs: but this seemed to be a changing situation. As to informal social situations, there was a mixture of opinion as to whether the single woman is at a disadvantage. Certainly it would be wrong in university teaching as now in school teaching to think of the unmarried woman in terms of the 'embittered spinster' stereotype. No such person was met with.

The unmarried women were, like the married, happy in their situation and in their work.

v) *Prejudice*

It might have been expected that the minority situation of women in university teaching and at professorial level would be found due to deep-rooted prejudices against women. In practice prejudice is very difficult to prove. It is also very difficult to discriminate between prejudices in society at large and specific prejudice within the university world — though universities were seen as more enlightened than society at large so far as equal rights for women are concerned.

It can be said that at least part of the explanation of university women teachers' situation does lie in society's prejudices in the past: in those social attitudes which judged higher education less suitable for females than for males. Such past attitudes were common to all the countries studied. Not that society had necessarily imposed official barriers to women's entry to higher education — the right to attend universities has long since been achieved — but influences in the schools and in some families taught girls that their aspirations should not go in certain directions. There have admittedly been some instances of overt barriers, in the limitation of entry to medical studies in Britain for some years: and in Germany, during the Nazi period, official difficulties in the way of female students' access to universities. But attitudes in society have in the past dominated so that the surge of enthusiasm for women's access to higher education in the early decades of the century was followed by many years during which women's position in universities was not consolidated.

In all the countries studied there has been recent growth in the proportions of female students admitted to higher education. There has also been public awareness and official recognition of the need to ensure equal opportunities for females. Thus in the countries studied there is now less likelihood of overt expression of opinions unfavourable to women in higher education (the amount of residual comment of this kind varying according to the country and the amount of 'official' condemnation of such attitudes): but there is also enhanced awareness among women that they have suffered from or may be suffering from prejudices against women on the part of male colleagues or male higher authorities in the universities.

Given the recognition that there have been in the past social influences impeding women's access to universities, to higher degrees, to university teaching, there was a widespread view that it is only a matter of time before the situation of women in universities rights itself. Thus many women would suggest that we are at present living out the effects of past prejudices: in some years' time there will be much greater representation of women on university staffs, especially at the higher levels. The increase in the numbers of women at the lower levels, especially at assistantship level in the continental universities, is pointed to as a sign of better things to come — though even women who hold this view usually express some doubt as to whether there will be *complete* equality: women may still be in a minority but in a much larger minority.

How rapidly the situation may change remains in fact doubtful. Since there is still evidence of prejudice in society outside the universities — in the UK, France, Finland, West Germany at least this is overt — girls growing up in society, and boys too, are likely to be affected by such attitudes and may internalise them. As many women remarked, it takes a long time for society to change: the removal of deep-rooted prejudices is difficult to achieve. Attitudes towards the working mother may be among the most influential and longest surviving of influences working against university women's advancement.

Schools may be regarded as one instrument of change but many women felt that schools could still do more to improve attitudes. Few if any of the women interviewed had received satisfactory vocational guidance in their schools. It may be that such guidance comes more effectively from parents — especially from parents who are enthusiastic about their daughters' education — but schools should not neglect this task, the more so as not all talented girls have educated parents or parents knowledgeable about and keen on careers for their daughters. Schools — in some instances cited — still need to give thought to whether a 'hidden curriculum' is transmitting old attitudes. (Coeducational schools are becoming universal: but many university women teachers have in the past been produced by girls' schools and speak well of them.)

Was there evidence of prejudice inside the university world? Again, it is difficult to prove. It was impressive that the great majority of women said they had personally not encountered prejudice. But there were some who were strongly of the opinion that they had not received appointments because they are women. It also seemed evident in some cases that women had suffered by prejudice without being fully aware of it. Such prejudice had expressed itself mainly as inaction; professors had failed to perceive that they were not giving the woman an opportunity to make her way in the academic world, they were allowing her to continue indefinitely at a subordinate level — presumably because they did not see a woman as a future professor or as someone with a career to make. Professors may have failed their women colleagues by not urging on them the need to work for higher qualifications or to widen their qualifications. At the same time many women indicated clearly how much they had been helped by their (male) professors. Such instances would outnumber instances of failure to see where help was appropriate — except of course that there may be many more cases of the latter kind among women not now teaching in universities.

In this problem of the definition of prejudice, how can one interpret the common belief that the university is a man's world? It is certainly a matter of attitudes: but the attitudes are not adopted out of prejudice against women. It is simply that men have been running universities for a long time and — although there are a few noteworthy exceptions of women in high university posts — men continue to run them. The structure of committees and the conduct of meetings have evolved in accordance with male preferences. This is not to say that women would necessarily produce or prefer a different structure: but it does mean that the woman in a minority in such organisations may have disadvantages simply because she speaks differently and might conduct business differently. More women's presence — not simply that of the token woman — would probably be the most effective way of improving this situation.

The situation of the 'man's world' may well differ within departments and between departmental perceptions and those of the university in general. In some departments where there is a good percentage of women members of staff, then the atmosphere is naturally much less that of a man's world, the more so as a goodly percentage of the students will also be female. In such cases too there may well be one or more female professors (in a large department) or it may be that the head of department or director of the institute is a woman (possibly elected for a limited term of office, as, e.g., in France). Even in such cases, the dictum concerning a man's world is likely to remain true for central university committees where the female professor or the female head of institute or other unit will again be in a small minority.

Yet it was not generally felt that women were purposely excluded from decision-making processes though there was some recognition that informal decision-making might well take place in men's social meetings. But this again depended on the individual university and on the woman's perception of social interactions: some women were insulated by their rank and department's location from such perceptions. Where women were excluded from top university committees because only those of professorial rank could be members this was regarded as something which should be reformed: it arose not out of prejudice against women, though, but out of traditional university structures: it just so happens that women are more likely than men to be excluded by such a requirement. In the French and German systems where participation by all ranks of university teachers has been formally introduced, women do not suffer from this kind of exclusion.

So far as expression of prejudice in everyday conversation is concerned, a fair number of women had noted such expression: but it was not generally something they took seriously (though it could be indicative of more deeply rooted attitudes). Usually they would regard it as an expression of individual peculiarity rather than a general trend: the most common reaction was to be amused at it.

Thus, although there is some perception of being excluded from decision-making processes — and resentment of such exclusion in some instances (including membership, in France, of high level professional committees) — there is not a general feeling that prejudice is a major factor here. Yet some women thought that, where membership of committees is a matter of being elected — as in Britain — there may be a failure of male colleagues to think of women as suitable nominees.

Altogether, while women university teachers are aware of past prejudices and of the continuation of these in society outside the university, they do not themselves generally feel they have been or are the victims of such prejudices. They consider too that prejudices are passing and that the younger generation of men in universities is likely to be free of prejudices which may still linger in the minds of older men in university teaching and lead to irritating paternalism towards attractive young women or more serious failures to see women as potential colleagues.

Attitudes and personality traits of women

Prejudices against women, stereotypes of females in society can affect the individual woman's self-concept and consequently her behaviour — in a way which will make her conform to the stereotype. There was a general recognition of the characteristics thought to be appropriate to the sexes and these characteristics were common to all the societies in question. But opinion varied as to whether women really are more diffident, more self-effacing, less confident about their own merits. A few women thought that such traits might indeed be biologically determined. But the majority considered them to be socially induced.

There was a fair amount of support for the view that women are less competitive and less aggressive: in the German phrase, they lack elbows. Women were also perceived as being less single-minded than men about their careers: expressed more positively, this trait arose because of their greater ability to enjoy what life has to offer in art, music, social relationships. They were also, in the view of some women interviewed, more likely to be critical of their own work.

But many women rejected the view of women as lacking in self-confidence. They did not think such an attitude affected women's willingness to publish their work or to seek recognition. They claimed the ability to evaluate their own work and to know that it was good. Where there was reluctance to publish or to seek higher rank, they would ascribe the behaviour to individual personality differences (idiosyncraciès of their own) rather than to general sex difference in attitudes.

Women differed too in their attitudes to interaction with colleagues in the university. Some took the line that women and men behave similarly. Others consciously took the view that a woman should exercise charm; they saw themselves, while functioning fully as efficiently and professionally as their male colleagues, as having this distinctive style of behaviour, being pleasantly reasonable and cooperative rather than firmly assertive. Thus, implicitly, while considering themselves fully equal to male colleagues, they attribute to themselves a role rather different from that of male colleagues — a way of behaving which in fact they consider better than that of more aggressive males.

(Other women, it may be mentioned, recognise the existence of charm of manner in some male colleagues too.)

Not all the typically female reactions are in the direction of being self-effacing. Since many women in a number of countries asserted that women have to be better than men to succeed in university careers (an indication that some prejudice must be lurking somewhere), it follows that many of the women do have considerable confidence in their own abilities and performance. And, as one or two noted, this can mean that some university women teachers are rather terrifying to their male colleagues.

Women's organisations

Attitudes towards prejudice and the evaluation of women's roles affect women's readiness to sympathise with or support actively feminist organisations. Here there did seem to be some difference between countries and between women within individual countries. In East Germany, given the official support for equal opportunities for women and the clear official pronouncements about the need to advance women, there was perhaps less feeling of urgency about giving support to feminist organisations. It was rather part of the social work which university women teachers, like teachers at other levels, engage in. But in East Germany as in other countries, there was rejection of appearing to be an aggressively militant, mannish feminist.

In France the involvement of the women in feminist organisations seemed to be greatest, even if in France there were many women who did not wish to be involved or who, while feeling sympathetic, did not find time or inclination to join a specific organisation. There was an impression of a more advanced state of feminist organisations in France than in the other countries even if this was said almost to have passed its peak. But of course this impression may be due to some selective factors in the groups studied.

In Finland the struggle for women's equality seemed already well established so that militant feminist organisations were not appropriate at this stage in development. As one woman put it, all that can be done by legislation has been done: it remains to change attitudes. Certainly some of the women were keenly interested in equal opportunties for women and were working in this field. Others, like women in senior posts in other countries, felt that they were best serving the advancement of women by being very good in their own work and thus encouraging younger women to follow the same path.

In Britain and in West Germany there was rather the impression of a developing interest in women's organisations, especially within the universities themselves. There had been perhaps a slower or later response among women there to disadvantages in women's careers. But the strength of response and the willingness to be actively involved in seeking better opportunities, both among staff and students, may be very much a matter of individual universities' populations.

In general, there was no doubt that the great majority of those interviewed sympathised with attempts to improve the situation of women and their career prospects. Many pointed out that they had been convinced feminists for years, at times when it was much less fashionable than today to be a feminist and be aware of the need to help women towards equal opportunities. There was, however, a small minority who were unsympathetic to feminist views and who would rather interpret modern movements to support women as the expression of individuals' dissatisfactions with their own lives and as unrealistic demands for privileges. In such cases, it was stated that women can get what they want if they are determined and put their minds to it.

But among the majority who are convinced feminists — some of whom point out that they have lived and are living as fully 'liberated' women — there are differences of opinion as to how improvement may be achieved. Some would insist that there is a need for concerted action through organisations. Some women feel that possibly this is so but they themselves have already too full a life to spare time from it to attend many — possibly frustrating — meetings. Others, as we have noted, take the view that individual example, making a success in one's profession, is likely eventually to be the most efficacious way of bringing about changes. Possibly, too, something may be done, they suggest, by trying to alter attitudes within one's own family circle and among social acquaintances — and through schools.

The absentees

In considering the effects of prejudice it must be remembered that the most telling evidence of prejudice has not been collected. It would have been found, in all probability, in the statements of those women who were earlier in university teaching or were highly promising graduates in their time but are not now in the university teaching profession. There are women who decided, because of social pressures, that they should give up their university work when they started a family. (In some cases obviously women make this decision because they themselves prefer to be at home with their children: it is not to them that reference is made here but to those other women whose upbringing, family, colleagues, friends made them consider the two roles incompatible.) Or there are the women who felt they must retire on marriage because that was the attitude or even policy of their university authorities. There are the women whose husbands objected to the division of the wife's attentions and interests so that the woman gave up her further studies or her university post. And then too there are the candidates who were interviewed for posts but, because they were women and might marry or have children or were women and were married and did have children, were seen as less suitable people to appoint to the post in question. Or there are the great numbers of women who have been invisible when appointments or nominations were under consideration — perhaps rendered even more so by the sparkle of an engagement ring. There have been students of high ability or junior members of staff of high ability who were not seen as people to encourage to embark on higher studies or to urge towards promotion because they did not fit the usual pattern: they were women, not men.

Obviously one cannot estimate the number of these absentees. But it is certain that they exist. Various women interviewed referred to past colleagues who came into one or other of these categories. There were present instances of women who were having problems with difficult husbands — not among the group studied themselves, but within their circle of acquaintances. There were young women whose continuation in university teaching was precarious because they were women. There were young women who had *not* been appointed to the new Hochschulassistenten posts of West Germany. There are departments which have never had any women assistants or who still have only one even though the number of female students has multiplied greatly. There are departments where female students may even be in the majority — or at least nearly equal in numbers with male students — and whose teaching staff remains exclusively or almost exclusively male: it cannot be that the ability to go into university teaching and the wish to do so have remained confined to the male students of such departments.

To understand fully the situation of women in university teaching, one should interview also those who are not university teachers. Possibly a follow-up of those who have left the profession before retirement age would throw some light on the situation: possibly some investigation of a cohort of both men and women graduates would also help. Certainly it must be kept in mind that the evidence which is obtained by interviewing the survivors is biased.

Let us note that there may be another kind of absenteeism, absence from higher ranks. Certainly there may be fewer women at professorial level because women simply do not choose to be there. It is true that some of those interviewed had turned down the chance of a Chair for personal reasons. It is true that some women disclaimed any ambition to become professors. One cannot tell to what extent such factors affect men also. Observation and casual conversation show that some male university teachers also do not want to be professors and do not join in the struggle for promotion. But is there likely to be quite such a great disparity between men and women in the wish to achieve top level appointments? Some disparity there may be because of the greater social pressures on men to make a career in this way. But surely there have been women distinguished in academic work who are simply missing from the ranks of professors — and women interviewed can speak of examples.

Differences between countries

Does the situation of women in university teaching differ from country to country? There are the obvious differences in the structure of the universities and in their arrangements for qualification and appointment. There are too some differences in the proportions of women appointed at the higher levels. But what is most striking is the similarity in situation and outlook of the women in the different systems.

There are even, it would appear, different types of university women teachers to be found in all the systems. There is the doyenne — metaphorically if not actually — who is in the older age groups, who is an eminent authority in her chosen field, internationally recognised, quietly confident and amiable in her authority. There are those who relate with enthusiasm and pride their work in building up the department or specialist study. There is the energetic, middle-aged woman, well qualified, enjoying not only her teaching duties but also invigorated by participation in administration, a function in which she is particularly successful. There are other middle-aged women who are not ambitious for promotion but who are devoted to their teaching of students and the advancement of their subject by this means. There are the keen research workers, accepting their due share of teaching and research but wishing above all to have the facilities and scope to pursue that research as they know they could pursue it. There are the women with young children, determinedly doing justice to all the demands made on them, living remarkably well organised and strenuous lives. And the young women, not sure yet whether their future will lie in university teaching but engrossed in their present academic work, accepting perhaps that theirs is a limited-term appointment. Such similarities cut across the countries' boundaries. So do similarities between those engaged in the same subject areas. And yet strongly distinguished individual personalities flourish in all the systems.

Future developments

Will the situation of women be different in universities in the future? The answer lies not only in possible changes within existing structures but in the ways in which universities themselves may change: new pressures are transforming European universities from inside and from outside. It is uncertain whether the university will be recognisably the same by the century's end.

So far as more conservative estimates are concerned, women in many cases viewed the situation with optimism. They foresee a better representation of women simply because of the increased numbers of females who now study at university and the increasing numbers who are now appointed at the lower levels of staffing. Whether this optimism is justified remains doubtful. Some improvement is certainly to be expected but it seems slow to manifest itself and there are a great many factors which can intervene between the lower levels of appointment (in most systems) and permanence in the career or appointment at the top levels. As we have noted, in four at least of the systems studied there is a period of little or no growth in university resources: this is likely to affect promotions in the immediate future and recruitment policies for some years to come.

A factor which might also contribute to an optimistic outlook is the spread in all the countries studied of concern for equal opportunities for women. Where prejudice against women's appointments may linger still, it may be counteracted by this public concern and younger generations may grow up without accepting the conventional stereotypes of male and female achievement potentials and personality traits. Greater sensitivity to the dangers of sex stereotyping may lead schools to improve their educational and vocational counselling and even to avoid some of the hidden curriculum which still transmits patterns of behaviour and occupational roles based on gender. Similarly, if social attitudes change, the attribution of domestic duties to females only and expectations that mothers will be almost wholly responsible for the care of young children may also disappear: and the freedom of women to pursue an academic career will be notably increased.

But such developments must be affected by the economic state of the country in which the universities are situated. In times of economic recession there is a tendency to revert to the view that women can be very happily occupied inside the home: acceptance of the right of women to take paid employment outside the home is not universal in Western European societies. In societies where the labour market needs all the skilled manpower (or womanpower) it can get, the attitude to women's employment and women's choice of jobs is very different.

Since there is currently, in the countries studied, a general acceptance of women's right to higher education and to employment commensurate with that education, the question arises whether more positive action can be taken to speed up or create greater access of women to university teaching posts and to promotion within that career. Should arrangements specially favourable to women be made?

One possibility would be positive discrimination in favour of women i.e. the decision to appoint a fixed quota of women, whether their qualifications reached the same level as those of male competitors or not. This solution would in all probability be rejected by the women in the system or likely to enter the system. It is no great advantage to be appointed simply because one belongs to a favoured sex. As it is, women resent being appointed to committees or other bodies simply because they are women: being the 'token woman' is unsatisfactory, however attractive some of the circumstances may seem, superficially. Moreover, women have no doubts that they are as capable as men of achieving the qualifications thought necessary for university appointments. It would be an unhappy change to move from a situation in which, according to many women, a woman has to be better than a man to get the job to one in which a woman could be less good than a man and get the job.

There might admittedly be the situation — more common in argument than in real life — where two candidates are equally well qualified. Whether the man or woman is appointed in such a case should depend on the proportion of male and female staff already in the department or university. It should certainly not depend on the belief that the man is more likely to be a reliable member of the department because a woman may have children. The problems of maternity leave are real — as has been indicated in all the countries studied — but these problems can be solved by means other than the automatic disqualification of any woman within child-bearing years. The major point here is that — since bearing children is of benefit to society — there should be adequate provision of staffing to provide assistance during the absence of women on such occasions or of men and women on the other occasions. It is a subtle form of discrimination against women to make their colleagues suffer overwork during maternity leaves. Hence, if candidates seem equal, a choice for one — or the other sex — should not instantly impose itself.

Do these arguments mean that there should be acceptance of the status quo in the Western European university system and that, apart from avoiding positive discrimination against women, no specific effort should be made to improve their position? Should everything be left to the slow process of education and social change? This laissez faire policy does not seem satisfactory. There would seem to be much to be said for something of the same policy as is being implemented in East Germany, the conscious analysis of the present situation of women teaching in the university and the explicit decision to help them to advance towards higher levels in their career. Whether it is desirable to go all the way to introducing a system of sponsored mobility — which undoubtedly could advance women, if there was a firm policy of increasing their numbers at the various levels of the university teaching hierarchy — is doubtful. There has been a tradition in universities of more open access (even if in the past assistantships have been very much a matter of professorial patronage): individual decisions are made as to whether an attempt on higher levels is appropriate. Sponsored mobility too may ultimately lead to a lowering of standards as well as to concurrent frustration on the part of those not sponsored. But action could be taken in individual universities to consider the position of each woman member of staff and to see what advancement she could make in qualification and whether there is any way in which she could be helped towards that qualification. Obviously a committee cannot determine whether the individual chooses to engage in research and to publish the results of that research: — though it could give facilities leaving the individual more free to pursue research or encourage departments so to reorganise their work. But the awareness that there was interest in the individual's progress and that eventual promotion was possible in certain conditions might well prove beneficial.

Similarly a university could look thoughtfully at the percentage of women employed within it in different subject areas and at different levels — indeed, it could look at non-academic as well as academic staff. It could also monitor the number of women applicants for positions, the number actually appointed and the levels of qualification of those not appointed. Within departments, members of staff could consider their policies in encouraging students to think of going on to higher level qualifications (even in those times when university teachers in some subjects consider that there is no point in anyone going on to further studies in the subject). Students may well have their own reasons for accepting such advice or rejecting it. What is important is that women as well as men should see themselves as possible recruits to teaching in higher education and to research in their subject specialisms.

Such proposals to monitor the situation may seem anodyne. But it is remarkable what a simple inspection of the present situation can do in shaping future policies. A problem which is clearly perceived sometimes goes away.

In all this the question must arise whether such actions would be unfairly discriminatory against men. Certainly in any self-respecting university department or unit there should be a policy of facilitating the progress in qualification and research of all members of the staff. Claims to relaxation of teaching duties so that research can be done should be considered so as to take into account the situation of all members of the department. But since women at present are so clearly under-represented at various levels and in some subject areas it does seem essential that specific action should be taken to see whether their position can be improved. The action taken is not necessarily going to be disadvantageous to their male colleagues.

It is also to be questioned whether such a committee in the university or such monitoring of progress would be an interference with individual privacy and freedom. This must depend on the constitution of the committee and how it sets about its work. It must clearly be an advisory rather than an executive committee. And it would be beautifully paradoxical if it were constituted in accordance with academic seniority and so showed the usual pattern of male dominance with possibly a token membership of women.

How such committees succeed in the DDR is something yet to be determined since as yet the situation of women has not been brought to the stage of development which is intended. But the explicit decision to improve the situation is something which might well be adopted in other systems of higher education.

Whether anything so decisive can be done at the secondary school level is doubtful. Yet if attitudes of confidence in their own academic achievements and potential are not developed in girls during this stage, later efforts by university teachers will be considerably handicapped. Some attempts are being made by universities in Britain to introduce girls, by means of Sixth Form conferences and open days, to the idea of studying in subject areas — notably engineering — where formerly they have been in a very small minority. The increase of such contacts could be valuable. They would certainly reinforce the growing tendencies in secondary schools to be aware of the limited range of occupations towards which girls have been guided — or have guided themselves — in the past.

Future structures of university teaching

Whatever changes may take place in attitudes and in attempts to improve the representation of women in university teaching, a great deal must still depend on the way in which that teaching is organised and how advancement and access are determined in that career. As it is at present organised, much depends on the foundations laid for the career in the late twenties and early thirties of the individual's life. Whatever decisions women may make about their time of childbearing, it seems inevitable that there will be some conflict between their role as mothers and as university teachers and researchers. Of course it is abundantly clear that many women do combine the two roles with outstanding success. But the demands placed upon them are considerable: it cannot be expected that all women who have the qualities necessary for university success will also have excellent health and cooperative husbands. And the combining of research and the care of small children depends very much also on the subject areas as well as individual domestic circumstances.

It would be helpful to women if success in university teaching as a career were not dependent on full-time continuation in the career from the time of taking the first degree onwards. (It is of course to be recognised that in some faculties success is achieved by having acquired practical experience in one's chosen specialism in earlier work outside the university: but the same conflict of interest and problem of continuity in full-time employment may arise for women in such work also.)

One development which might improve the situation from the woman's point of view is the greater use of part-time posts. This solution does not always work out well, especially when there is failure to define precisely what half-time means. In poorly organised part-time arrangements, the woman finds herself doing considerably more work than she is paid for: she may be expected to take part in various informal aspects of the department's work — student counselling, working groups, sub-committee meetings: and she may in fact engage in these willingly and with good grace — but to the detriment of her own more important work. Or she may be so loaded with teaching and administration that she has no time for reading and research. On the other side, she may appear to full-time workers in the department to have a remarkably easy life, the administrative work connected with her teaching being left as an additional load for her full-time colleagues. If then there is an extension of part-time posts, the work load must be very carefully considered and defined. But if this kind of arrangement is well done it has the advantage of releasing some of the woman's time for family commitments while still keeping her in touch with developments in her own specialist subject and allowing her to develop her knowledge and teaching, even if at a slower rate than the full-time workers. What also needs careful definition is the effect of some years of part-time work on access to higher salary scale levels when the woman returns to full-time work again.

The prospect of shared jobs would seem particularly promising for women at this stage of their career but it remains doubtful whether this kind of arrangement is going to become generally accepted. The adminstrative complications it offers are often exaggerated. It seems to have much to commend it.

Possibly an alternative form of part-time teaching could be introduced with advantage into more university systems — the 'docent' type of post. It is interesting to see how the office of docent or Dozent has evolved in Finland, East Germany and West Germany: and it is perhaps a matter of regret that it seems to have been phased out in West Germany — or be in process of being phased out there. But the East German development of making it a full-time post, lower in rank only to a professorship, does not seem the most useful form for the advancement of women. The Finnish example rather, with the flexibility it offers as to the amount of teaching to be done in a department, seems to have advantages to offer. It could conceivably be — as the Privatdozent position was in some ways in West Germany — a kind of temporary arrangement before the woman moved back into full-time university work. It would also have advantages in years when universities are finding their teaching resources limited because of scarcity of full-time posts, as a way of supplementing their teaching — certainly it would involve some financial costs but less than would be incurred in providing for special interests by full-time appointments: it could also give some lightening of the teaching load when funds are not available for full-time posts.

As we have noted, definitions of tenure are being widely considered in universities. Assuming the more radical proposals are not implemented, the point at which tenure is achieved may materially affect the situation of women. Where, as in the continental systems, tenure is not assured to those holding the 'assistant' (in British terms, lecturer on the lower points of the scale) type of post, there may be considerable wastage of women when their tenure of this kind of post comes to an official end. Such termination may coincide with an increase of family demands so that the woman retires from university teaching not too reluctantly. Or it may be that some kinds of prejudice operate in favour of renewing appointments for men ('with families to support') rather than for women, if only a limited number can be re-appointed. If more radical changes take place and the system of life tenure is replaced by one of limited-term tenure, there are two types of predictable consequences for women. One is that women might be more willing than men to accept a limited-term contract: they might still be willing to embark on a career where prospects could not be reliable until the late twenties or early thirties. Men, especially in professions where well-paid appointments are available outside the university, might thus be diverted from university teaching. This would not necessarily be a good way of increasing the proportion of women who teach in universities. The other consequence is that decisions about giving tenure might come precisely in the years when women are most likely to be faced with competing demands from their young children. This might well reduce the proportion of women who would go on from an initial short-tenured appointment to a longer-term or 'permanent' tenure post.

Much has been said about the under-representation of women at professorial level. Various women have asserted that they do not particularly want to become a professor and that really appointment to such posts would make little difference. But is the post of professor likely to remain the same in the universities of the future? Or can the problem of access to professorial rank be solved by doing away with professorial rank? There have already been changes from the Golden Age of professors when the professor enjoyed godlike authority within the department. Processes of democracy have now intervened, in some universities and some departments, at least to reduce the authority and to limit the professor's power to determine the use of resources and the organisation of departmental work. The East German system emphasises the collective nature of departments even if professors still enjoy considerable prestige and authority. France is indicating the change of status by changing titles and conditions of work. Similarly too in West Germany the title of professor now covers appointments at different levels. In Britain, there are two kinds of professor, those holding an established Chair and those given the title of professor because of academic distinction. In Britain too the fashion is spreading of having rotation of the responsibilities of head of department, with the possibility of such responsibilities going to a non-professorial member of staff: similarly in France responsibilities in the UER may devolve on a non-professorial (old terminology) member of the unit.

It may be that the separation of functions is going to increase so that professors will no longer have the power to determine the affairs of their department. Their formerly automatic and exclusive presence on the major committees of universities is giving way to democratic processes of electing members of staff at other levels. In such developments, while the professorial position might become much more attractive to those academics who do not want to spend many hours on administration and in committee meetings the question of its continuing existence might be raised. It is of course true that in small departments, responsibility for administration might not be so easily delegated: yet there are also strong arguments for rationalising the situation within countries by combining in one or two universities the teaching formerly scattered among a large number; or by combining small departments into a more coherent school or faculty within a university. Thus the title of professor might signify as once it did — before universities became quite so complex administratively — simply eminence in the academic discipline. But it is not a title necessary for directing important research projects. The functions of the professor in future might be more those of present-day titular professors in Britain. These would still be questions of the most equitable way of awarding the title — the Finnish system seems to have something to commend it — but the onus of administration and power would be removed. So, presumably, would be higher salaries and better conditions of work.

Whether changes are radical or less so must depend on government policies, on centralisation and manpower planning. In East Germany there is a clear commitment to such central decision-making. The populations of the universities are adjusted to what are calculated as being the needs of society for trained people with various qualifications. In France and Finland there is clear central control by the Ministry of Education or Higher Education at least with regard to funding of universities and the establishment of posts; and in France too there have been governmental decisions as to which university courses to validate and decisions to control the supply of certain trained specialists (through the Grandes Ecoles as well as through the universities — and greater governmental coordination is now proposed here). In West Germany there have been developments, since the establishment of a Federal Ministry of Education in 1969, to take over from the individual states some of their regulating of their own universities. The Hochschulrahmengesetz typifies this, even if its implementation has still been a matter of legislation in individual state parliaments. In Britain, although there is apparently considerable autonomy for the individual university it has been increasingly clear that developments of courses of study and numbers of students admitted is a matter in which the UGC — and through it, the Treasury — has a decisive voice. Thus the trend would seem to be towards greater centralisation and greater decision-making by governments as to what the population of universities shall be and what subjects shall be studied there, and for how long. One notes, of course, that central government control is not new in continental systems, nor state control in Germany. But recent events show a greater specificity in planning student numbers and types of studying.

In such centralised decision-making one further factor particularly influencing women should be noted. When manpower planning takes effect there is often a tendency to reinforce the study of applied sciences or at least courses which have a clear vocational outlet. Similarly research in such studies rather than in 'pure' sciences and social sciences may be encouraged and funded — recent pronouncements in Britain illustrate this all too clearly but some of the pre-Mitterand governmental reforms and closures of courses in France showed a similar trend. Now it is in the social sciences and the Arts that women staff and students are most commonly found. Unless there is explicit determination to avoid reducing the numbers of female students and female staff, a move towards manpower planning and increased vocational orientation of universities might well reduce again the proportion of women within them — unless of course there is a radical revolution in vocational choices by girls at secondary and higher education levels.

Governmental control might also provide the answer to a question noted earlier — whether to continue to combine teaching and research in universities. Centralised policy might find a more satisfactory solution in having research conducted by research institutes. In practice many university teachers find that, as the amount of time required for teaching grows (both because of increased numbers and because of modern teaching methods), research is postponed or fitted into an increasingly smaller proportion of the year. Continuity and concentration on research are harder to achieve. The problem could be solved by a more effective system of 'internal leave' — the clear designation of periods of time during which the individual is freed from teaching and administrative duties to engage in research: but such a system demands high staffing resources. Alternatively, the decision could be to divorce the two functions, as just suggested, and leave universities simply as teaching institutions. It has of course been argued that research and teaching invigorate each other. But in practice many students have little if any knowledge of their teachers' research interests: the teaching could be done equally well — or even better — by people who have not carried out research in the area. Much research is carried out at a level which is not appropriate to or of interest to students at the undergraduate stage. If the individual teacher has little or no control of the content of the courses to be taught then reference to the individual's own research is ruled out. Yet if the two functions were separated, both women and men members of university staffs would — in the majority of cases — deeply regret the loss of one function. But it may be that in continuing to think of the two as conjoined we are perpetuating a medieval tradition — where 'research' was scholarly erudition or what passed for it — or a nineteenth century tradition where research had not yet reached its present levels of specialisation and needs for team work and expensive resources. The separation would still cause dismay.

The problem of university women teachers may thus be a vanishing problem as universities themselves change and are transformed. Present problems may be unexpectedly solved: new problems arise. But whatever the shape of future institutions of higher education it remains essential that women as well as men should engage in scholarly activities, in thinking clearly and honestly about their special interest, in discovering and integrating as much knowledge as possible about it and in transmitting that knowledge to the rest of society: and that they should have the opportunity to develop and practise their special abilities in such thinking and communication.

BIBLIOGRAPHY

L. Adolphs: *Die Beteiligung der Frau an der Wissenschaft* (Walter Braun Verlag, Duisburg, 1981).

H. Anger: *Probleme der deutschen Universität* (J.C.B. Mohr (Paul Siebeck), Tübingen, 1960).

Arbeitsgruppe am Max-Planck-Institut für Bildungsforschung: *Das Bildungswesen in der Bundesrepublik Deutschland* (Rowohlt, 1979).

Bundesminister für Bildung and Wissenschaft: *Statistiches Material zur Bildungssituation von Mädchen und Frauen* (Bonn, 1978).

Carnegie Commission on Higher Educatino: *Opportunities for Women in Higher Education* (McGraw-Hill, 1973).

Central Statistical Office of Finland: *Position of Women* (Helsinki, 1980).

Central Statistical Office of Finland: *Statistical Yearbook of Finland* (Helsinki, 1980).

Committee appointed under the chairmanship of Lord Robbins: *Higher Education* (HMSO, 1963).

M. Cordier: 'La situation des femmes dans les cadres professoraux de l'Université' (*Diplômées*, 11, déc. 1979).

Department of Education and Science: *School Leavers CSE and GCE 1981* (HMSO, 1981).

Department of Education and Science: *Statistics of Education 1965* (HMSO, 1966).

Department of Education and Science: *Statistics of Education 1972* (HMSO, 1974).

Department of Education and Science: *Statistics of Education 1975* (HMSO, 1977).

R. Drucker: 'Zur Vorgeschichte des Frauenstudiums an der Universität Leipzig' in *Vom Mittelalter zur Neuzeit*, ed. H. Kretschmer (Rütten und Loening, Berlin, 1956).

F. Euvrard: 'Travail des Femmes et Revenu Familial' (*Informations Sociales,* mars, 1980).

C. Führ: *Education and Teaching in the Federal Republic of Germany* (Inter Nationes, Bonn-Bad Godesberg, 1979).

Gemeinschaftsarbeit: *Das Bildungswesen der DDR* (Volk und Wissen, Volkseigener Verlag, Berlin, 1979).

Johann Wolfgang Goethe-Universität, Frankfurt am Main: *Vorlesungs- und Personenverzeichnis für das Sommersemester 1981.*

A. Grandke: 'Zur Entwicklung von Ehe und Familie' in *Zur gesellschaftlichen Stellung der Frau in der DDR* (Wissenschaftlicher Beirat bei der Akademie der Wissenschaft der DDR, 1978).

E. Haavio-Mannila, R. Jallinoja: 'Changes in the Life Pattern of Families in Finland' (Department of Sociology, University of Helsinki, 1980).

B. Heyns, J.A. Bird: 'Recent Trends in the Higher Education of Women' in P.J. Perun (ed.): *The Undergraduate Woman: Issues in Educational Equity* (Lexington Books, 1982).

Das Hochschulwesen, Zeitschrift für des Hochschulwesen der DDR (VEB Verlag, Berlin, 1982).

Erich Honecker: *Bericht des Zentralkomitees der socialistischen Einheitspartei Deutschlands an den X Parteitag der SED* (Dietz Verlag, Berlin, 1981).

J. de Jong (Kontaktfrau): 'Memorandum und Dokumentation zur Situation von Wissenschaftlerinnen an den Hochschulen von NRW and Vorschläge zu ihrer Verbesserung' (Ruhr-Universität Bochum, Juni, 1980).

I. Kandolin, H. Uusitalo: 'Scandinavian Men and Women: a Welfare Comparison', (Research Group for Comparative Sociology, University of Helsinki, Research Reports, No. 28, 1980).

R.K. Kelsall, A. Poole, A. Kuhn: *Six Years After* (Higher Education Research Unit, Department of Sociology Studies, Sheffield University, 1970).

H. Kuhrig, W. Speigner: 'Gleichberechtigung der Frau — Aufgaben und ihre Realisierung in der DDR' in *Zur gesesllschaftlichen Stellung der Frau in der DDR* (Wissenschaftlicher Beirat bei der Akademie der Wissenschaft der DDR, 1978).

Minister für Wissenschaft und Forschung des Landes Nordrhein-Westfalen: *Handbuch Hochschulen in Nordrhein-Westfalen* (Dusseldorf, 1979).

Ministère de l'Education, Service des Etudes Informatiques et Statistiques: 'Les Principales Caractéristiques des Enseignants en Fonction dans les Etablissements d'Enseignement Supérieur, Année 1978-79' (Paris, 1979, Note 79-34).

Ministère de l'Education, Service des Etudes Informatiques et Statistiques: 'Année 1979-80: Effectifs Post-Baccalauréat' (Paris, 1981).

Ministère de l'Education, Service des Etudes Informatiques et Statistiques: 'Statistiques des Examens du Baccalauréat d'Enseignement Général, du Baccalauréat de Technicien et du Baccalauréat Expérimental, Session 1980 — Résultats Définitifs' (Paris, 1981, Note 81-05).

Ministerium für Hoch und- Fachschulwesen: *Hochschulen und Fachschulen der DDR: Statistischer Überblick* (1980).

Ministry of Education: Committee Report, June, 1982, quoted in letter (Helsinki, 1982).

J. Minot: *L'Enseignement Universitaire* (Ministère de l'Education — Ministère des Universités, 1979).

Le Monde de l'Education: 'Treize ans de résultats à Paris: la palme aux lycées de filles' (mars, 1983).

National Programme of Finland for Promoting Equality between Women and Men (Helsinki, 1980).

O.E.C.D.: *Reviews of National Policies for Education: Finland* (Paris, 1982).

Joël-Yves Plouvin: *Le régime juridique des universités depuis la Loi d'Orientation* (Economica, Paris, 1980).

Ruhr-Universität Bochum: *Personal- und Vorlesungsverzeichnis* (Wintersemester, 1980/81).

C. Schmarsow: 'Women in Higher Education — Some Information on the Situation in the Federal Republic of Germany' *Higher Education in Europe* (CEPES, Bucharest, Oct.-Dec., 1981).

Scottish Education Department: *Statistical Bulletin, School Leavers* (HMSO, 1983).

I.Sommerkorn: *On the Position of Women in the University Teaching Profession in England* (Revised edition of Ph.D. thesis, University of London, 1969.)

Staatsverlag der Deutschen Demokratischen Republik: *Statistisches Jahrbuch der DDR 1980* (Berlin, 1980).

K. Starke: *Junge Partner: Tatsachen über Liebesbeziehungen im Jugendalter* (Urania Verlag, Leipzig-Jena-Berlin, 1980).

R.Szreter: 'Opportunities for Women as University Teachers in England since the Robbins Report of 1963', *Studies in Higher Education* (1983, vol.8,2).

Unesco: *Higher Education: International Trends, 1960-70* (Paris, 1975).

Unesco: *Statistical Yearbooks* (Paris).

University Grants Committee: University Development from 1935 to 1947 (HMO, 1948).

University Grants Committee: *Returns from Universities and University Colleges in Receipt of Treasury Grant, Academic Year 1961-62* (HMSO, 1963).

University Statistical Record: *University Statistics 1980* (1982).

University Statistical Record: *University Statistics 1981-82* (1983).

M. Wander: *Guten Morgen, Du Schöne!* (Verlag der Morgen, Berlin, 1977).

Wissenschaftlicher Beirat bei der Akademie der Wissenschaften der DDR unter Leitung von H. Kuhrig, W. Speigner *Zur gesellschaftlichen Stellung der Frau in der DDR* (Verlag für die Frau, Leipzig, 1978).